Engaging the Six Cultures of the Academy

Engaging the Six Cultures of the Academy

Revised and Expanded Edition of the *Four Cultures of the Academy*

William H. Bergquist
Kenneth Pawlak

JOSSEY-BASS
A Wiley Imprint
www.josseybass.com

Published by Jossey-Bass.
A Wiley Imprint
989 Market Street, San Francisco, CA 94103-1741 www.josseybass.com

Jossey-Bass books and products are available through most bookstores. To contact Jossey-Bass directly call our Customer Care Department within the U.S. at 800-956-7739, outside the U.S. at 317-572-3986, or fax 317-572-4002.

Jossey-Bass also publishes its books in a variety of electronic formats. Some content that appears in print may not be available in electronic books.

Library of Congress Cataloging-in-Publication Data

Bergquist, William H.
Engaging the six cultures of the academy : revised and expanded edition of The four cultures of the academy / William H. Bergquist, Kenneth Pawlak.—2nd ed.
p. cm.—(The Jossey-Bass higher and adult education series)
Rev. ed. of: The four cultures of the academy. 1st ed. c1992.
Includes bibliographical references and index.
ISBN-13: 978-0-7879-9519-5 (cloth)
1. Universities and colleges—United States—Administration. 2. Organizational behavior—United States. 3. Educational anthropology—United States. I. Pawlak, Kenneth, 1953- II. Bergquist, William H. Four cultures of the academy. III. Title.
LB2341.B476 2008
378.1′010973—dc22

2007026551

Printed in the United States of America
SECOND EDITION

HB Printing

The Jossey-Bass

Higher and Adult Education Series

Contents

Preface

It has become increasingly fashionable during the past two decades to describe organizations as *cultures*. Anthropologists, management consultants, organizational psychologists, and other social scientists have become enamored of this concept and helped popularize the notion that cultural analyses yield important insights into the life and dynamics of an organization. The definitions of organizational culture and the methods used to study it are as diverse as the disciplines involved (see, for example, Pettigrew, 1979; Deal & Kennedy, 1982; Peters & Waterman, 1982; Schein, 1985, 1992; Kotter & Heskett, 1992; Cameron & Quinn, 1999; Alveson, 2002; Martin, 2002). Unfortunately, most analyses of organizational culture are intriguing but not very useful. They provide vivid descriptions, but they rarely provide the historical underpinnings suggesting how the culture came to be what it now is. Even more important, they provide little guidance to the organizational leader who must live with and in this culture—or, more accurately—the many cultures that make up a living organization.

Culture plays an important role in shaping people and the structures they create. In this book we look at culture's impact on postsecondary education, where it plays a major role in defining patterns of perceiving, thinking, and feeling about the nature and scope of education. A culture helps identify reactions to things that are important to people living and working in that culture. In this book, we propose that there are six key cultures operating in higher education institutions: *the collegial culture*, *the managerial culture*, *the developmental culture*, *the culture of advocacy*, *the virtual culture*, and *the tangible culture*. Each one has much to say about the educational mission, vision, values, and purposes and about roles to be played by instructors, students, administrators, trustees, and even the general public. In addition, each of the organizational cultures offers specific hypotheses about the best ways in which to meet the emerging challenges of twenty-first-century life in the academy.

Purpose of the Book

Engaging the Six Cultures of the Academy provides an analysis of the six organizational cultures found in academic institutions. We offer a framework to guide leaders and inspire new courses of action to further improve functioning within these complicated institutions. Specifically, we offer an exposition of ways in which to use (or not use) the concepts of organizational culture so that those who work in academic institutions can improve their daily lives as leaders, administrators, faculty members, trustees, and concerned stakeholders.

Contemporary pragmatism often seems to dictate that we find a use for every concept; furthermore, contemporary organizational leaders frequently appear to need a strategy for change when confronted with the notion of culture (for example, Cameron & Quinn, 1999). In this book, we offer a counterperspective: what is required most is not a set of recommendations about how to change or mold a culture to meet one's own needs; rather, we must determine how to work with and use the strengths and resources of the existing organizational culture to accomplish our goals. We must, in other words, learn to appreciate rather than annihilate cultures.

Audience

This book is aimed at participants in contemporary academic life—in particular those leaders, faculty members, and other members of twenty-first-century colleges and universities who are living in one or more of the six cultures that we describe and inevitably work with those who live in one or more of the others. Specifically, this book is intended for those reflective practitioners (Schön, 1983) in higher education who want to know more about the organizational dynamics of the academy that they find most perplexing or frustrating.

Considering this potential benefit for readers, we offer several suggestions that may initially seem rather outlandish. First, we suggest that you not read this book in an orderly fashion—moving from chapter to chapter. Rather, we suggest that you turn first to one specific chapter that provides an analysis of the culture that you *least appreciate.* This is the culture that most often evades your understanding. You find it most difficult to relate to representatives of this culture. You either avoid or frequently confront colleagues who are most closely aligned with this culture. Your own efforts at institutional improvement are most often thwarted by those who seem to embrace the values and perspectives associated with this culture. We suggest that you turn first to this troublesome culture and only then to the other cultures, those with which you work easily and those with which you most often align yourself.

To get this self-reflective process started and help you decide the order in which you will choose to read the chapters contained in this book, we pose the following questions:

1. From the brief chapter descriptions that follow, which do you find most confusing or understand least well?
2. With which people, aligned with which culture, are you most likely to be in opposition?
3. Which set of cultural assumptions do you find least acceptable or least compatible with your own perspective on life in the academy?
4. Which culture do you know least about when it comes to its history, justification, and values?

5. When you think about the people in your institution with whom you are least likely to affiliate, which culture are they likely to align with?
6. Which culture is most likely to be a focus of negative humor and criticisms, and to be referred to as "those people," when you are talking with your friends and colleagues?
7. On an institutional level, which of these cultures is most likely to be blamed when things go wrong?
8. On a personal level, were you once aligned with any of these cultures but have since "abandoned" or reappraised it in recent years?

In addition to addressing these questions before proceeding further, you may also wish to take the Academic Cultures Inventory that you will find at the back of the book. For at least two reasons, you may decide to take the inventory both before reading the book and afterward. First, taking the inventory ahead of time will give you a cognitive link to the concepts in the text. Second, a view of your own data (and data from your colleagues) may be instructive.

We hope that this book assists you in your reflective endeavors and that you will be better able to engage all six cultures of the academy after reading our description of and our own reflective analyses of them.

Chapter Overview

After an introduction in which we set a framework for our analysis of organizational cultures in the academy, we devote the next six chapters to a description and analysis of each of the distinct cultures that we believe exist in American and Canadian higher education. We examine the distinctive history, perspectives, and values of each one. We agree that there is no type or classification aligned with specific cultures; indeed, a person's views may change over their careers.

In Chapter One we focus on the collegial culture. This culture finds meaning primarily in the disciplines represented by faculty in the institution. Those aligned with this culture value faculty research and scholarship as well as the quasi-political governance processes of the faculty. They also tend to hold assumptions about the dominance of rationality in their institution and conceive of their institution's primary enterprise as the generation, interpretation, and dissemination of knowledge, and as the development of specific values and qualities of character among young men and women who are future leaders of our society.

The managerial culture is featured in Chapter Two. Those aligned with this culture find meaning primarily in the organization, implementation, and evaluation of work that is directed toward specified goals and purposes; they value fiscal responsibility and effective supervisory skills; they hold assumptions about the capacity of the institution to define and measure its goals and objectives clearly; and they conceive of their institution's enterprise as the inculcation of specific knowledge, skills, and attitudes in students so that they might become successful and responsible citizens.

The developmental culture is described in Chapter Three. This culture finds meaning primarily in the creation of programs and activities furthering the personal and professional growth of all members of the academic community. Those aligned with this culture value personal openness and service to others, as well as systematic institutional research and curricular planning; they hold assumptions about the inherent desire of all men and women to attain their own personal maturation while helping others in the institution become more mature. From the perspective of the developmental culture, the institution's enterprise is conceived as the encouragement of potential for cognitive, affective, and behavioral maturation among all students, faculty, administrators, and staff.

The last of the four cultures originally presented by Bergquist (1992)—the culture of advocacy—is described in Chapter Four. This culture finds meaning primarily by establishing equitable and egalitarian policies and procedures for the distribution of resources and benefits in the institution. Those aligned with this culture value confrontation and fair bargaining among constituencies, primarily management and faculty or staff, who have vested interests that are inherently in opposition. They hold assumptions about the ultimate role of power and the frequent need for outside mediation in a viable academic institution; those aligned with this culture also conceive of the institution's enterprise as either the undesirable promulgation of existing (and often repressive) social attitudes and structures or the establishment of new and more liberating social attitudes and structures.

In Chapter Five we introduce the first of two new cultures. The virtual culture is one in which meaning is found by responding to the knowledge generation and dissemination capacity of the postmodern world. The global perspective of open, shared, responsive educational systems is valued in this culture, and those aligned with it hold assumptions about its ability to make sense of the fragmentation and ambiguity that exists in the postmodern world. Those aligned with the virtual culture also conceive of the institution's enterprise as linking its educational resources to global and technological resources, thus broadening the global learning network.

The tangible culture is described in Chapter Six. Depending on one's own perspective, this culture is either very old or quite new (emerging as a response to the virtual culture). The tangible culture finds meaning in its roots, its community, and its spiritual grounding. Those aligned with this culture value the predictability of a value-based, face-to-face education in a stable physical location and hold assumptions about the ability of established systems and technologies to instill the institution's values.

They conceive of the institution's enterprise as the honoring and reintegration of learning from a local perspective.

Finally, in Chapter Seven we offer specific suggestions on ways to engage the six cultures by taking an appreciative perspective and through the ironic management of the paradoxes and polarities that are inherent in the interactions among these six cultures. From appreciative and ironic perspectives, we suggest that any organizational change process should involve a greater understanding of contending points of reference, and as a result, a change in these points of reference. Members of the academy must change the ways in which they view paradoxes and polarities before attempting to somehow resolve those that they confront. In this final chapter we encourage readers to view and understand their academic institution from the point of view of those with whom they are most likely to disagree before attempting to overcome these disagreements. Given the strength of the six academic cultures we analyze in this book and the contentious relationships that often exist among them, both an appreciative and an ironic perspective seem appropriate and necessary.

Acknowledgments

A book of this length and scope requires the helping hands of many colleagues. We first wish to thank our colleagues from the Canadian higher education cohort group at the Professional School of Psychology: Linda Coyle, Anne Cumming, Jan Lindsey, Julia Martin, and Margo McMahon. Over the past eight years these academic leaders have been sources of both ideas and inspiration for the two of us. We also wish to thank participants in the focus group that was held on July 11, 2005; they offered a collaborative critique of this book in one of its early full drafts.

We are also intellectually indebted to Walter Truitt Anderson, who offered us many insights into the postmodern condition and introduced us to the work of Richard Rorty, which sets the stage for the last chapter of the book. Finally, we wish to express our deep indebtedness to our families. Our wives, children, and grandchildren have been there—waiting patiently for our attention—throughout the long hours of writing and rewriting this book.

About the Authors

William H. Bergquist is a widely published author, researcher, and scholar who has conducted research and scholarship in North America, Europe, and Asia. His forty-three published books (often with Jossey-Bass) and fifty plus articles address such diverse issues as the struggles of men and women recovering from strokes, and the experiences of freedom among the men and women of Eastern Europe following the collapse of the Soviet Union. *The Postmodern Organization* has been identified as one of the fifty classics in organizational theory, while *In Our Fifties* (with Klaum and Greenberg) was featured on *Good Morning America*. *The Vitality of Senior Faculty* (with Carole Bland) received the annual research award in 1998 from the American Educational Research Association, while *Designing Undergraduate Education* (with Gould and Greenberg) and *A Handbook for Faculty Development* (with Steven Phillips) have been widely acknowledged and cited as seminal publications in the field of higher education.

Serving as an international consultant, coach, and trainer to leaders in more than one thousand colleges, universities, corporations, government agencies, human service agencies, and churches over the past thirty-five years, William Bergquist has cofounded the *International Journal of Coaching in Organizations* (now in its fifth year of operation) and the International Consortium for Coaching in Organizations (a major collaborative initiative involving senior level leaders and organizational coaches from countries and diverse institutions throughout the world).

Dr. Bergquist has served as professor and educator in the fields of psychology, management, public administration, organizational development, and public policy in more than two dozen colleges, universities, and graduate institutions. The postsecondary institutions in which he has taught range from the University of California in Berkeley, California, to the Tallinn Polytechnic Institute in Tallinn, Estonia, and College One, an experimental liberal arts summer college held for three years at Bowdoin College in Brunswick, Maine.

Kenneth Pawlak is a teacher, consultant, and author. He was originally hired by Langara College to instruct in and supervise its program to prepare teacher assistants to work in special education settings in the public schools. He also worked for some time in employee development. More recently, he has been division chair, working with a variety of divisions in areas as diverse as nursing, human services, criminal justice, human kinetics, and creative arts.

Dr. Pawlak is the founder of the ParaEducators Network of British Columbia, an organization dedicated to the professional development of teacher assistants in the province. His background in the education of children with special needs has given him the opportunity to examine learning in close detail. He has been a regular participant on the B.C. Naramata Conference Committee on Inclusion. For thirty years, this conference gathered educators, governmental officials, and union representatives from across the province to examine their work with children with disabilities.

Dr. Pawlak is an instructional skills facilitator, has a certificate in executive coaching from the William James Institute, and an appreciative inquiry facilitator certificate sponsored by the League of Innovation and the Company of Experts. He initiated the British Columbia Appreciative Inquiry Network, an informal group of appreciative inquiry consultants who meet to communicate best practices and to share their applications of appreciative inquiry and the appreciative process in a variety of organizational settings.

He has consulted with higher education institutions on topics such as continuing education staffing, identity development for a higher education foundation, predicting educational futures, student engagement in learning, the student experience, curriculum development, learning outcomes, and prospect management.

Engaging the Six Cultures of the Academy

Introduction

In *The Four Cultures of the Academy*, Bergquist (1992) identified four different, yet interrelated, cultures found in North American institutions of higher education. These cultures have had a profound impact over the past half century on the ways in which campus leaders view their work in the academy, as well as the ways in which faculty members, administrators, and students perceive the potential for personal career advancement and institutional change. These four cultures also influence how those outside the academy perceive the purposes and appropriate operations of academic institutions, and how they believe they themselves should interact with these institutions.

Two of the four cultures may be traced back to the origins of North American higher education. They were identified by Bergquist as the *collegial culture* and the *managerial culture*. The other two have emerged more recently, partially in response to the seeming failure of the two original cultures to adapt effectively to changes in contemporary colleges and universities and partially in response to the changing status of academic institutions in today's society. The first of these more contemporary cultures was referred to as the *developmental culture* and the second was referred to as the *negotiating culture* (which in this volume we have renamed the *advocacy culture*).

In the current book, we propose that additional external influences in our global culture are pressing down on the academic institution, forcing it to alter the way it goes about its business, and two new cultures are now emerging as a result of these global, external forces. These two cultures interact with the previous four, creating new dynamics. The first of the two, the *virtual culture*, has been prompted by the technological and social forces that have emerged over the past twenty years. The second culture, the *tangible culture*, has perhaps existed in some form for quite some time, but has only recently been evident as a separate culture partly in response to emergence of the virtual culture. We include both U.S. and Canadian academic institutions in our analysis, in order to help make comparative sense of these six cultures, though we fully realize that in using the term *North America* we are neglecting higher education institutions in Mexico.

Three Social Structures in Interaction

We now live in a world that supports three different types of social structure: premodern, modern, and postmodern (Bergquist, 1993). Each of these social structures exists in the twenty-first century and often operates alongside the other two—thereby making our world particularly challenging with regard to the topics considered in this book: organizational culture, leadership, and higher education. *Premodern* social structures have been present for many centuries and exist today in both Western and Nonwestern countries. A vast majority of the people now living reside in this type of social structure. *Modern* social structures are also prevalent in all nations and have provided the base for most contemporary economic, technological, and higher educational systems. While *postmodern* social structures are also prevalent today throughout the world, we are not yet fully aware of the implications these social structures hold for our economic and technological systems during the remaining decades of the twenty-first century, nor can we yet be very definitive regarding the long-term implications for higher education institutions. Given that we will be engaging the concepts of premodern, modern, and postmodern throughout this book, we will briefly describe each one as it relates to the fundamental social structures of contemporary life.

Premodern Social Structures

This social structure goes by many names: traditional, primitive, developing, third world, agrarian, and neo-feudal. We have chosen to use the term *premodern* in large part because other terms tend to be value-laden or restricted to non-Western countries. Although some premodern (hunter-gatherer) societies are very loosely structured and formed around nomadic patterns of living (the gathering rather than extraction or cultivation of nature resources), most premodern societies that exist today are found in small villages or other close-knit communities and focus on the cultivation or extraction of natural resources (for example, agriculture, lumber, fish, minerals). Premodern societies are typically dependent on extended family systems. The extended family serves not only as the primary economic unit of the community, but also as the primary source of most social services, including education. There are no medical plans, disability plans, retirement plans, or social security systems in premodern societies—family members are expected to take care of their injured relatives and aging parents.

Bartering is the main unit of economic exchange in the premodern society. Premodern governmental institutions are typically minimal in size and scope—usually focusing exclusively on the protection of national boundaries against invasion. There may be a rudimentary community government system, such as a gathering of elders, a village council, or town hall meetings; but the primary authority resides within the family and in the informal control exerted by the most economically powerful families in the community. While most premodern societies are established in small communities, relatively large cities existed throughout the world long before the nineteenth-century advent of industrialization in Western Europe. Minimal effective government exists in these urban centers. Rather, tightly knit ethnic neighborhoods and religious organizations (as represented by cathedrals or temples) provide most of the order and services in the city.

Modern Social Structures

The shift from premodern to modern was made possible through the invention and availability of new technologies. The modern society was a by-product of Western industrialization. Extended families from premodern communities are broken up as younger members of the family are lured by the prospect of money and material possessions to the new urban centers of industry. A new form of community has been created (the suburb) and the new industrial worker has embraced a new commodity (money). Whereas banks exist in premodern societies primarily to serve the upper class, they play a much larger role in modern societies, serving not only as a safe repository for saved money but also as a source of unearned money. Monetary leverage becomes a valuable entity in these societies. Industrial workers substitute employment in modern institutions for their premodern reliance on the extended family. The modern worker also begins to look to government for basic social services: education, health, retirement. Citizens no longer look primarily to their family or to their church or other charitable institutions for support. Thus, we find in the modern society expansion not only in the size of private industrial institutions but also in the size and scope of public institutions.

With mass production comes a shift in focus from quality to quantity. Profit can only be made if there are large-volume sales to offset initial costs associated with purchase of mass production equipment. Where the premodern artisan typically only makes a product when it is requested and tends to custom-make each one, mass production processes call for uniformity of product and for interchangeable parts. The new emphasis on uniform production and marketing and sales sets the stage for new organizational roles that are not directly connected to the production process. These nonproduction roles in marketing, sales, and production control are soon complimented by another organizational role (manager), which is associated with the overall coordination of organizational functions.

Postmodern Social Structures

The new social structures into which the more privileged people of the world are moving offers a remarkable mosaic of the premodern, modern, and postmodern. New communities are being formed that in some ways resemble the premodern villages of olden times—yet these new communities are formed around electronic communication systems and the new digital economies of the twenty-first century and the ways in which these technologies have us interact with one another. The big businesses of the modern era continue to exist, but are now competing against or cooperating with small e-commerce businesses of the postmodern world. Economies exist not just nationally and internationally but also globally. Our new postmodern world comes to us with great promises, such as universal education, abundant food sources, and new forms of energy, as well as daunting challenges, including overpopulation, environmental collapse, virulent plagues, and destructive outsourcing. Each of these promises and challenges is global in nature and scope.

A level of cooperation that was never achieved in either the premodern or modern era between nation-states is now required. The new global village must create a new vision of the world and discover new strategies and answers while also honoring the wisdom and values of past eras. Our emerging postmodern era is perhaps best described as an *edgy* experience: we are poised on the edge of both chaos and order. We know something will come, yet do not know exactly what form the *new* will take.

In many cases, technology is the common element in bringing about the transition from premodern to modern and from modern to postmodern. New machine-based technologies created the industrial era, which transformed the ways in which people lived. Similarly, new digital technologies have encouraged or even required a postmodern transformation in the way people live and relate to one another. The most important of these breakthroughs have made workers and capital more productive, and brought us unprecedented wealth, unprecedented connectivity, and unprecedented confusion. This is the state in which we find ourselves today—and the state in which contemporary colleges and universities find themselves.

Transformations and Hybrids

The profound nature of the transformation premodern societies have gone through in their shift to modern social structures is being matched by the profound transformation that is required in the shift from modern to postmodern. Furthermore, the transformations from premodern to modern and from modern to postmodern are essentially irreversible. We can never go back to a former world—though we can (and inevitably will) borrow from previous social structures as we seek to create new forms to meet emerging needs and serve new functions. Although the past fifty years might best be described as an era of adjustment to new social conditions, the new era will not be composed entirely of new societal elements. Rather it will offer a hybrid of some of the very old, premodern elements of society, modern-day elements (as exemplified in many colleges and universities that reached their zenith during the second half of the twentieth century), and newly emerging elements that bear little similarity to either their premodern or modern day precursors.

Multiple Cultures in Interaction

In this book, we wish to move beyond a mere exposition of six organizational cultures. We wish to explore the mixture of these cultures in most academic institutions and the value of this mixture. Although most colleges and universities, and most faculty and administrators, tend to embrace or exemplify one of these six cultures, the other five cultures are always present and interact with the dominant culture. This is a particularly important premise for readers to consider, because some analysts of organizational culture believe that hybrid cultures are undesirable or symptomatic of a fragmented, troubled institution. William Tierney (1988, p. 7), for instance, states that "strong, congruent cultures supportive of organizational structures and strategies are more effective than weak, incongruent, or disconnected cultures." Toma, Dubrow, and Hartley (2005) similarly argue that a strong, coherent, and unified institutional culture greatly benefits an academic institution.

Ironically, in arguing for a strong, unified institutional culture, and documenting the case for such a culture through case studies and references to other studies, Toma, Dubrow, and Hartley are writing from their own particular cultural perspective: the managerial culture. Although we agree that a unified institutional culture can be of great value in strengthening an academic institution, we would caution against building a unified institution that is dominated by one culture (in this case, the managerial culture) and fails to honor the legitimate claims and considerable benefits provided by the other five cultures.

In making the case for multiple cultures inside an academic institution, we can point to the work of Robert Birnbaum (1988). Although not specifically a study of organizational culture, Birnbaum's richly textured analysis of four kinds of institutions identifies ways in which various types can be effectively integrated. Like Birnbaum, we believe that differences in institutional type are important and that variations in cultural composition underlie them. We acknowledge that the six cultures we have identified are often at odds with each other, yet all six must be brought into any dialogue aiming to create a *self-correcting, cybernetic* institution (to use Birnbaum's terms).

Bergquist suggested in *The Four Cultures of the Academy* (1992) that each culture has an "opposite" on which it depends and with which it shares many features and assumptions. Thus, the developmental culture, which has evolved primarily in response to faults associated with the collegial culture, is nevertheless dependent on the collegial culture and shares with it many values and perspectives. Similarly, the advocacy (negotiating) culture grew out of faculty opposition to the managerial culture but looks to it for identity and purpose and shares values and perspectives with it. In *Engaging the Six Cultures of the Academy* we similarly suggest that the tangible culture has reared its head in opposition to the virtual culture's lack of acknowledgment of the value of face-to-face or historical contact, but that they both need each other.

Organizational Cultures and Organizational Improvement

Interest in the study of organizational cultures is understandable because cultures provide a framework for creating order out of the complex and often baffling dynamics of organizational life. In the field of anthropology, culture is the conceptual foundation on which field observers base their explanations of the orderliness and patterning of individual and collective life experience. In organizational theory, culture has assumed a similar explanatory role. The term *culture*, however, is still vague and ill defined; hence, this term is not yet adequate to provide direction for an organization's managers, researchers, or consultants. More definitive categories must be identified that enable leaders to focus on and use tangible, observable phenomena. Because postsecondary educational institutions (and in particular, colleges and universities) have considerable influence on the character of a society's overall culture (Parsons & Platt, 1973), it is particularly important that we identify and attempt to understand the nature of these institutions' deeply embedded cultural properties.

Cultural Dynamics of Academic Institutions

The current book is informed by three definitions of culture that come from differing eras and perspectives. The first is offered by a noted cultural anthropologist and social historian, Bronislaw Malinowski (1948, p. 36). He defines culture as "an integral whole consisting of implements and consumer goods, of constitutional charters . . . of human ideas and crafts, beliefs and customs . . . a vast apparatus, partly material, partly human, and partly spiritual, by which man is able to cope with the concrete, specific problems that face him."

A second definition comes from an analyst of corporate cultures, Ronnie Lessem (1990, p. 8), who offers a developmentally oriented approach: "[An organizational culture] has to cultivate a humanly fulfilling context—a space and time—within which the production and consumption of needed, worthwhile, and quality products and services can take place." Our third definition comes from Edgar Schein (1992, p. 12), an organizational consultant and theorist, who articulated one of the most inclusive definitions of organizational culture: "[A] pattern of shared basic assumptions that the group learned as it solved its problems of external adaptation and internal integration, that has worked well enough to be considered valid and, therefore, to be taught to new members as the correct way to perceive, think, and feel in relation to those problems."

What do these seemingly disparate ideas have in common? Several features are noteworthy. All three definitions suggest that culture provides meaning and context for a specific group of people. The culture holds the people together and instills in them an individual and collective sense of purpose and continuity. This, in turn, helps reduce organization-induced anxiety (Bergquist, Guest, & Rooney, 2004). Academic institutions, in particular, are in the business of conveying and providing meaning not only to their students but also to their faculty and administrators—and ultimately to society as a whole.

All three definitions also suggest that a culture helps define the nature of reality for those people who are part of that culture. It provides lenses through which its members interpret and assign value to the various events and products of this world. If we are to understand and influence men and women in their daily work inside academic institutions, then we must come to understand and fully appreciate their implicitly held models of reality. Schein agrees with this view. "The bottom line for leaders," he writes (1992, p. 15), "is that if they do not become conscious of the cultures in which they are embedded, those cultures will manage them. Cultural understanding is desirable for all of us, but it is essential to leaders if they are to lead."

The final concept shared by these three definitions is perhaps the most important. It is that the culture provides guidelines for problem solving, and more generally, serves an overarching purpose—a dimension that is often ignored in cultural analyses. A culture is established around the production of something valued by its members. A culture does not exist for itself; rather, as Lessem (1990) notes, it exists to provide a context within which the primary intentions of the organization are fulfilled.

In preparing our own analyses of organizational cultures in the academy, we have built on a few preliminary analyses of organizational culture that have set the stage for our study. William Tierney (1988, 1990) has done a superb job of surveying existing research in the assessment of academic cultures (and climates) and identifying some of the critical tasks to be accomplished in establishing a body of literature in this field. Much of the other work done to date has focused either on the tools and concepts that are needed to do an adequate job or on the analysis of the culture that operates in a single institution at a specific point in time—usually in highly distinctive or innovative colleges (for example, Clark, 1970; Riesman, Gusfield, & Gamson, 1970). The present work builds on Tierney's recommendations, while moving beyond the preliminary, single-institution analyses.

Containing the Anxiety

In addition to understanding the cultures themselves and how they are formulated, it is important to consider how academic cultures can best be engaged—and this requires, in turn, that we appreciate the underlying purposes being served by these cultures. We propose that the containment of anxiety is the fundamental purpose for the formation and maintenance of organizational cultures. There is, of course, diffuse anxiety when faculty members work with students. Significant learning is never simple or easy. There is also anxiety at a second level, when the assumptions of one culture collide with those of other cultures—and these collisions are particularly prevalent when an academic institution is confronted with changing internal and external environments. A group forms assumptions and thus develops a culture as it learns to adapt to changing external circumstances and establish internal integration. When faced with the challenge of institutional change, those in the group feel better because the culture provides a solution, a way of perceiving, thinking, and feeling about the challenge they face.

Cultures do not change easily for a variety of reasons. Not the least of these reasons is the ability of cultures to assuage the anxieties and fears that develop as we adapt to external influences and internal change initiatives and as we seek internal integration. If the assumptions on which our culture is based are challenged through either external or internal situations or through an organizational change process, we tend to resist the challenges. We seek cognitive and emotional stability. We avoid the fear and anxiety of instability because they provoke pain, and we avoid pain. So we avoid change. Edgar Schein (1992) specifically suggests that people develop anxiety when their basic assumptions are unstable. The human mind needs cognitive stability. Therefore, any challenge to or questioning of a basic assumption will provoke anxiety and defensiveness. In this sense, the shared basic assumptions that make up the culture of a group can be thought of at both the individual and group levels as psychological defense mechanisms that permit the group to continue to function.

Culture provides a container. It establishes roles, rules, attitudes, behaviors, and practices. It describes ways for people to be safe. Culture provides predictability and ascribes importance to one's actions and one's presence in the world. It says that when you participate in this culture you are not alone—you are important! There are specific roles and responsibilities. A student should be able to depend on the faculty member's allegiance to the fundamental values of an academic culture. A faculty member should be able to rely on her colleagues. Culture provides meaning. In some higher educational institutions, education is expected to provide an opportunity for transcendence and personal growth; in others, it is something to be endured and gotten past as soon as possible in order for one to be formally certified or licensed. It is the faculty member's responsibility to ensure that meaning is borne in some way to the student. The faculty members' culture allows them to do their job—to work with students, to create new knowledge, and to share it with others.

The fundamental interplay between the containment of anxiety and the formation of organizational cultures was carefully and persuasively documented by Isabel Menzies Lyth (1992). She wrote about ways in which nurses in an English hospital cope with the anxiety that is inevitably associated with issues of health, life, and death. Menzies Lyth noted how the culture of the hospital in which the nurses worked helped ameliorate or at least protect the nurses from anxiety. She suggested that a health care organization is primarily in the business of reducing this anxiety and that on a daily basis all other functions of the organization are secondary to this anxiety-reduction function.

Reducing the Anxiety

Somehow a college or university that is inclined to evoke anxiety among its employees and students must discover or construct a buffer that both contains the anxiety and addresses the realistic, daily needs of its employees and students alike. How exactly does anxiety get addressed in organizations? Menzies Lyth suggested that it gets addressed through the "social defense system"—that is, the patterns of interpersonal and group relationships that exist in the organization. In his analysis of organizational culture, Schein (1999) suggests that the culture of an organization is the residue of the organization's success in confronting varying conditions in the world. To the extent that an academic organization is adaptive in responding to and reducing pervasive anxiety associated with the processes of teaching and learning, and related functions of the educational enterprise, the existing cultures of this organization will be reinforced, will deepen, and will become increasingly resistant to challenge or change.

Perhaps the leaders of contemporary colleges and universities can best reduce the fear of their faculty, administration, students, trustees, and community through bringing together the diverse perspectives of their institutions. Taken in isolation, each of the six cultures provides a vehicle that is only partially successful in reducing the fears and anxieties of people about their own learning and the processes of change in which they must engage. Furthermore, even when successful, each culture alleviates only the symptoms of the anxiety—not its ultimate source. Fear and anxiety will only be fully addressed when people feel they are being freely served with the skills, knowledge, strategies, and resources of all members of the academy—regardless of culture.

We believe that it is crucial to understand all six of the cultures so that one can operate effectively within and among them. With this knowledge one can also more effectively influence and improve the quality of change that is required in contemporary higher education. The message that we hope to convey in this book is not about eliminating or even criticizing any of the cultures. Rather, we seek to foster an appreciation of the unique features found in each culture and how these six cultures interact. If there is a sense of appreciation, each culture can become a force for improvement rather than destruction in our academic organizations and systems. Each culture can contribute to the learning of educators rather than reinforce limiting and inflexible assumptions about the nature and direction of the higher education enterprise.

1

The Collegial Culture

> *The collegial culture:* A culture that finds meaning primarily in the disciplines represented by the faculty in the institution; that values faculty research and scholarship and the quasi-political governance processes of the faculty; that holds assumptions about the dominance of rationality in the institution; and that conceives of the institution's enterprise as the generation, interpretation, and dissemination of knowledge and as the development of specific values and qualities of character among young men and women who are future leaders of our society.

Since American and Canadian higher education were first inaugurated in the colonial college, faculty members have worked predominantly in a collegial culture. Today, the collegial culture continues to hold sway over the norms and values of most North American colleges and universities. This culture encourages diverse perspectives and a relative autonomy in one's work. Relationships are informal, nonhierarchical, and long-term. Men and women who are successful in this culture usually are actively involved in or support from the outside the faculty governance processes of their institutions. Alternatively, they hold positions of high prestige based on scholarly activities, research, or longevity on the faculty. Leadership emerges from committee and deliberative group activities or from autonomous academic activities. While most employees in North American colleges and universities who are fully aligned with the collegial culture tend to come from the faculty, many members of the administrative and support staff often embrace and even help to sustain this culture.

Leadership that is based on scholarship and research became dominant with the emergence of the German-style research university in the United States in the mid-1800s and the Scottish university in Canada (modeled after Edinburgh) in the late 1800s. Leadership that emphasizes collaboration and quasi-political activities is directly influenced by the original colonial liberal arts college, which in turn is designed after the British universities at Oxford and Cambridge (often referenced by the contracted phrase *Oxbridge*). In Canada Edinburgh once again serves as the primary model for the liberal arts. The collegial culture in Canadian and American colleges and universities is thus based on the English, Scottish, and German models of higher education. Interdependence and collaboration are more actively supported by the British model, whereas faculty autonomy is more prevalent among institutions resembling the German and Scottish universities.

The British and Scottish Collegiate Models in Colonial North America

It is not surprising that colonial Americans and Canadians looked to Oxford, Cambridge, and Edinburgh when designing and establishing their first colleges. As Frederick Rudolph (1962) noted in his excellent history of American higher education, the original British university contained many elements that served as guidelines for the formation of Protestant (often rural) colleges in North America.

The British Model in Colonial America

Many characteristics of the collegial culture in Britain transferred to virtually all colleges and universities in both the United States and Canada. Several characteristics, however, were unique to the United States, whereas others were unique to Canadian colleges and universities. Parochialism, a focus on quality, and an emphasis on the liberal arts were much more prominent in early American higher education institutions than in their Canadian counterparts.

Controlling Environment. One of the most prominent characteristics of both the British university and early American colleges and universities was total control over the environment in which the young students lived and learned. Cohen (1998, p. 66) has suggested that "the concept of in loco parentis does not accurately describe the disciplinary measures the colleges attempted to install because most of them were considerably more stringent than parents would have prescribed." Residential living at the university was a given in both England and the colonial United States: "It is what every American college has had or consciously rejected or lost or sought to recapture.... Adherents of the collegiate way... pointed with satisfaction to the extracurriculum, to the whole range of social life and development, to the benefits of religious influence and orientation" (Rudolph, 1962, p. 89). Faculty members in America were expected to engage with their students in all aspects of life at the university, because a complete liberal arts education incorporated heart and muscle as well as mind. According to Rudolph (1962, pp. 136–137), the American colonial college "became an arena in which undergraduates erected monuments not to the soul of man but to man as a social and physical being."

Focus on Quality. In the United States a second characteristic—one that continues to be influential—was the English university's emphasis on complexity of thought and the educational process. Faculty and students were judged on their manner of thought and discourse rather than on the basis of any specific body of knowledge. Quality counted more than quantity.

The faculty was suspicious of any curriculum that was too practical, concrete, or contemporary.

Attention was directed, in particular, to the cultivation of quality in the students attending the American institution. In his study of the impact of the Oxbridge model on American colleges and universities, Alex Duke (1996, p. 46) notes that the Oxford or Cambridge man of the eighteenth century "displayed social and intellectual skills far beyond those of the typical American undergraduate. . . . [T]he exemplary Oxonian or Cantabridgian was at ease in social gatherings, well read, well spoken, and dedicated to assuming a position of leadership in his nation's service."

Emphasis on the Liberal Arts. It was assumed that the young men attending Oxford or Cambridge were already in a social position to obtain work after graduation. (And indeed, in those days, it was young men; very few women attended college.) Similarly, in the American colonial college, emphasis was placed on liberal education. The proponents of a liberal arts education who wanted to educate the whole individual agreed with Woodrow Wilson, then serving as president of a prestigious liberal arts institution, Princeton University, that "the college ought to cultivate the students' intellectual and spiritual life. 'What we should seek to impart in our colleges,' Wilson maintained, 'is not so much learning, but the spirit of learning.' In this vein, they saw the totality of college life, not just the classroom, as an instrument of personal development" (Duke, 1996, p. 40).

Although liberal arts colleges currently account for less than 5 percent of all baccalaureate degrees awarded in the United States, the foundations of higher education in the United States were laid down in the colonial liberal arts colleges. One can even declare, as have Koblik and Graubard (2000), that the liberal arts college has become uniquely American, for the British institutions soon grew much too large and embraced much too diverse a set of educational purposes to be defined anymore as a pure liberal arts college. Thus, although the American colonial college initially emulated the British liberal arts tradition, it soon stood alone in promulgating this tradition—and was soon to lose out (as in England) to the pressures of scientific research and technologies, the emergence of the course elective system, the demise of residential life on many campuses, and eventually, the democratizing emphasis on career preparation (Duke, 1996).

The Scottish Model in Canada

In Canada the collegial culture has its roots in the Anglican-dominated colleges and universities of eastern Canada. Generally speaking, the early colleges in Canada were religious and the universities were secular. There was a strong influence from the Scottish university model—and specifically the University of Edinburgh—in Canada, since the influential leaders were Scottish. Although a few American universities were also influenced by life at the University of Edinburgh (William and Mary) or the University of Aberdeen (College of Philadelphia) (Cohen, 1998), the English schools held sway during the early years of the American colonial college.

The Anglican church dictated the design of colonial institutions in British Canada, as well as their curricula. The Family Compact left the Anglican clergy in control of much of the early decision making in colonial Canada. They were in a minority even among the Protestants, but they were able to infuse an Anglican bias in Canadian colleges and universities. Different characteristics were borrowed by the colonial Canadians from the British universities—primarily because Canadians tended to emulate the University of Edinburgh rather than either Oxford or Cambridge. More like the German research universities, Canadian institutions relied on a curriculum that focused on the pure and applied sciences. Like the University of Edinburgh, Canadian universities and colleges focused on memorization and development of facts, and relied on lectures as the chief means of instruction. Furthermore, like the University of Edinburgh, Canadian universities tended to be less elitist, and from their founding, more democratic than either the Oxbridge or colonial American institutions.

Leadership in the Colonial College

Various properties of the English and Scottish academic culture were appropriated intact by leaders of the first colonial colleges in both America and Canada. Several characteristics of these colleges, however, were unique and not specifically borrowed from their distinguished sister institutions in Great Britain. The first colonial colleges—notably, Harvard and Yale—were led by strong presidents who dominated their institutions and considered faculty members to be hired underlings. Typically, the president of a colonial college himself taught the final course in the students' senior year to ensure that students left with the correct philosophy of life and appropriate ethical standards.

Jencks and Riesman (1968, p. 6) noted that college presidents in early American institutions were "far more domineering than they are today, carrying the business of the college around in their briefcases or even in their heads, entrusting very little to committees of faculty members or lower-level bureaucrats, and imposing their personal stamp on the entire college.... The vision of a college professor as an independent expert with a mission transcending the college where he happened to teach was almost unknown." Thus, in the early history of American and Canadian higher education, a precedent was set for strong administrative leadership and weak faculty influence. Rudolph (1962) even suggests that faculty in these institutions were extensively exploited by presidents and the boards of trustees that these presidents effectively controlled.

This precedent of having controlling presidents was soon overturned as the colonial institutions were secularized in both

Canada and the United States. The faculty in these institutions matured, became more firmly established, and began to influence the curriculum that they were asked to teach and monitor. Nevertheless, the role of a strong administrator, who rules by moral force and even fiat, continues to influence the professional lives of many leaders in contemporary postsecondary institutions. There is still room in many colleges and universities for a strong president—especially in those institutions that preserve a religious heritage, such as was found in the colonial colleges. This kind of strong collegiate leader gains authority because of his or her quality of thought and character. To use Max Weber's (1947) term, the effective colonial leader held *charismatic* power, rather than attaining authority from the presence of specific administrative expertise. Just as colonial college presidents taught the final course, so, according to the dictates of the colonial culture, ideal college presidents led their institutions by educating fellow administrators and faculty members and serving as an example to them. There is still the presence of (or at least the yearning for) charismatic leadership in many twenty-first-century colleges and universities.

The Colonial College's Relationship to Other Educational Institutions

Another distinctive characteristic of the colonial college in the United States (and a difference between it and Canadian colleges and universities) was its isolation from primary and secondary schools. When the American colonial college was being established, the only existing educational programs were offered to young men (and a few young women) who needed a rudimentary introduction to reading and writing in order to conduct commerce and read the Bible. Colonial colleges were established for older students, in part to provide teachers for those young students. These "college preparatory schools" filled the gap by expanding on the rudimentary elementary programs the young people had attended. They were, therefore, the precursors to today's high schools and junior high schools. Thus, an important characteristic of the American colonial college was its autonomy from lower levels of education. In general, administrators and faculty members in those colleges had not previously been employed in either elementary or secondary schools. Rather, they were specifically educated and prepared from the beginning (at first through the undergraduate colleges and later through graduate programs) to assume positions in colleges or universities. In Canada there was a stronger link with the secondary schools—representing the egalitarian spirit inherited from Edinburgh.

The Influence of the German Research Model

Clearly, certain aspects of the North American colonial college influenced the collegial culture of contemporary colleges and universities. Other powerful forces, however, had an even greater impact on these institutions, and in particular, their collegial culture. In the mid-nineteenth century, just at the time when the North American public, through its federal and state representatives, was expressing an increased commitment to higher education and giving newly formed universities a big boost (Cohen, 1998)—through the Morrill Land Grant College Act of 1862 in the United States—the leaders of many North American institutions were becoming enthralled with the achievements of German research universities. Brubacher and Rudy (1958, p. 171) noted that "the impact of German university scholarship upon nineteenth-century American higher education is one of the most significant themes in modern intellectual history. Just as the American college has derived its structure from an English prototype, so the American graduate school [and university] has taken its pattern from the Philosophical Faculty of the German university." Although there was some interest in the French university model, many North Americans were apparently turned off by

French liberalism and were enamored with the promise of major scientific and technological advances through the formation of powerful new universities (Cohen, 1998).

Unfettered Scientific Research and Faculty Dominance

The essential concept behind the German university system was that an institution of true higher learning should be, above all, the workshop of free scientific research. This university, unlike the American and Canadian colonial college, was dominated not by a willful president but by a willful and autonomous faculty. In their pursuit of knowledge for knowledge's sake, German faculty members were given great freedom in their selection of course offerings and their choice of scholarly projects. The German university, similar to the Scottish institutions, emphasized not only the liberal arts but also the sciences. Paradoxically, the German university—and later the American and Canadian research university—was both more theoretical and more practical in orientation than either the British university or the American colonial college.

The strange mixture of theory and application became even more pronounced in the American and Canadian university. The reputations of major midwestern research universities, such as the University of Michigan, the University of Wisconsin, and the University of Minnesota, and the University of Saskatchewan and the University of Alberta in Canada, were built on a solid record of technical achievement as well as scholarly excellence (Brubacher & Rudy, 1958).

Faculty and Discipline Focus

Another important characteristic of the German research university was its emphasis on the discipline and work of faculty members rather than the education of young people. Whereas

British universities and American colonial colleges were expressly devoted to educating their young students, the German research professors often found undergraduate education to be a nuisance. Leaders of the German research universities typically directed their most valuable educational resources to produce more researchers and scholars in order to expand their own influence and that of their particular fields of study.

In some ways, however, the German university resembled the British, Scottish, and American colonial institutions. Usually, only an established scholar or researcher was allowed to preside over these academic institutions. The German university also remained independent of elementary and secondary educational institutions. General education was considered the prerogative and responsibility of these lower-level institutions. In the United States, many nineteenth-century leaders of major research universities actually argued for the adoption of a six-year secondary school plan, such as was found in Germany. Such a plan would eliminate the first two years of undergraduate education at the university. This scheme led to the creation of two-year junior and community colleges (to which we turn in describing the managerial culture).

The Decline and Fall of the British Collegiate Model

Although the British and American colonial college models remained dominant in the small American and (to a lesser extent) Canadian liberal arts colleges through the mid-twentieth century, the German research university model reigned at most large, tax-supported universities and even at the larger, more prestigious private universities. The prevalent notion of quality among American and Canadian college and university leaders was built during the colonial era on the image of Harvard, Yale, Stanford, McGill, and other prestigious universities. These universities, however, converted from the British to the German prototype by the beginning of the twentieth century, and the notion of quality shifted in alignment with this conversion.

Shifting Role of Higher Education Institutions

The shift in the notion of quality occurred not only because the prestigious universities were changing their own orientation but also because the old elitist model of quality proved irrelevant in the design and creation of new colleges and universities that were serving an increasingly diverse population of young men and women:

> Once fully integrated into the American college—by the late nineteenth century—the blend of British, Scottish, French, and German influences combined with America's own Jeffersonian democratic ideals to produce in the twentieth century a new conception of college education based upon meritocratic standards. . . . More emphasis was placed on the development of intellectual skills so that college graduates would be able to keep up with an expanding body of information and facts. Moral training and education for personal growth became less prominent in the college. [Gaff, Ratcliff, & Associates, 1997, p. 56]

Whereas the more practical, career-oriented approach to college education was becoming more prevalent and putting the traditional British college out of business, the ultimate demise of not only the elitist liberal arts college model but also the British criteria of educational institutional quality can be blamed on the German research university. Jencks and Riesman (1968) note that the university college model, which emulates the German research university and defines its primary purpose as the preparation of students for graduate work, dominates North American higher education, even in the small state-supported and private colleges and universities where such a model is inappropriate.

Much of the growth in American higher education occurred during or immediately after the satellite *Sputnik* was launched—the 1950s—partially in response to the need for trained scientists and partially in response to the baby boom. As a result, a large proportion of the faculty members who now teach in American and Canadian colleges and universities received graduate training at a time when the German research university model was particularly prominent. Consequently, many of the tacit assumptions about the role of faculty in a postsecondary institution and about the proper place of an academic's discipline, scholarship, and research are based on the German model (Parsons & Platt, 1973).

Although the leaders of many smaller colleges and universities imitate the British university model because they are unable, financially or intellectually, to create a first-rate research university, they are inclined to view their own institutions as second-class. In his study of eight postsecondary institutions varying widely in size, programmatic emphasis, and structure, Warren Bryan Martin (1969) offered convincing evidence almost forty years ago on the extent to which the research university prototype—and more broadly, the collegial culture—dominates the consciousness of American faculty and academic administrators. Martin found that these academicians shared attitudes about "educational assumptions, values and goals; the criteria for institutional excellence; and the prospects for professional or institutional change" (p. 206).

The Elitist Backlash: Closing of the North American Mind

Although we must declare the British model of elitist education to be in profound decline, we cannot yet announce its death, for periodically there are groundswells of support for a traditional, highly selective liberal arts–based approach to undergraduate and graduate education. This elitist backlash is noteworthy in the popular writings of former U.S. Secretary of Education

Edward Bennett, in Allan Bloom's best seller *The Closing of the American Mind* (1988), and in the movement away from special focus programs (most often programs begun during the 1960s—such as women's or African American studies) to programs that emphasize the often Western culture–oriented "fundamentals."

In his sharp critique of contemporary American education, Bloom (1988) encouraged college and university leaders to reconsider their core requirements, the proliferation of electives, and an emphasis on career preparation. Although educators rarely harken back to the colonial roots of American higher education, they do reinvoke many of the values and aspirations of the colonial college and dress these values and aspirations in contemporary clothes (Garcia & Ratcliff, 1997). Although Bloom's work has been declared racist and elitist, it has opened a valuable dialogue about the values of traditional liberal arts education.

Living and Working in the Collegial Culture Today

What about life in the twenty-first-century college and university? Are there any sustained patterns in academic institutions that may be explained through understanding of the collegial culture? What about those institutions that are shifting way from this culture?

In most academic institutions, although its strength is diminishing, the collegial culture is still very powerful and has a strong influence on the ways in which faculty members interact, as well as on what they value and reward. We will explore several dimensions of the contemporary collegial culture to see how old patterns persist.

Disciplinary Orientation

Initially, the colonial college and university were institutions that welcomed teachers and students who wanted to explore many fields. However, the collegial culture soon began to place great value on faculty work directed toward disciplinary scholarship and research and the inculcation of a disciplinary orientation in students. This led to what Arthur Cohen (1998) called the *centrifugal curriculum*—with the compelling movement away from a coherent, universal core curriculum to a curriculum dominated by disciplinary requirements and electives. John Millett, president of Miami University, once spoke of the dominance of disciplinary specializations: "It is often said that faculty members have a major loyalty to their discipline or professional field of knowledge rather than to the college or university in which they practice their profession" (1962, pp. 70–71). His observations may still hold true today in many colleges and universities that are strongly influenced by the collegial culture. It is not just a matter of loyalty to a specific discipline but also a matter of diverse perspectives. Or to borrow from Cohen, it is a matter of "centrifugal" (divergent) professional identities among faculty members in different disciplines.

The study of intellectual revolutions by Thomas Kuhn (1970) suggests that disciplinary paradigms create a powerful identity among practitioners in a specific field of study. Rice (1986) similarly writes about this powerful identity (which he labels the "assumptive world of the academic professional") and describes ways in which faculty members are socialized in their discipline. The power of the discipline seems to be further reinforced and amplified by the housing of the discipline in a specific organizational structure—that is, the academic department. As Gumport and Snydman (2002) suggest, the academic structure of an institution plays a big role in shaping the boundaries and character of knowledge for those who work in the institution.

Although there is an overall pull toward disciplinary identification in most colleges and universities that are strongly influenced by the collegial culture, there are important differences in the strength of this identification among the various academic disciplines that affect all aspects of a faculty member's professional life, both inside and outside the classroom (Donald, 1997). Colbeck concluded:

> [T]he degree of paradigm consensus influences social relations among faculty and expectations for faculty behavior within a discipline . . . . Hard disciplines [physical sciences] are characterized by widespread agreement about curriculum content, research collaboration, competition for recognition and funding, clearly defined intellectual boundaries, and gate keeping of those boundaries by a powerful elite . . . . In contrast, low paradigm consensus or "soft" disciplines [humanities] consider knowledge as recursive; scholars use new lenses to explore intellectual territory already mapped by others . . . . Soft disciplines are characterized by idiosyncratic curricula, weak boundaries, independent research efforts, and tolerance for unusual ideas or methods. [1998, p. 651]

Colbeck comes to a particularly important conclusion: opportunity for integration of teaching and research is much greater among faculty in the soft disciplines than among faculty in the hard disciplines. "The knowledge and social structures of hard disciplines," according to Colbeck (1998, p. 651), "appear to define faculty work behavior more rigorously than the knowledge and social structures of soft disciplines. Faculty in hard disciplines, therefore, may have fewer opportunities to integrate teaching and research than faculty in soft disciplines."

Research and Scholarship Orientation

The search for a way to integrate teaching and research has long been postponed because of the collegial culture's long-standing emphasis on research and scholarship, usually at the expense of teaching. Faculty members in many colleges and universities still find it very difficult to integrate their interest in research and scholarship with their teaching interests, and the latter suffered when these faculty members were given the opportunity, through their various grants, to do more of the former. Why the long-standing emphasis on research? We believe that the dominance of research is due in large part to the emergence of the German research university as the prevalent model of prestigious higher education, and the reinforcement of this status by the collegial culture that continues to pervade most institutions of higher education.

This shift is not inevitable. Twenty-first-century faculty members can integrate their diverse interests in teaching, research, and scholarship. There has been renewed interest in integrating teaching and research. This renewed interest began with Ernest Boyer's (1990) proposal on the scholarship of teaching, and the growing interest among academics in using research methodologies to improve the quality of their teaching (Cross, 1990). This recent emphasis on scholarship and research associated with teaching flies in the face of the collegial culture's emphasis on research (particularly in the hard disciplines) and scholarship (particularly in the soft disciplines), and reinforces the interdisciplinary orientation of the developmental culture (to which we turn in Chapter Three). Although the bow to teaching is certainly in keeping with the British tradition and the soft disciplines, it requires a shift in attention away from one's home discipline, unless one's discipline is education or the behavioral sciences. This is unacceptable, because all elements of the collegial culture veer toward a disciplinary orientation. Ultimately, research and scholarship are placed at a higher point in the hierarchy than either teaching or community service, which are the other two elements in the traditional collegiate trinity.

When viewed from the perspective of the British and German models of higher education, the strong emphasis on disciplinary loyalty in the collegial culture seems to have produced a division in the lingering influence of these two models based on the faculty member's discipline (Kreber & Cranton, 2000). Faculty members in the hard disciplines seem to adhere to the German research model, with a relative deemphasis on teaching and upholding strong paradigmatic strictures and structures. Conversely, faculty in the humanities seem to be the keepers of the British flame, emphasizing teaching as it intermingles with their own interests in research and scholarship, and leading in recent years to the new, so-called scholarship of teaching and greater attention to classroom research.

Faculty Autonomy

No matter whether they emphasize research, scholarship, or teaching, all members of the collegial culture value autonomy. They value it so much that, unlike most other professional groups, faculty members have never appealed to their local, state, or federal government for regulation or for assistance in monitoring admission to the field. There are no medical exams, bar exams, or licensing requirements for faculty members (Cohen, 1998). This kind of autonomy parallels the more general and unique autonomy of American colleges and universities in our society (Ben-David, 1972). When academics in the collegial culture are reviewed for promotion and tenure, their accountability rarely extends to direct observation of faculty performance in the classroom or to assignment of priorities to specific research or scholarship activities. Many faculty members in the collegial culture would take great offense at being asked, let alone required, to accept an observing colleague in their classrooms. Ironically, even though classroom teaching is certainly a public event, it is considered an intimate exchange between faculty member and student. This exchange might be profoundly disrupted if observed and judged by another faculty member.

The value of autonomy is particularly manifest in and reinforced by the doctrine of *academic freedom*. This is one of the dominant norms of the collegial culture. It originates, according to Millett (1962, p. 56), in the distinctive role of American colleges and universities as vehicles for social change in our society: "The whole concern in the United States and in the Western world with academic freedom is an effort to acknowledge the unique relationship between higher education and society. Higher education is dangerous." Statements like this are reinforced throughout the collegial culture by its emphasis on "pure scholarship" and reason. Faculty members are given the freedom to choose the area in which they will conduct research as long as it lies within their disciplinary domain. If colleges and universities are truly sources of change for contemporary society, then academic freedom becomes essential to safeguard the society as well as the academy. Unfortunately, this freedom and the underlying assumption about the academy as an agency of social change and a moral force in society are upheld at a price. They tend to isolate the academy and its faculty members from mainstream life in North America. Both perpetuate a destructive isolation of the academic from the nonacademic world.

Academic freedom translates on a daily basis into an emphasis on independent work and the right to be different in dress, manner, and even professional interests. Millett (1962, p. 62) identified the strength of this individualism in the collegial culture and related it directly to the basic mission of the postsecondary institution: "The goal of the academic community is to provide an environment of learning, not a product of learning. Knowledge is acquired by individuals." Millet further suggested: "The goal of education is realized in individuals. It is conceivable that the learning process could be carried on with just one scholar and one student" (1962, pp. 68–69). For many faculty members, one of the most attractive features of the collegial culture is this tolerance for and even encouragement of autonomous activity. Whereas the other academic cultures, and most of the other dominant cultures in our society, reinforce collaboration and corporate activity, the collegial culture nurtures the "lone wolf," the "eccentric," and the socially oblivious "absent-minded professor." In his humorous but thoughtful book titled *The Academic Tribes*, Hazard Adams (1976, p. 13) notes that in higher education, "eccentricity is not merely tolerated, it is positively admired."

Prestige and Dominance of Large Research Universities

An even deeper and (some would say) pernicious aspect of the collegial culture is its alignment with values and perspectives that are decidedly male-oriented. Eisler (1987) describes two worlds, one of them forged on the masculine anvil of competition and hierarchy, the other forged on the feminine anvil of collaboration and egalitarianism. She uses the metaphor of the blade (quest for dominance) and the chalice (search for a holding and supportive environment) to distinguish these two worlds—while suggesting that neither is occupied solely by one gender (see, for example, Gilligan, 1982, and Belenky et al., 1986, in their studies of feminine and masculine epistemology).

Quite clearly, the traditional collegial culture is a world of the blade, with a strong emphasis on often subtle but nevertheless quite powerful competition and striving for prestige and dominance. During the twentieth century this competitive commitment occupied the primary attention of many traditionally male faculty members who could rely on a wife (and other family members) to fulfill most domestic obligations (Gappa, Austin, & Trice, 2007). Apparently, this division of labor has not completely died with the liberation of gender-based roles: "The traditional academic career leading toward tenure continues to be one that is based on a male model and on men's normative career path [which requires that the faculty member] is free from competing family responsibilities because those are handled by someone else" (Gappa et al., 2007, pp. 75–76). Because this career path is still normative—especially for faculty on tenure track—the female faculty member often faces the prospect of abandoning hopes for marriage and children.

The blade (and not the chalice) prevails at the institutional level as well as at the individual faculty member level. It is not just a matter that some faculty members succeed by devoting their lives to the pursuit of tenure and disciplinary status, it is also the case that entire institutions compete with one another and can be placed on a hierarchy from high levels of prestige to low levels—and the general public is very aware of this hierarchy. The large research university is placed at the top of the collegial culture's pyramid, and the liberal arts college, along with other types of colleges, including community colleges and vocational colleges, are placed at much lower points on the pyramid. There is something inevitably attractive about university status for any postsecondary institution that is saturated by the collegial culture.

Research Is King. The prestige and dominance of the research university comes not just from the triumph of the German model of higher education over the British liberal arts education model but also from other factors that are directly aligned with the values of the collegial culture and the aspirations of those members of the academy who dwell in this culture. First, it is important to note that there is no national university in either the United States or Canada. Although there have been numerous proposals over the years for a "federal" university in both countries, this has never occurred. Instead, there are a few highly visible private and state-supported public institutions that serve a national and even international purpose. To claim this greatly expanded leadership role in American and Canadian higher education, these institutions must do something better than any other institutions do—and this something is basic research. Quite clearly, major universities are more successful in sponsoring research and scholarship than most liberal arts or community colleges. Since research is at the top of the list in the collegial culture, it stands to reason that those universities which are held in high regard by the general public should also be those that are saturated by the collegial culture.

Powerful Academic Disciplines. Not only is research king in the highly prestigious universities, but academic disciplines are the powerful fiefdoms in which this research reigns supreme. The disciplinary orientation of the collegial culture is likely to be nourished more in the traditional university than in the traditional liberal arts college—and much more than in the two-year community college or vocational college. This is a second reason why universities hold the top position in the collegial pyramid. It is much more likely that each discipline will have its own department in a large university than in a smaller (and often financially strapped) liberal arts or community college.

Autonomy. The third reason why research universities tend to hold a higher position than liberal arts and community colleges in the collegial culture involves the norm of autonomy. Faculty members are more likely to be left alone to do their work in a large university than in a college. Even in a large community college or liberal arts college, faculty members usually have heavy committee assignments and live in a much more "intimate" and engaging setting than faculty members who work in more disengaged, or even alienating, universities.

Collegially Oriented Leadership. A fourth reason for the prestige of the large research universities is the collegially oriented leadership found there. Frankly, the high-level "administrators" in most universities are not required to do much administration. Those who actually run the university are often substantial in number and highly competent, since they are often well-paid and have considerable job security in these well-heeled institutions. Conversely, the administrators of liberal arts colleges often have to serve as real-life administrators, monitoring expenditures, managing staff, and overseeing the implementation of institutional policies and procedures. The administrative staff in these often financially strapped colleges is usually small in number, overworked, and insecure about the college's future. The emphasis on administrative tasks is even more the case in community colleges—where the managerial culture is more prominent and academic administrators are more oriented toward this type of work.

Ability to Carry Out Research. The fifth reason for the prestige of the research university aligns directly with the collegial culture's deemphasis on teaching—especially undergraduate teaching. The university is much more likely than either the liberal arts college or the community or vocational college to have substantial external revenues that are not directly tied to the teaching and learning enterprise. Universities are likely to have large endowments, receive research grants and funds to conduct scholarly activities, and support various profit-making ventures, such as "big-time" college athletics and many forms of continuing education. Independent liberal arts colleges are usually dependent on tuition. Even public universities are much less tied to governmental appropriations, which are usually aligned with teaching, learning, and career preparation, than are either public community colleges or private (or public) liberal arts colleges. The government funds that private colleges receive—in the form of government-sponsored student loans—are tied directly to student satisfaction with their education.

Bigger Is Better. The remaining three reasons for the prestige of the big research universities concern the relationship between the postsecondary institution and society. These reasons involve not only the collegial culture's values and priorities but also the broader social context in which this culture operates—and ultimately the emphasis on dominance and prestige that characterize Eisler's masculine culture ("the blade"). Universities are usually bigger than the colleges against which they are compared—and that means that they are seen as better in a society where "big is always better." The collegial and managerial cultures tend to agree in this one area, thereby adding even more weight to the prestige factor. When we turn in Chapter Six to one of the two new cultures—the tangible culture—we will see yet another expression of this preference for large size. The tangible culture values the physical assets that usually accompany the large university: an expansive and beautifully landscaped campus, imposing buildings, and substantial library holdings.

Public Expectations of Postsecondary Institutions. The seventh reason for the university's pride of place concerns the multiple expectations held by the general public in both the United States and Canada about the purposes to be filled by postsecondary institutions. Universities are much better equipped to handle the many different demands of the society in which they are situated than are colleges. Furthermore, they can handle these demands without sacrificing the fundamental values of the collegial culture. Money from one source in a university can often be diverted to support other programs—those most valued by the collegial culture. Most universities have traditionally been able to use profits from their high-priced (but prestigious) career-oriented programs to support the humanities, and they can afford endowed chairs, special library and museum collections, and distinguished visiting professorships—all of which are greatly valued by members of the collegial culture—because they were generating substantial funds through many diverse sources. Very few liberal arts colleges or community colleges can afford these academic luxuries, nor have they been able to be "all things to all people."

Ability to Broaden Scope. Finally, the university has been able to outperform and overshadow the liberal arts college and community college—at least from the perspective of the collegial culture—because it can readily broaden both its internal and external scope of operations. Universities can not only expand laterally, by adding more departments and special programs, and expand vertically, by adding higher-level degree programs, but can also expand outward from their home bases. Universities are often positioned to offer a broader range of field placements, internships, and residencies than can most liberal arts and community colleges. This capacity for breadth places the university at a distinct advantage from the perspective of the collegial culture. It takes some pressure off faculty members who are oriented to research and scholarship rather than teaching. To put it bluntly, many collegially aligned faculty members would love it if their students could "learn from someone else for a while!" The broad outreach of the university also engenders more financial support, which, in turn, means that faculty members can expect greater administrative support, fewer student contact hours, and more funds for events that bring prestige to the university.

The Collegial Pyramid and the Megauniversity

Major public universities in both the United States and Canada that are funded by state or provincial dollars have taken the place of nationally funded institutions. The large tax-supported universities are accompanied by large private universities that were once affiliated with a religious denomination but are now funded by a mixture of private and public dollars. Such megauniversities as Harvard, Yale, the University of Michigan (and other Big Ten schools), the University of California and UCLA in the United States, and McGill, the University of Toronto, and the University of British Columbia in Canada began to serve regional, national and international needs by the middle of the twentieth century. These institutions, which probably number fewer than fifty in all, now serve as de facto national universities for both the United States and Canada.

There is even greater breadth today in these megauniversities as they become international in scope, serving the research, scholarship, educational, and community service needs of people in many different countries and representing many different societies and cultures. It is not uncommon to read that a newly inaugurated leader of a Third World country received his or her education at a North American university. Young men and women from many countries around the world—even those that are hostile to American interests—are sent to American or Canadian universities for a prestigious education. Research contracts and scholarly projects in North American universities are often global in perspective or are focused on regional issues from outside the North American continent, and in these cases, often funded by the outside sources.

All of this is directly aligned with the values of the collegial culture and the academic aspirations of those who are aligned with this culture. The international scope of the megauniversity adds to its prestige, while leaders of the university further diversify sources of funds and its faculty members are provided with an even broader range of opportunities for research and scholarship. The potential for international travel and study makes the university more attractive to prospective students. Although students choosing to attend a major university may have to sit through some dull lectures taught by graduate students in very large lecture halls, they anticipate a chance to study or work in an exotic location and interact with other students from many other countries. Whether or not this expectation will ever be realized, prospective students enroll in the university with a willingness to tolerate an environment that is dominated by the collegial culture—a culture that is led by faculty members who are unlikely to place any of them at the top of their list of priorities.

Thus, the collegial culture thrives, and the megauniversity becomes a world that is highly attractive to many people, and not just academicians. This academic sanctuary seems in many ways to be a throwback to another place and time. As Brent Ruben (2003, p. 27) suggests: "The ivory tower presents an image of the academy as a place that is different and disconnected, a sort of academic fantasyland where students prepare for their transition into the so-called real world. It's an interesting image."

Institutional Influence and Change

How is influence exerted and how is change initiated in institutions with strong collegial cultures? Is the answer to be found in leadership? Faculty members who dwell primarily in a collegial culture generally assume that effective leadership is exerted through the complex give-and-take of campus politics. General education programs are created that serve to protect disciplinary turf. Negotiations take place inside and outside interminable and frequent curriculum committee meetings. Personnel reviews of faculty occur in multitiered, unpredictable committee meetings that incorporate both subtle horse trading and thoughtful discussion about the ultimate merit of the diverse activities and accomplishments in a faculty member's portfolio. The successful faculty leader at any institution dominated by the collegial culture will have learned how to live in and even enjoy these committee meetings and will have gained power by working skillfully inside this structure as well as working outside it by meeting individually with colleagues and making artful use of memoranda, agendas, action-oriented proposals, and multiple e-mails.

These political skills are not easily gained, and a faculty member's credibility is not readily built. As a result, most faculty members do not gain much power until they have served in a specific higher education community for many years. Until the late 1970s, the result was that each college and university had its own built-in hierarchy. Old, skillful, knowledgeable faculty members sat at the top of the pecking order and new, inexperienced faculty members sat at the bottom.

Several factors are now disrupting or soon will disrupt this hierarchy. First, with the decrease at most institutions in new positions and the severely reduced mobility of most academics, there are fewer young, inexperienced faculty members to take their place at the bottom of the pecking order. Second, this static situation may be short-lived, because as many senior faculty members begin to retire there will inevitably be an influx of new faculty members (Bland & Bergquist, 1997). Third, even with the influx of new faculty members, it is not clear that they will have much power in their institution because many of them may be part-time and may not be appointed to tenure-track positions. We turn more fully to this issue in our discussion of the virtual culture in Chapter Five.

A faculty member who tacitly accepts the norms, values, and rules of precedence of the collegial culture will usually assume that institutional change takes place primarily through—and power resides in—the quasi-political, committee-based, faculty-controlled governance processes of a college or university (Millett, 1962). All faculty members expect that all members of their community will recognize the important role played by them and offer them dignity and consideration. Faculty members do not think of themselves as employees of a college or university. Because of the real or imagined power of faculty governance, collegial academics believe that the road to increased influence comes through assuming leadership—usually acting as chairpersons of major college or university-wide committees. On many campuses, a faculty senate presides over the affairs of the institution. On other campuses, one or more faculty members sit on the president's cabinet as the university's central decision makers.

Conclusions

Faculty members in a collegial culture face a formidable task: how to judge the effectiveness, let alone worth, of subtle and complex endeavors such as basic research, service to other people, and in particular, classroom teaching. It is very tempting for these faculty members to search everywhere for some clear indicators of achievement and quality—even if these indicators seem at times to be trivial or a bit off the mark. In keeping with the German research university tradition, many college and university faculty members look primarily to non-teaching-related criteria, even if their institutions are primarily in the business of teaching and learning.

These faculty members tend to see themselves and their colleagues as effective if they have established a strong publication record in refereed journals, a large percentage of their undergraduate students decide to attend and are accepted into prestigious doctoral programs in their discipline, they have chaired major institution-wide committees or wielded informal influence in their deliberations, and their teaching is heavily oriented toward advanced undergraduate or graduate courses. Some faculty members and academic administrators (particularly those from the developmental culture) suggest that publications play a major role in faculty review procedures precisely because publication outputs are readily quantifiable and enable a faculty member's colleagues to avoid making qualitative judgments. It is this ambiguity about accountability in the collegial culture that has moved many administrators, and faculty too, both often under pressure from a demanding citizenry, toward a quite different culture—the managerial culture.

2

The Managerial Culture

> *The managerial culture:* A culture that finds meaning primarily in the organization, implementation, and evaluation of work that is directed toward specified goals and purposes; that values fiscal responsibility and effective supervisory skills; that holds assumptions about the capacity of the institution to define and measure its goals and objectives clearly; and that conceives of the institution's enterprise as the inculcation of specific knowledge, skills, and attitudes in students so that they might become successful and responsible citizens.

The managerial and collegial cultures stand out as the twin pillars of twentieth-century higher education in the United States and Canada, with the managerial culture holding up an increasingly larger proportion of the weight during the last half of this century. Much as the collegial culture is a hybrid of the British, Scottish, and German university models, the managerial culture originates in several types of postsecondary institutions in the United States and Canada. One of the points of origin for the managerial culture is the Catholic college and university in the United States and Canada. The other is the Canadian and American community college.

Although the rural, Protestant colonial college actually preceded and helped determine the nature and purpose of the colonial high school—as was noted in Chapter One—the urban Catholic college in America was an extension of the established elementary and secondary schools. These schools were run by various teaching orders of priests and nuns, originally to prepare individuals for religious service, and then to serve city youth from the lower socioeconomic classes. Coming out of the elementary-secondary school tradition and building on the accepted hierarchy of the teaching orders and the church, the Catholic college was created based on the assumption that lines of authority should be clear and that formally designated administrators of the institution should have control over the planning and managerial functions of the college.

Similarly, community colleges in the United States and Canada grew out of the elementary and secondary school systems of their communities. They were managed like other educational institutions in the local school system. Faculty members were trained as teachers rather than as scholars or researchers. Administrators were just as likely to have received their advanced degrees in higher education as in a specific academic discipline. Offering courses in areas where clear curricular guidelines could be defined and where the desired competencies of students could readily be specified, these colleges focused on vocational preparation, as did many of the Catholic colleges. First established in the latter part of the nineteenth century, community, or junior, colleges have become a major component of American and Canadian higher education over the past sixty years. Together with Catholic colleges and universities, community colleges have been the primary source of the managerial culture in higher education. This culture, in turn, has become increasingly influential in Canada and the United States and has generally become as prominent as the collegial culture.

In the managerial culture, educational outcomes can be clearly specified and criteria for judging performance can be identified and employed. Faculty members are effective as leaders if they are successful in fiscal and personnel management—often in the role of department chairperson. Academics in this culture often assume that the best way to influence their institutions is through movement into an administrative position. Usually, these faculty members do not bother with faculty governance processes and consider these processes to be inefficient and a waste of time. In preparation for a future role as administrators, managerially oriented faculty members argue from the perspective of cost containment, feasibility, and specifiable outcomes.

Faculty members in the managerial culture often teach using instructional materials that have been prepared by other people. The act of instructional design is frequently separated from the act of teaching; these two sets of skills are often viewed by the managerial faculty member as distinct. In their broader instructional role, managerial faculty members are inclined to devote considerable time and attention to specifying educational objectives or outcomes, sequencing autonomous instructional units, and selecting and using instructional methods that draw on resources extraneous to them. The faculty member's teaching role may even be considered dispensable, and the faculty member may act instead as instructional systems manager or facilitator.

Origins of the Managerial Culture I: The Catholic Church

Catholic higher education first began to play a significant role in Canada and the United States during the mid-nineteenth century, when many immigrants arrived in North America and either settled in the major cities of the East or migrated to the West. "With the massive immigration of the mid-century, the founding of Catholic colleges accelerated," observed Philip Gleason (1967, p. 17). "The single decade of the 1850s saw as many new institutions as had been founded in the previous sixty years."

Serving the Underserved and Unassimilated

North American Catholic colleges and universities were clearly committed from the first to serving the underserved. They also served those immigrants who were not easily assimilated into mainstream North American society because of either language or culture. As with the hospitals and welfare agencies it created, the Catholic church adopted various paragovernmental functions after it found that the formal governmental agencies of the cities were not serving their parishioners effectively (Jencks & Riesman, 1968). The existing suburban Protestant colleges were not accessible to the impoverished (or even wealthy) Catholic parishioners, more because of geographic location and cost than because of any religious discrimination. As a result, the teaching orders of the Catholic church themselves established colleges and universities for both men and women.

In Canada a division of language and culture accompanied the religious division. The Protestants were predominately English-speaking, and their colleges were controlled by the Anglicans even though Anglicans were a minority of Protestants. The Catholics were predominately French-speaking. French colleges were allowed, but they were not supported by state funds. This meant that the government could not control their curriculum, and for many years their credentials fell short of governmental requirements. Though Catholic colleges in Canada offered schooling to the urban poor and disadvantaged, there was very little public appreciation of or support for these valuable services.

Similarly, in the United States, Catholic colleges aided the Catholic church in supporting ethnic minorities who found little government support—in large part because they wielded little political power. Only when the number of Irish immigrants reached a critical mass in American society and readily accepted Protestant-American customs, in part because they already spoke English, did Catholic institutions and Catholic immigrant needs receive much public support in the United

States. As Philip Gleason noted, the Catholic immigrants themselves often did not help matters:

> The cultural assimilation of the church was delayed for generations by the coming of the immigrants because they made it an entirely different kind of social organism. Instead of remaining a small group much like other Americans in social background and outlook, little disposed to call attention to themselves in matters where they differed from the majority, Catholics became almost overnight a throng of foreigners who were poor, uncultivated, and sometimes aggressive in demanding that their religious rights be respected. [1967, p. 20]

The isolation of their institutions was further enforced by the desire of Catholics to support their own independent educational institutions. Although their support fueled the creation and maintenance of these institutions, this support led, as in Canada, to the assignment of second-class citizenship to these institutions (Gleason, 1967).

Assimilation and Isolation

Unlike Protestant institutions, the Catholic college served mainly as a vehicle for the upward mobility of its students. Whereas Protestants initially tended to come to North America to escape religious or political persecution, Catholics sought vocational and economic improvement (Jencks & Riesman, 1968). The Catholic colleges of North America reflected this orientation. From the first, they directed their efforts to occupational preparation. The traditional, gentlemanly liberal arts of the Protestant colleges never caught on in Catholic institutions. The skills being taught in the Protestant liberal arts curriculum were meant for youth whose parents had already guaranteed their place in society. Catholic college students had not found their niche and expected the college to give them an opportunity for social mobility.

This push toward social mobility was clearly a move toward assimilation into the dominant North American culture. Ironically, as Catholic-sponsored institutions, the colleges that existed primarily to support this upwardly mobile assimilation also continued to support social and cultural isolation through the promulgation of both Catholic and ethnic traditions and values. Again, Gleason offers great insight in this regard:

> Insofar as the schools dealt with the past, the immigrant's desires were anti-assimilationist in tendency—the knowledge, values, and traditions he wanted to see preserved and transmitted were those of the ethnic group. Thus the young would grow up with a sense of common identity and an awareness of the links that bound them to the generation of their fathers. But in respect to the preparatory function of education, the immigrant's expectations were assimilationist in tendency—he wanted schools that would give children the best preparation for success in life, and to do that the schools had to transcend the narrow horizons of ethnic consciousness. Just as the individual immigrant was torn between the drive to improve his status and the desire to maintain the familiar ways of the past, so the schools of the immigrants were called on to meet two conflicting requirements—to keep alive an alien past and to prepare the young for the unpredictable demands of a strange and novel society. [1967, p. 23]

We will see this dilemma frequently recur in the history of the managerial culture in North American postsecondary education. Through both the Catholic church and community colleges, the managerial culture has always been in the business of promoting upward social mobility through vocational education and the granting of credentials and degrees. However, there has always been a counterbalancing desire to keep the new graduates in the local community as advocates for and leaders of the socioeconomic or distinctive ethnic or racial groups the institution serves.

The advocacy culture broke off from the managerial culture in part because of this tension: If a college or university is seeking to move its graduates "up and out" of their current social class, then is the sponsoring community truly being served by these goals? Individuals who are aligned with the advocacy culture often propose that upward social mobility meets individual student needs but not the needs of the sponsoring community. As the advocacy culture gets stronger, the managerial culture retreats from its paradoxical position: it can now abandon its concern for the interests of the community, because they are in the capable hands and heart of the advocacy culture. Thus, colleges that are dominated by the managerial culture are free to focus on upward social mobility for all of their students—they can focus on outcome measures of success and quality—and on the enhancement of their own societal prestige, often resulting in efforts to shift from college to university status. The community may be sacrificed, but the needs of the college or university and its students are met.

Because Catholic colleges primarily served poor students who lived nearby, usually in urban environments, there was also less inclination to make the undergraduate experience residential. Although many Catholic colleges had dormitories, these institutions primarily served commuter students who lived at home and often worked in addition to attending college. The *collegiate way* that Rudolph describes in conjunction with the Protestant college (and the collegial culture) was simply not among the experiences of a great majority of students in Catholic colleges. Rather, to play on Rudolph's term, this was the *commuter way* (Rudolph, 1962). Early Catholic colleges more closely resembled urban rectories than ivy-covered, rural colleges. Most of the Catholic college student's learning took place in the college classroom, not through extracurricular activities. Even more was learned through the combination of classroom knowledge and experience gained out in the world. Students learned as much from their parents, who were without a college education and often had a limited command of the English language, from jobs, and from contemporaries who were not attending college, as they did from their instructors and fellow students.

Catholic Leadership

The Catholic college differed from Protestant institutions in the extent of clerical control over its academic and nonacademic affairs. After the early colonial years, during which ministers were often presidents, lay presidents typically ran Protestant colleges. These institutions were also governed by lay boards of trustees. Laymen were attractive because they had money and were expected to provide financial support to the college. By contrast, Catholic colleges and universities were led in many instances by clerics (priests and nuns); moreover, the boards of trustees at these institutions were, until very recently, populated by other clerics from the teaching order that had founded and provided funds for the college.

Catholic colleges have never established a tradition of direct lay financial support, relying instead on financial support from the church, which, in turn, elicited funds from the laity. In being directed by clerics, the Catholic colleges, more than the Protestant institutions, embraced the governance and administrative structures of the sponsoring church. Because the Catholic church was even more hierarchical and authority-based than most Protestant churches of the nineteenth century, the Catholic college became much more hierarchical and authority-based than comparable Protestant colleges.

The leadership role of Catholic women, both as administrators and trustees, is particularly noteworthy. Women who were members of religious orders often received extensive training and education in preparing for leadership in Catholic women's colleges in North America. They often knew more than their male counterparts in both religious and secular institutions and came into office through carefully crafted succession plans. Furthermore, as David Riesman (1967, p. iii) observed, these women were usually among the most innovative and "adventurous" educational leaders "perhaps because of their second-class citizenship vis-à-vis priests." We should also mention that these women were free from the traditional expectations for a secular woman's role in family and society. One need only point to the exceptional leadership of visionary nuns at Immaculate Heart College in Los Angeles during the 1960s and at Alverno College during the 1980s and 1990s to see that this tradition continued through the twentieth century.

The Jesuit Influence

Another feature of the Catholic college in North America during the nineteenth century is noteworthy and distinctive. The Jesuits were by far the most influential teaching order in North American Catholic higher education. They were strongly influenced by the European seven-year curricular model for post-primary education (Gleason, 1967). The distinction between high school and college was not drawn; rather, the first three years of college were considered preparatory and the final four years more specialized. In view of this curricular orientation, Jesuit educators found the North American distinction between high school and college to be artificial and unacceptable. The blending of secondary and postsecondary educational culture was further encouraged. The Jesuit influence on the Catholic college was particularly strong in Canada.

A Focus on Undergraduate Education

The educational enterprise in Catholic colleges and universities has traditionally been directed toward the welfare of the student, not the promotion of a specific discipline. Whereas undergraduate education in the Protestant college was considered preparatory to graduate school, the undergraduate education of the Catholic college student was considered the culmination of an integrated secondary (high school) and postsecondary (college) educational program.

The emphasis in Catholic colleges and universities on the importance and dignity of undergraduate education helps account for the relatively small focus on graduate education in these institutions (Gleason, 1967) and for the failure of the German research university model to have an influence on them. Whereas the Protestant colonial college was forever influenced by the German concentration on graduate education, research and scholarship, and faculty autonomy, the Catholic college was influenced by its major rival, the Canadian and American community or junior college. Only in the case of some prestigious Jesuit-run universities do we find Catholic higher education competing with their Protestant counterparts.

Origins of the Managerial Culture II: Community and Junior Colleges

The community or junior college shares several characteristics with the Catholic college, even though the former is a public, two-year institution and the latter is a private institution usually offering a four-year degree. Like the Catholic schools, junior and community colleges were first administered by people who had previously worked in secondary schools and were trained to serve the less privileged populations in the United States and Canada (Cohen, 2003). William Rainey Harper, the first president of the University of Chicago, is usually identified as the father of the junior college movement in the United States (Hillway, 1958). Arguing that the pedagogical distinction between the first and last two years of college is greater than that between high school and college, Harper advocated for the division of undergraduate institutions into "junior" and "senior" colleges.

Two junior colleges were established on the basis of Harper's model: the Lewis Institute in Chicago (1896) and the Bradley Polytechnic Institute in Peoria, Illinois (1897). Although several private junior colleges—notably, Lasell Junior College (formerly Lasell Female Academy) in Newton, Massachusetts—were founded in the 1800s (Landrith, 1971), the junior and community college movement is usually considered a mid-twentieth-century phenomenon. From a total of 207 junior colleges in 1922 (137 of which were privately supported), the United States witnessed a growth in the number of junior colleges to more than 600 mostly public schools by the time World War II ended (Cohen, 1998). During the second half of the twentieth century, community colleges became the first tier in many three-tier higher educational systems in the United States, and more recently in Canada. Although the Catholic college has become a secondary player in most parts of the United States and Canada, the community college has become prominent, enrolling "around 45 percent of all first-time freshmen, and more than 20 percent of those who complete at least four courses transfer to in-state, public universities within four years of matriculation" (Cohen, 1998, p. 313).

A Legacy of Parochial Innovation

The community college and the Catholic college share aspects of the managerial culture, at least during its early manifestation. Catholic and community colleges are both parochial—focusing in particular on local needs and interests. In the case of both Catholic and community colleges, increased student access is based primarily on geographic proximity. Men and women of all ages usually attend a community college not because of its reputation, cost, or curriculum, but because it provides education in their own neighborhood (Cohen, 2003).

Both Catholic and community colleges are also parochial when it comes to governance and control. A Catholic college is usually run by the local, autonomous teaching order of the church, with few directives coming from above. Similarly, the community college is by definition financed and controlled by the local community, usually through a board of elected officials. Although governance of universities is vested, in part, in a senate of faculty, community colleges are "accountable to external boards whose sole preoccupation should be to ensure that the college operates in conformity with the board members' perception of the public interest" (Dennison, 1986, p. 154). Community colleges embrace institutional cohesion. They integrate what they do through established internal bureaucratic processes and firmly established external board monitoring (Cohen 2003). "Good universities are indeed loose federations of co-existing faculties and departments; community colleges are not. To be most effective, [community] colleges need to place the greatest possible emphasis on the integration of what they do, rather than on the separateness of the activities" (Dennison, 1986, p. 155).

Catholic and community colleges are similar in another way, too. They both stress instruction more than scholarship or research, share an orientation toward commuter students from lower socioeconomic levels, and share a commitment to promotion of social mobility rather than merely acknowledging the ascribed status (as Protestant colleges do). As Cohen (2003) has noted, the community college has flourished over the years and to this day precisely because it has been willing to respond to the increasing number and diversity of demands citizens are placing on educational institutions in their own backyards. Because most academic institutions—dominated by the collegial culture during the nineteenth century—were indifferent or even hostile to the articulation between secondary and postsecondary schools, it was essential that a new kind of institution be formed to provide this bridge. Furthermore, the new urban workers, who could not afford and probably did not need a liberal arts education, had to be given access to an occupationally oriented educational program beyond high school (Medsker & Tillery, 1971). North America was being populated by immigrants who came primarily from Europe. Education was a way to assimilate these new citizens into the North American culture. There was a strong desire to be different from Europe and to offer North

American citizens a more democratic choice in their lives. There was a gap between the ability of the citizenry in their schooling, their desires and the existing university model (Dennison, 1986). Along came the community college during the 1890s.

The term *innovative* is used to describe both Catholic and community colleges—largely as a result of their shared commitment to educating the underserved and accomplishing their mission through the use of nontraditional modes of teaching and learning. Community colleges, in particular, began purposively as innovative alternatives designed to serve nontraditional students. As Terry O'Banion (1989, p. 1) has noted, "The community college as an institution is one of the most important innovations in the history of higher education." Similarly, we can look to many Catholic colleges, such as Immaculate Heart and Alverno, as significant sources of new ideas in North American higher education.

Leadership and Authority

In their close articulation with the secondary school sector, the community and Catholic colleges resemble one another in yet another way. Like Catholic college faculty and administrators, those who lead the junior and community colleges have until recently come from high school teaching, counseling, or administrative positions (Medsker & Tillery, 1971). Moreover, in many areas of the United States, community colleges are now (or at least until recently have been) governed by boards that also oversee the operations of primary and secondary school systems. It is not uncommon for gifted high school students to be taking courses in their local community colleges or even for some college remedial courses to be offered at local high schools. Many community college faculty and administrators prefer to identify themselves primarily with colleagues in four-year institutions—the community college often being considered an extension of secondary schools (Cohen, 2003). Many others, however, are inclined toward reverse snobbery and align themselves with those who serve all of the citizens without "academic pretensions"—that is to say, with their high school and vocational education colleagues.

The similarities and differences that have been drawn between Catholic and community colleges reveal several of the most important and often intractable tensions in the managerial culture. First, there are differing opinions about the source of authority in colleges and universities that are dominated by this culture. On the one hand, at Catholic colleges authority is usually vested in the president, who in turn receives authority from the church, or more recently, from the college's board of trustees. Typically, this board, like that of the Protestant college, consists of members who hold office for many years. Furthermore, these board members usually select most, if not all, of their successors. On the other hand, community college presidents are usually beholden to a board elected by the local community. Members of the board and the president must therefore be responsive to other community leaders, pressure groups, and concerns. Faculty members in community colleges normally perceive themselves to be employees of public agencies; conversely, academics at Catholic colleges are more likely to see themselves as part of a corporate-type setting, with major control being exerted by an invisible, but powerful, governing board.

Teaching Mission and Load

Because both the community college and Catholic postsecondary institution are often under financial pressures, the founding commitment to serving the underserved student is easily lost. The teaching mission of these institutions is often no longer interpreted as a commitment to high-quality instruction, nor is it focused on the distinctive needs of underserved students. Attention shifts from quality to workload. Do faculty members at a specific institution have an appropriate teaching load? Is the load too heavy? In many instances, faculty members do not have time for research or community service. In some instances, a community college becomes teaching-oriented not because it wants to be but because its faculty members have no time to do anything but teach (Grubb & Associates, 1999).

In the case of the Catholic colleges and universities, this pressure toward heavy teaching loads comes not only from limited financial resources but also from a shift in the composition of core faculty over the past three to four decades. In many of these institutions the core faculty was for many years composed of low-paid secular instructors and often unpaid faculty members from the sponsoring religious order. Then, in the 1950s and 1960s, the core faculty in most cases shifted to an exclusively secular faculty. This shift did not end here. Because of the financial vulnerability of these Catholic institutions, many part-time instructors were hired at a low rate instead of full-time faculty members who would be paid more highly. The same part-time faculty situation exists in many urban community colleges. We see a compounding of the heavy teaching load problem because of the hiring of so many part-time faculty members. These men and women teach a large number of courses at multiple institutions—receiving very low pay and no benefits in compensation for their heavy teaching load. (We have much more to say about part-time faculty members in Chapter Five.)

The Managerial Way

With the emergence of multipurpose, multiconstituency, multilevel universities in the 1960s—signaled by the successful reception of Clark Kerr's *The Uses of the University* (1963)—North American higher education felt it had found the answer to many of its pressing problems. The *collegiate way* was replaced by the *managerial way*. In the same year that Kerr's book on the "multiversity" was published, a second major book, *The Age of the Scholar*, was published. This book, written by Nathan Pusey, then president of Harvard University, received far less attention than did *The Uses of the University. The Age of the Scholar* was written more from the traditional collegial point of view and warned of some of the dangers lurking in Kerr's multiversity. The world of North American higher education was not ready to hear these warnings. Its leaders were enamored of the prospect of large-scale, efficient universities that could meet a variety of educational needs occasioned by the coming baby boom.

This movement toward large-scale, efficient—and public—universities required and enhanced the ascendancy of the managerial culture. Arthur Cohen (1998, p. 187) describes this shift in twentieth-century higher education as a process of "secularization." Although he was referring specifically to the increasing proportion of institutions that were public rather than private (and to a decrease in the number of liberal arts colleges), his term could also be applied, perhaps even more appropriately, to a reduction in the direct affiliation of many private colleges and universities with religious denominations, and to a reduction in the number of faculty and administrators who were members of religious orders.

The secularized higher education institution, and in particular Kerr's multiversity, depended on exceptional managerial skills. As Cohen (1998, p. 247) observed, "[T]he role of the president shifted notably from leader of the education program to manager of the bureaucracy." Budgets were more complex than in the simpler institutions of the past. Increased administrative support services were required to handle the diverse demands being placed on these large, multipurpose institutions. In part because of these diverse demands and the inability of university administrators to meet them, the golden age of the multiversity was quite short (Cohen, 1998). With the strident calls of Mario Savio and his followers at the University of California (Clark Kerr's own multiversity), the age of student discontent began. Students and many sympathetic citizens deplored the indifference of vast educational systems to their unique needs. They complained of complicity between big business, big government, and big university; they demanded a renewed focus on teaching rather than a preoccupation with research and publishing. They articulated a reengagement with social values and reform. The student protests did not overturn the multiversity, but they did tarnish its image. Furthermore, these activists did not diminish the managerial culture's impact on modern colleges and universities. But they did provide fertile ground for the growth of two other cultures: developmental and advocacy.

The managerial culture was enhanced by the rapid growth in the 1960s not only of multiversities but also of megasystems. Higher educational systems were spawned that encouraged statewide planning of facilities, development of sophisticated cost-finding procedures, and demand for comparability in the description, budgeting, and evaluation of academic programs. The term *postsecondary* emerged in the 1960s as a way to define these new systems. Previously, *higher education* referred only to education after high school. This meant public and private universities and colleges. The term *postsecondary* embraced not just higher education but also trade, technical, and vocational education after high school, and adult education (Dennison, 1986). Although the new Postsecondary Commissions (also called the 1202 Commissions) that were required in the U.S. Congress's 1972 higher education amendments never got off the ground, the concept reinforced the desirability of statewide coordination and monitoring of all institutions of higher education—public and private, proprietary and nonprofit. Even major research universities were now often under the jurisdiction of a statewide board. Supposedly, this centralized coordination and governance would not just reduce expenses but also provide for equitable distribution of funds to participating institutions (Cohen, 1998). Management culture "centralists" argued that all higher education institutions would benefit. Rather than individual colleges and universities fighting one another for a piece of the allocation pie, they could approach their state legislature with a single unified message and thereby expand the size of the overall pie.

Although many of the benefits promised by the managerial centralists never came to pass, statewide and provincewide planning has had a profound impact on the management of budgets and strategic planning processes in contemporary North American colleges and universities. Another centralizing government initiative has had an even greater impact. Federal regulations in both the United States and Canada concerning hiring, firing, and performance review have transformed personnel management. Affirmative action guidelines, equal employment mandates, and related federally imposed restrictions have required administrators in higher education to gain new knowledge and skills in the management of people. An academic leader from the collegial culture is ill prepared to deal with this new reality of legalities and regulations. A specially trained corps of managers is required to keep a college or university out of the courtroom and in the good graces of federal funding agencies.

Another factor has contributed to the growth of the management culture in contemporary colleges and universities: lack of financial support. There was a relative reduction in federal, state, provincial, and private philanthropic support for colleges and universities during the late 1970s, 1980s, and 1990s. Public discontent with higher education institutions began to increase as the ideals of higher education by the mid-1960s were found to be something of an illusion. The student protests of the late 1960s also damaged the cause of higher education in many circles of influence and wealth. Colleges and universities had to do some severe belt tightening during the 1970s, 1980s, and 1990s. Retrenchment has become an all-too-common condition among many institutions, which had been characterized by growth and prosperity during the 1960s and early 1970s. Effective management does not seem to be an imperative under conditions of growth. It is imperative, however, when there is retrenchment and declining resources. New demands for accountability on the part of skeptical publics combine with new planning initiatives that are required of institutions facing scarce resources. Both factors encourage the emergence of strong managerial leadership and discourage the laissez-faire collegial leadership that was acceptable and dominant until the 1970s.

A final reason for the expansion of the managerial culture is the significant increase in part-time faculty and the resulting diminution of influence of academics in the daily operations of colleges and universities. In many North American colleges and universities, part-time faculty members teach more than half of the courses offered. These institutions have become increasingly centralized, with control resting in the hands of a few full-time faculty members and administrators. The collegial culture tends to wither away when part-time faculty appointments are prevalent. Part-timers simply do not have sufficient time or interest to participate in campus politics, lengthy committee meetings, or the informal negotiations that typify the collegial culture. And because many of the part-time faculty are themselves also working in corporations that support a managerial culture, they are accustomed to a strong, top-down structure. They also feel it is appropriate to delegate academic administrative matters to a few full-time faculty members, who become increasingly involved themselves in management.

Living and Working in the Managerial Culture Today

What would it take for leaders with a managerial orientation to be effective in bringing about improvement on their campuses? We will look, as we did in our analysis of the collegial culture in Chapter One, at the nature and potential of institutional leadership in the managerial culture. In this culture, highest value is assigned at the instructional level to the learning of students—particularly learning that can be assessed quantitatively and attributed specifically to a planned educational event. We find the strong influence of Catholic and community college education in the managerial emphasis on tangible educational goals that are primarily directed toward the student's vocational roles and responsibilities as a citizen. A second instructional value, however, seems to contradict the first: teaching is supposed to be fiscally efficient. Bowen and Douglass (1971, p. 6) articulated this when they spoke of "efficiency in liberal education" and listed various instructional strategies that could reduce costs. Their list of cost-cutting strategies not only specified the managerial culture's priorities but also defined the nature and scope of the clash between the values and goals of the collegial culture and those of the managerial culture. Their list also suggested many of the points of contention raised by faculty who have embraced the advocacy culture.

Thus, the key words of the managerial culture seem to be efficiency and competence. The successful leaders are the ones who are realistic and efficient and competent administrators or teachers. We see this focus on efficiency and competence in many of the more recent publications intended for new academic leaders (for example, Diamond, 2002); furthermore, the same managerial perspective seems to be embraced whether the discussion is about administration or about teaching. The criteria for judging efficiency and competence in administration tend to be borrowed from corporate settings, whereas those used to define efficient and competent instruction are often derived from the military and high-tech industries. We shall briefly examine each of these sets of definitions.

Academic Administration

As the managerial culture has become more dominant in North American colleges and universities, administrators of these institutions are expected to be efficient and effective managers of people and money. As an efficient manager, a college or university administrator is expected to employ corporate management theory. As Cohen put it, "[J]ust as large business enterprises were emphasizing functional organization and efficiency, the universities were incorporating such practices" (1998, p. 154). Two of the most influential managerial theorists from the corporate sector, Robert Blake and Jane Mouton (Blake, Mouton, & Williams, 1981), applied their "grid management" theory to the academic setting. Their analysis is still quite salient, though the tools of organizational development that they advocated are not widely used. They acknowledged that "to attain excellence a college or university must develop an organizational model for itself," and "cannot be led or managed like a business" (p. 29). Nevertheless, they perceived the chief responsibilities of academic administrators in traditional corporate terms that readily offend those aligned with the collegial culture: for example, "administering the activities that result [from a clearly formulated mission]," "managing the academic personnel function," and "managing external relations" (p. 301).

Blake, Mouton, and Williams are not alone in failing to account for the collegial culture when transferring corporate management theory to colleges and universities. Other attempts to transfer procedures from corporate settings to colleges and universities have often been similarly insensitive, and as a result, have been received with hostility and profound skepticism: "Although they may not appear to have a political purpose, academic management fads are solutions that further specific ideologies. Academic management fads have not themselves degraded the narrative [about virtues, civic participation, democracy and social justice, the idea of higher education as a social institution], but they are technical vehicles that contribute to the degradation" (Birnbaum, 2000, p. 227).

Birnbaum suggests that most of the managerial fads in higher education in recent years are based on and have contributed to a common managerial culture–based narrative:

> Business and industry are highly efficient and effective; higher education is not. Higher education could improve if it adopted the management techniques of business.... But intransigent

> faculty will not permit it because they are protecting their own selfish interests, and academic managers are too timid to stand against them. The solution to the problem is to free managers to be entrepreneurial and market driven. The simplicity of this narrative is its power, and the story of a small, privileged elite that benefits at the expense of the public is an evocative story that taps into the American [and Canadian] psyche. So is the narrative of a fad that pledges to right the wrong and put the university [and college] in its place. [Birnbaum, 2000, pp. 227–228]

Birnbaum believes that these narratives from the managerial culture, like all carefully crafted narratives, are particularly compelling. We believe that Birnbaum's management-oriented narratives and the accompanying corporate models have been wholeheartedly accepted primarily in those institutions where the managerial culture is pervasive.

Managerial Instruction

A successful faculty member in the managerial culture is an efficient and competent teacher and manager of the instructional process. Because administrators or faculty in administrative roles are given responsibility for management and because the primary product of a college or university is supposed to be education, faculty members should exhibit leadership primarily in their classroom performance and in their collaboration with other faculty members in the design and implementation of an appropriate sequence of course offerings. Faculty are able to influence the educational outcomes of an institution first and foremost through teaching and course design, rather than by serving as members of faculty committees or as chairs of the faculty senate. There is neither room nor time available for academic politicos who spend all their time wheeling and dealing in the academic corridors, or for eccentric lone rangers or designers of boutique courses (Bates & Poole, 2003) who work in isolation and consider their classroom to be a private fiefdom.

In his insightful analysis of the community college culture, Howard London (1978) noted that a faculty member who works in an institution infused with a managerial culture is likely to find intellectual identity primarily through teaching rather than through either independent research and scholarship or interaction with fellow faculty members: "Teaching in the community college [is] seen [by faculty members] as a way to maintain both the intellectual commitment and the accompanying self-image" (London, 1978, p. 39). Unfortunately, many of the faculty members studied by London found very little intellectual stimulation in the classroom; they felt compelled to "popularize" their concepts and to entertain rather than instruct. Put succinctly, "teachers [have] to preserve or acceptably modify their identities as intellectual beings in the face of an unreceptive, skeptical audience" (p. 115).

According to London, faculty members in a community college face a dilemma:

> Having internalized the value of disinterested inquiry, whether in the classroom or through research or scholarship, [community college faculty find] themselves organizing, preparing, and teaching in reference to the popular functions. The collision of the two functions [disinterested inquiry and popularized teaching], for which most faculty were unprepared, . . . threatened self- and role definitions; in a subtle yet critical way these were assaults on the teachers' identities, and as such, had to be repelled . . . . [T]he manner in which this was done [through highly rigid and punitive modes of teaching] was, for some of their students, like salt in an open wound: It challenged the very sense of worth and ability [that the students] already doubted. [1978, p. 52]

London (1978, p. 53) states that successful instructors "are able to specify the educational objectives or outcomes of the courses they are teaching and are able to implement an appropriate, instructional design in a humane manner that does not pour salt into student wounds. Furthermore, the competent instructor can and will use an instructional method that most efficiently and effectively conveys a body of knowledge related directly to these objectives."

Borrowing from the work done in military education on the use of criterion-based instruction (for example, Popham, 1978), efficient and competent faculty are expected, from the managerial culture's perspective, to design programs that move all students toward competence rather than set up competitive (grading-on-the-curve) systems that require some students to succeed while others fail (Diamond et al., 1975). In contemporary twenty-first-century higher education, the managerial culture generally encourages faculty members to be acquainted with new instructional technologies that have recently become available at relatively low cost (Bates & Poole, 2003).

Professionalized Students

Successful students in the managerial culture are efficient and competent learners. They have demonstrated a high level of achievement in specific skills, knowledge, and attitudes. Rather than attempting to influence school policy by means of student councils (let alone petitions or demonstrations), these students are aware of the existing lines of authority and do not seek to move from their role as students to the role of administrator or member of a decision-making body in the academic setting. Instead, they become efficient learners inside the academy (maximum acquisition of competencies with minimal expenditure of time and money) and look for a role outside the academy as breadwinners, management trainees, or professionals. As Bledstein (1976) noted in his poignant assessment of the rise of a professional culture in North America, there may not be a traditional social class structure in the United States (or in Canada), but in its place is an overwhelming concern for establishing one's place in society by obtaining an academic degree, a license, or some other earned pedigree. To achieve a professional position, a student must be an efficient and competent learner.

Typically, "professionalized" students are steeped in the managerial culture. They are not troublemakers. They learn to be patient and respectful of the institutional and instructional processes through which they must pass in order to obtain a degree and, thereby, increased economic prosperity. Students attracted to or accepted by colleges and universities dominated by the managerial culture often come from middle-class or lower-middle-class backgrounds. We have known for many years that these students are more likely to be vocationally oriented and less intellectually inclined than students in elitist colleges and universities where the collegial culture continues to rule (Medsker & Tillery, 1971). Students in the managerial culture firmly believe in the academic institution as a vehicle for upward mobility—as the royal road to a respectable profession. These students are readily absorbed into large, complex corporate structures that discourage attempts at influencing policy by employees who are near the bottom of the organizational ladder.

The Myth of Upward Mobility

In his classic case study of a junior college, Burton Clark (1960) described the myth of upward mobility. He noted that all democratic societies must provide certain institutions that not only hold the myth of upward mobility but also provide the mechanisms for "cooling off" (Goffman, 1952) those who discover that the myth will never be realized for them. According to Clark (1960, p. 151), community colleges are in the business of building mechanisms to "deflect the resentment and mollify the disappointment of those to whom opportunity is denied [in order] to induce them to take less rewarding work . . . through the gradually accumulated evidence (achievement tests, vocational aptitude tests, course grades, teachers' recommendations, counselors' advice) that they ought to change to a terminal vocational curriculum rather than transfer to a four-year institution."

Cohen (2003) takes a somewhat different perspective in addressing the assumption of upward mobility in community colleges. He notes that educational equality should be based not on the success of individual students in moving to higher socioeconomic levels but rather on the success of groups who have been subjected to discriminatory practices to move upward. "If equal opportunity means allowing people from any social, ethnic, or religious group to have the same chance to enter higher education as people from any other group, the goal [of upward mobility] is both worthy and attainable" (p. 388).

Because an increasing number of community colleges today function as the first two years of a four-year college program, Clark's and even Cohen's analyses are a bit dated; however, they do accurately identify an important emphasis in both community colleges and Catholic colleges on programs that seek to improve employment opportunities for underserved populations primarily by emphasizing skills development and the assessment of competence. These emphases give the appearance of democratizing the college and the classroom. On the one hand, each student is given an opportunity to succeed and move ahead with career aspirations, regardless of background or status. On the other hand, as Clark states, the managerial culture becomes a repressive setting in which old socioeconomic distinctions are reinforced rather than broken down (Bergquist, 1995).

Conclusions

In essence, in the managerial culture we find a quest for efficient and competent administrators, faculty members, and students who respect and work in a formal, hierarchical structure; this structure in turn encourages clarity of communication, specificity of roles and outcomes, and careful delegation of responsibilities.

The goal of leadership is attained when a competent person fills a clearly specified role. General and somewhat vague notions about charisma and leadership by example are more likely to be found in colleges and universities that emphasize the collegial or developmental perspectives.

In the managerial culture, one influences and changes the academy by being a skilled manager of people and money. It is in the careful attention to the generation of revenues and the regular administrative duties of a college or university that one has an effect on the institution's operations. Enrollments are now "managed" rather than left to the unpredictable and ill-defined tendency of students to stay in school because they like a particular faculty member or feel comfortable talking to their student service advisor (Hossler & Anderson, 2005). Lengthy discussions among faculty members are often seen as esoteric by members of the managerial culture. "At times, faculty participation in decision making can be notoriously detailed, deliberate, and slow. Faculty members are experts in their disciplines but are not necessarily efficient as committee members" (Gappa, Austin, & Trice, 2007, p. 162). Irrelevance and inefficiency seem to pervade committee meetings. Senate hearings are viewed with disdain. These are the "games" that grown faculty members must play to "massage their egos," "avoid work," or "delude themselves" about the amount of influence they really exert on the life and goals of the college or university. Instead, faculty members must join with their administrative colleagues in focusing on the bottom line. The search for truth in higher education institutions is rivaled by a search for revenues and entrepreneurship (Newman, Couturier, & Scurry, 2004; Gappa et al., 2007).

Members of the managerial culture believe that one becomes more influential by moving up through formal lines of authority and being responsive to pressures for accountability. A faculty member becomes department chair, then division chair or dean, then academic vice president, and finally president. The ability to move up through the organization is assumed to be based at least in part on a rational appraisal by superiors of the individual's managerial competence: "Can she work effectively with people?" "Can he manage a budget?" "Can these administrators successfully plan for and implement a new program?" "Can these potential faculty members be held accountable for their work, and can they meet the challenge of this accountability?"

One also gains the capacity to influence and control events by acquiring and using valid information. How one manages information is a critical ingredient in every contemporary organization, but it takes on special importance and meaning in the managerial culture. Information is not only needed to make a thoughtful decision but is also required if one is to be accountable and receive attention from peers and superiors. If managers are not in control of the facts, they will not be heard. If they cannot demonstrate their success through numbers, then they are not accountable and are therefore not credible. Data—not charisma—seems to play a critical part in the managerial culture. For faculty members this means a "ratcheting up" of their multiple roles in the academy: "[E]xternal calls for greater accountability and demonstrable outcomes, institutional pressure for faculty to generate revenue, and the necessity of keeping up with the never-ending expansion of new knowledge all conspire to create seemingly endless demands and expectations of faculty members" (Gappa et al., 2007, p. 17).

Institutional research has become increasingly important in many colleges and universities for this very reason. One must understand and appreciate one's own institution to be an effective academic leader. The administrator or faculty member who has received and can understand budget reports, student attrition figures, and employment projections commands more respect than the administrator or faculty member who has other abilities but has no access to this information or does not understand it.

Agencies such as the National Center for Higher Education Management Systems, which specialized during the 1970s and 1980s in the development of sophisticated information systems, often offered training programs that were attended only by college and university administrators. Faculty members rarely attended these seminars, even though decisions that had a profound impact on academic life were made on the basis of information generated with procedures and tools introduced at these seminars. Today, when faculty members in the managerial culture have access to these techniques, they usually exert greater influence in their colleges or universities—especially if they are assisted in this endeavor by faculty members who are aligned with the developmental and advocacy cultures. We turn now to these two, newer cultures of the academy.

3

The Developmental Culture

The developmental culture: A culture that finds meaning primarily in the creation of programs and activities furthering the personal and professional growth of all members of the higher education community; that values personal openness and service to others as well as systematic institutional research and curricular planning; that holds assumptions about the inherent desire of all men and women to attain their own personal maturation, while helping others in the institution become more mature; and that conceives of the institution's enterprise as the encouragement of potential for cognitive, affective, and behavioral maturation among all students, faculty, administrators, and staff.

For all its strengths—specifically, its encouragement of deliberation and open communication—the collegial culture suffers from a lack of organization and coherence. These deficiencies are particularly important in a postsecondary institution facing limited financial resources and a changing student constituency. In response to these problems, some collegial faculty members have advocated a more deliberate mode of planning and development that retains faculty authority and a democratic spirit while avoiding the political infighting of the collegial culture. Under several banners—faculty development, curriculum development, and long-term institutional planning—these faculty members, and some administrators, have created a new culture over the past forty years. We have called this culture *developmental.*

Rationality is particularly important in this culture, just as it is—at least on paper—in both the collegial and managerial cultures. Organizations and procedures are redesigned by the developmentalists to accommodate more effectively the particular needs of the institution ("form follows function"). Institutional research is brought to bear on issues of institutional planning. Faculty members are asked to examine their own assumptions about teaching, learning, and student needs so that they can make better decisions and plan successful programs. Members of this third culture tend to be relatively naive about the political process of a college or university and often are viewed by faculty members and administrators with a managerial orientation as too idealistic and ill equipped to implement a carefully conceived program.

Until recently, we would also say that the developmental culture, like the collegial culture, was faculty-focused, and like the British wing of the collegial culture, student-focused. We must now revise this generalization, for we are seeing examples where the professional development programs in some institutions are less focused on either faculty or students and are more aligned with aims that all employees can pursue (Watts, 2002). As the demands on colleges and universities increase, new purposes and delivery formats for professional development will inevitably emerge. The developmental culture is still evolving as a relatively new reality in North American higher education.

Origins of the Developmental Culture

During the student movement of the 1960s, there was a growing sense among many faculty and academic administrators that traditional postsecondary institutions (and the dominant collegial culture) were not responsive to the needs of either students or society. Student life and its improvement required greater emphasis. Furthermore, postsecondary institutions needed to be more committed to and clear about many of the less tangible aspects of human growth and development—such as moral development and critical thinking—that often seemed to be lacking among contemporary citizens.

The work of Nevitt Sanford and his colleagues, represented in the classic *The American College* (Sanford, 1962), pointed the way to specific strategies directed at addressing these needs. Sanford focused not only on the classroom but also on the extracurricular aspects of student life. He and his colleagues offered new concepts of teaching and learning and directed the attention of faculty and academic administrators to areas of student life that previously had been considered the exclusive domain of student counselors and directors of student service programs. Distinguished academicians such as Joseph Katz (Katz & Associates, 1968) asked what role colleges and universities should play in the more complete development of students. The research of Arthur Chickering on student growth in small colleges and his description of central aspects of student development drew attention from both scholars and those working directly with students. Along with Sanford's *The American College* (1962), Chickering's *Education and Identity* (1969) became a best-selling book in American higher education. The work of William Perry (1970) on the stages of students' intellectual and ethical development further refined the dialogue about student development during the late 1970s and 1980s.

The new, intense attention directed at students and their specific needs required an equally forceful statement about the teaching skills of postsecondary instructors and their growth and development. It also drew attention to the requirement for new forms of institutional research aimed not just at readily quantifiable items, such as finance, student enrollment, and resource allocation, but also at more elusive aspects of student learning and campus morale. Students are affected by all aspects of campus life; consequently, each of these initiatives produced the need for a more comprehensive program of institutional change and development (Bergquist & Shoemaker, 1976). We will briefly consider three of the primary developmental initiatives: faculty development, institutional research, and organizational development.

Faculty Development

Many conversations about the failure of American colleges and universities to respond to the needs of either students or faculty were sparked by the publication of *Faculty Development in a Time of Retrenchment* (Group for Human Development in Higher Education, 1974). The authors of this work suggested that faculty development might be an appropriate, though only partial, response to these concerns. The issue is not only training; the practice of any art generally benefits from colleagueship, knowledge about the effects of the art, rewards for good work, support for special projects, arrangements for collaboration, and a knowledgeable audience.

The field of faculty development emerged in part from a growing academic concern for student development. Jack Lindquist (1978a, p. 12), a major figure in this field, observed: "In the early 1970s, many of the same developmentalists who had urged attention to the person of the student urged institutional attention to the person of the professor. Professors are developing adults who face such strains as a very tight job market, classrooms too full of extremely diverse students, institutions rife with adversarial clashes, and personal transitions which raise serious questions about identity and future directions." New attention to faculty concerns and welfare also emerged because of demands that postsecondary institutions do a better job (Group for Human Development in Higher Education, 1974).

In one of the first books written on the topic of faculty development, Bergquist and Phillips (1975, p. 3) concluded:

"Institutions of higher education face the harsh realities of decreased funding, steady or declining enrollment, and limited faculty mobility, together with demands for accountability voiced by students, parents, and state and federal officials. Since the teaching enterprise is central to higher education, faculty members in particular are being asked to reexamine their personal and professional attitudes toward classroom instruction and toward their relationships with their students. Many faculty are also being asked to consider training in new classroom procedures, as well as possible reorganizations of departmental structures and governance systems."

By the late 1970s, faculty development had become quite large and complex. It was offered in some form by approximately half of all colleges and universities in the United States. Several highly regarded foundations (most notably, the Kellogg Foundation and the Lilly Endowment) supported major faculty development initiatives. The Professional and Organization Development Network in Higher Education, a national association, was initiated to provide a forum for discussion of new approaches to the field. Newsletters and workshops were prepared and disseminated by many colleges, universities, centers, and consortia. A major series of handbooks on faculty development was produced by the Council for the Advancement of Small Colleges (CASC; now the Council of Independent Colleges) (Bergquist & Phillips, 1975, 1977, 1981), and several interinstitutional projects were conducted by national higher education associations, such as CASC and the Association of American Colleges (Gaff, 1978).

In the area of instructional improvement, the faculty development practitioner—a product of the developmental culture—diverged significantly from the practitioner of instructional development—a product of the managerial culture. Instructional development practitioners—most notably Robert Diamond (1976) of Syracuse University—concentrated specifically on student learning and often recommended instructional methods that eliminated the need for a faculty member's physical presence. They have even proposed instructional materials that are "faculty-proof." By contrast, those in the faculty development field have generally focused more on the faculty member than on the student, although the field emerged in response to student needs and concerns. Those with a faculty development perspective believe that, by enhancing a faculty member's skills through training programs and encouraging renewed interest in teaching and student advising, the quality of learning for students is ultimately improved. In moments of candor, many who take this perspective will admit that they are ultimately more interested in the faculty member as learner than the student as learner. As sophisticated, adult learners, faculty members offer faculty development practitioners a greater challenge and sense of shared goals than traditional college-age students.

Because of this primary interest in faculty learning and because of the developmental field's retention of the collegial culture's skepticism about quantifiable evaluation, the outcomes of faculty development projects have often been less than satisfactory for funding agencies and those community leaders who had expected faculty development initiatives to benefit students directly. Several major funding agencies, such as the Fund for the Improvement of Postsecondary Education, never supported faculty development programs in and of themselves; they were always more interested in faculty development as integral to some other purpose, usually related to the improvement or expansion of student learning opportunities. Other agencies, like Kellogg and Lilly, which had initially funded faculty development activities, soon became less inclined to do so unless these activities supported some other goal, such as curriculum reform. Thus, a basic assumption in the developmental culture about the inherent compatibility of personal and institutional welfare was called into question by those who could most influence institutional priorities from outside—namely, the funding agencies.

Institutional Research

Accompanying the emerging emphasis on faculty development was an intensified interest in institutional research. This interest was not limited to the budgeting devices of the managerial culture; rather, attention was directed more broadly to generating information about institutional climates and culture, student learning styles and stages of development, and institutional goals and priorities. The Educational Testing Service (ETS) developed a series of institutional research tools (an educational environment scale and institutional functioning inventories, for instance) that provided an overview of institutional life at a college or university. ETS also developed an institutional goals inventory that assessed perceptions about the desired state of the institution and the extent to which the institution was successfully moving toward this desired state. Comparable instruments were developed at other institutions and by other testing organizations (Bergquist & Shoemaker, 1976).

Other instruments were developed during the early 1970s to assess student learning styles—based on the assumption that recognition of diverse learning styles not only empowers the students but enables faculty members to design curricula and engage instructional techniques and technologies that both challenge and are intentionally aligned with the preferred styles of each student (Bates & Poole, 2003; Kuh et al., 2005a). Riechmann and Grasha (1974) devised a means of evaluating the interpersonal preferences of students in a learning environment; Joe Hill (n.d.) from Oakland Community College (Michigan) developed a cognitive mapping method to analyze the appeal of certain media, as well as numerous other factors. David Kolb (1976) provided a learning style inventory that measured preferences for certain cognitive functions. Through interviews with students, an assessment of both developmental stages and tasks was possible (Chickering, 1969; Perry, 1970; Knefelkamp, Widick, & Parker, 1978). Moving beyond stylistic preferences, over the past decade Howard

Gardner (1993, 2000) identified a cluster of "intelligences" that spawned a series of experiments at the primary, secondary, and postsecondary levels of education on alternative ways to present class content that might fully engage (or help enhance) specific intelligences, such as linguistic, logical-mathematical, and spatial. Although only one of Gardner's intelligences—personal intelligence—has received widespread attention, being renamed *emotional intelligence* (for example, Goleman, 2005, 2006), his work complements the research and assessment tools associated with stylistic preferences and offers guidance for any educator who wishes to meet the challenge of diversity in the postsecondary classroom.

Much more important than the proliferation of testing procedures and instruments, however, is the linkage made between these efforts at institutional research and those at planned institutional change. Harold Hodgkinson (the Center for Higher Education at the University of California) led a group of nationally known consultants in proposing that institutional research be coupled with action plans that furthered the systematic movement toward institutional goals and kept in mind institutional climate and style. The largest and most extensively documented of the combined work on research and planned change was mounted by Arthur Chickering and Jack Lindquist in their project called Strategies for Change and Knowledge Utilization (Lindquist, 1978b). Working intensively with seven colleges, and less closely with about a dozen others, Lindquist effectively demonstrated that knowledge about an institution's life and culture that has been systematically acquired can enhance the quality and success of its change efforts.

The engagement of postsecondary institutions in a blending of institutional research, planning, and professional development, unfortunately, was in most cases short-lived. Many colleges and universities continue to conduct institutional research, but it is usually focused once again on finance, student enrollment and attrition, and resource allocation. The shifting of institutional research back to traditional areas of concern may also be short-lived, however, as more governmental and regional accrediting agencies begin to push for the assessment of student learning outcomes on an institution-wide basis. Furthermore, the new developmental push toward "student success" (for example, Kuh et al., 2005a) makes an impressive claim that "powerful learning environments and significant learning outcomes can be achieved no matter what the institution's resources or student preparation" (p. 89). Student success, however, can only occur if leaders of the institution, and those aligned with the developmental culture in particular, find ways to increase the "amount of time and effort students put into their studies and other activities that lead to the experiences and outcomes that constitute student success," and find ways in which to allocate resources and organize learning opportunities and services "to induce students to participate in and benefit from such activities" (p. 9).

Organizational Development

Faculty development and efforts to bring about institutional change in the early 1970s were complemented by organizational development initiatives. These initiatives borrowed heavily from the lessons learned by corporations about organizational change and development at the National Training Laboratories for Group Development (NTL Institute). Ron Boyer and Tony Grasha at the University of Cincinnati and Walter Sikes of the Center for Creative Change in Yellow Springs, Ohio (Sikes, Schlesinger, & Seashore, 1974), began to conduct workshops, provide consultation, and write about the need for effective organizational functioning (decision making, problem solving, conflict management) in higher education institutions. Founded in 1947, the NTL Institute, headquartered in Alexandria, Virginia, with a facility in Bethel, Maine, is a not-for-profit educational company of members and staff whose purpose is to advance the field of applied behavioral sciences and develop change agents for effective leadership for organizations of all types. (See *http://www.ntl.org/about.html* for more information.)

Several faculty development practitioners (such as Bergquist and Phillips) and advocates of institutional research (such as Lindquist) urged that organizational development be closely linked with other developmental efforts. They also proposed and were actively involved in the formulation of administrative development efforts that would further strengthen these initiatives. Borrowing from the work of Watson and Johnson (1972), Bergquist and Phillips proposed strategies targeted at three domains: structure, process, and attitude. *Structure* is changed when the organizational chart, the reward system, or institutional policies and procedures are modified. Changes in *process*, by contrast, involve alterations in the way that people operate and relate to others in the existing structures of the organization. Process changes entail shifts in communication patterns, modes of decision making or conflict management, or styles of management. The third domain, *attitude*, has to do with how people feel about working in the existing structures and processes of the organization. Changes in attitudes usually involve modifications in organizational culture. Concerns about change in all three of these areas are evident in many American colleges and universities. Structural change, for instance, can be seen in the widespread debate about faculty contracts, merit pay programs, and new governance models. Process-oriented change is evident in discussions about consensus building, collaborative management, and conflict resolution. Change directed toward shifts in attitude is to be found in a focus on organizational culture and images of leadership and faculty renewal.

Although Bergquist and Phillips make extensive use of the Watson and Johnson model of organizational change, Lindquist relied on the work of Ronald Havelock (1971), who conducted research during the 1970s on the processes of change and innovation in various human service settings. Working out of the

Institute for Social Research in Ann Arbor, Michigan, Havelock focused on strategies for the dissemination and use of knowledge in educational institutions. He proposed three different strategies: *rational planning*, *social interaction*, and *human problem solving*. Lindquist (1978b) added a fourth strategy to Havelock's list, which he called the *political approach*. Lindquist applied Havelock's three models and his own fourth model to a major analysis of change and innovation in American colleges and universities.

For many contemporary colleges and universities—or at least for their leaders—rational planning reigns supreme. As noted in our discussion of the collegial culture (see Chapter One), colleges and universities in particular are inclined to be perceived by those inside and out as strongholds of reason and rational deliberation. The higher education leader who believes in rational planning will devote a significant amount of time, money, and energy to collecting quantifiable information about such aspects of the institution as student enrollment and attrition, unit costs, projections of changing student or community needs, and student learning outcomes. This approach is exemplified in the work of the National Center for Higher Education Management Systems (Boulder, Colorado), Educational Testing Service (Princeton, New Jersey), and American College Testing (Ames, Iowa).

Havelock and Lindquist identify the social interaction strategy for planned change with Everett Rogers's (2003) description of ways in which new ideas and technologies are diffused in communities and organizations. Lindquist (1978b, p. 4) observes, "We live in social networks . . . . We can gain security, status, and esteem from these informal systems, just as we can from formal organizations. Some researchers maintain that these contacts are essential to change, for new ideas get communicated and validated through social networks." Taken together, Rogers's five-stage chronology represents a portrait of planned change that is very different from the one usually found in the literature and the experiences of many who support the rational planning process. Often, those who advocate rational planning draw very few distinctions between the various audiences that must be considered in presenting a new idea or product. They may overestimate the amount of information that the early adopters need to convince them to try out an innovation or offer the wrong kind of information in the dissemination process to those in the late majority.

Havelock's third strategy, human problem solving, is often specifically identified with the field of organizational development (OD). It relies on the improvement of interpersonal relationships and the critical role played by human emotions and group dynamics. Contemporary colleges and universities increasingly find themselves facing changing environments and internal transitions. OD is a concept and process that leaders can use to deal with these internal changes and with the personal and interpersonal stress they cause. Despite their use of organizational development strategies, few colleges or universities today have made use of this valuable behavioral science tool. There have been a few minor exceptions (Boyer & Crockett, 1973; Sikes et al., 1974; Lindquist, 1978a, 1978b; Bergquist & Armstrong, 1986). Twenty-first-century postsecondary institutions certainly experience the stresses associated with change. Furthermore, these colleges and universities are filled with men and women who advocate the values of participation and meaningful work and are experiencing the alienation associated with rampant individualism—the primary conditions that usually lead to the use of OD strategies. So why have these strategies not been used by many college or university leaders?

When we examine the academy's resistance to the principles and practices of organizational development, three main hindrances become apparent. First, as we noted in our discussion of the collegial culture, higher education is the bastion of rationality in North American society (Parsons & Platt, 1973). The collegial culture holds sway over the norms and values of most North American colleges and universities. Our students learn about the importance of rational thought and discourse; they are repeatedly taught that irrational, intuitive decision making has disastrous consequences in the laboratory, as well as in the halls of Congress, Parliament, and the White House.

This focus on rationality seems to contradict the emphasis on feelings and relationships that is found in the field of organizational development, and more generally in the developmental culture. Many academicians firmly believe that carefully researched and formulated policies and procedures will win over rational, dedicated colleagues. Lindquist (1978b, p. 2) clearly articulates the assumptions underlying this strategy: "Since we change on the basis of reason and evidence, the best way to obtain alterations in attitudes and behavior is to invest in systematic research and development of new knowledge, new practices, and new products. Apply a rational process to attain a rational end. If the research is correct and the development sound, the proposed change will sell itself." Any attempt to formulate a strategy for presenting a new idea that takes into account the personal interests and expectations of other parties, or that involves group review and negotiation, is considered a retreat into the undesirable realm of "campus politics," or worse yet, "groupthink."

Second, the concept of autonomy, another ingredient of the collegial culture, is widely accepted in American and Canadian colleges and universities and is reinforced by the collegial, virtual, and tangible cultures. Many faculty and administrators enter North American colleges and universities precisely because they wish to be left alone to pursue their own teaching, research, writing, or ideas. OD requires and promotes too much interdependence for most academicians' tastes. Finally, the colleges and universities of Canada and the United States often do not have sufficient financial resources to mount a major organizational development effort. Other human service agencies that are also strapped for funds somehow find the funds to support organizational development, but colleges and universities, under the guidance of the managerial culture, often encounter so many other demands for limited and often declining funds that they have little interest in taking the major risks associated with establishing an organizational development program. Thus, we find that the colleges and universities that provide many organizational development consultants for North American corporations, hospitals, churches, and schools do not themselves make use of such services. The prophet remains unheard and misunderstood in her own institution.

Given that organizational development is often blocked by financial realities, by the images that academicians hold about this behavioral science technique, and by the collegial and managerial cultures, how are we to create conditions for the use of these tools? We have three choices. First, we can ignore the six cultures of the academy and push ahead with organizational development strategies. The resistance of at least five of the cultures (the developmental culture being quite supportive of this approach) can perhaps be overcome by particularly skillful organizational consultants, usually from outside the institution. Second, we can attempt to alter one or more of these six cultures through the use of organizational development techniques. We have few examples to date that would lead us to expect that either of these approaches might be successful.

A third approach holds more promise. By appreciating and making use of the unique perspectives and strengths of each culture, we can actively engage all six in the processes of organizational development. To take this approach, however, requires an alteration in the ways that organizational development is usually conducted. We must use new tools and concepts regarding organizational change, stabilization, innovation, and analysis that are compatible with the six cultures if we are to engage them in the processes of institutional improvement.

Lindquist's (1978b) fourth strategy, the political approach, looks neither to the quality of the idea being offered nor to the nature of the interactions among those who are developing or implementing the idea. It focuses instead on the distribution and use of power in the postsecondary institution. Lindquist identifies one of the basic tenets that underlie this approach as the need to be sensitive to the wants expressed by various constituencies and the necessity of bringing these to the attention of influential members of the community or organization. Change will take place if the expressed wants are clearly articulated and are relevant to those who have influence in the community: "Unless these various wants are felt strongly by influential people, and the people who hold them bring together various subgroups, no change is likely" (p. 7).

According to Lindquist, it is critical for those who are concerned to make authorities take notice that a more desirable state of affairs is possible, even with existing resources and expertise. He says that a gatekeeper must bring proposals to the agenda of the authorities, where they get reviewed, modified, revised, and worked over: "Important to the survival of change proposals in this river of nibbling piranhas are the persistent efforts of highly influential 'issues sponsors' who are determined to carry the change through" (Lindquist, 1978b, p. 8).

Though this political strategy may, on the surface, look just as systematic as the rational planning strategy, it involves a considerable amount of intuition (like the human problem-solving approach) and a thorough knowledge of the diverse needs of the various constituencies that make up the community or organization (like the social interaction approach). The close connection between a political approach and the advocacy culture is readily apparent, whereas that between the political approach and the collegial culture is less apparent but no less important. Although the political processes associated with the advocacy culture are normally public and legalistic, allowing for negotiations that take place behind closed doors, those associated with the collegial culture are likely to be more informal and legislative in nature.

The variety of strategies that have been generated by the developmental culture illustrate the diversity of approaches that must be taken when addressing the complicated organizational cultures and problems now facing our colleges and universities. Bergquist and Phillips (1975, 1977, 1981) speak of the importance of bolstering any instructional or professional improvement program (process) with organizational (structure) and personal (attitude) components if they are to be successful. Similarly, anyone seeking to improve the academy must view the settings in which they work as communities, rather than just organizations—in other words, rational planning and human problem solving must be supplemented with Havelock's social interaction and Lindquist's political strategies. At the heart of the matter is the commitment of organizational leaders to a climate of learning that all members of the organization embrace (Argyris & Schön, 1974). As a "learning organization" (Argyris & Schön, 1978, 1996) with an "improvement-oriented ethos" (Kuh et al., 2005a, p. 133), a postsecondary institution must engage, learn about, and learn from all the strategies presented during the 1970s and 1980s by organizational development practitioners such as Bergquist, Phillips, and Lindquist. These strategies and perspectives are still relevant.

If contemporary campus leaders are preoccupied with the managerial, advocacy, virtual, and tangible cultures, they are likely to be preoccupied with structural solutions and with rational planning as the chief means of employing knowledge. As a result, they will often ignore important information about, or be oblivious to needs associated with, changes in process or attitude. They may also fail to take into account the political and communal nature of the institution in which they are trying to effect change. Similarly, twenty-first-century campus leaders from the collegial or developmental cultures are frequently ineffective when they look at an organization's problems only through the lens of either process or attitude or through the use of problem solving, social interaction, or political processes. They tend to ignore the substance of the change, while plotting complex public relations campaigns.

Those favoring attitude modification believe that real change only occurs when the heart has been transformed. By contrast, process-oriented change strategists propose that change will endure only if it involves relationships between people. Structural change advocates suggest that what counts is the financial outcome. For advocates of rational planning, the quality of the evidence and the message should be sufficient for any academic audience. Those who believe in human problem solving and social interaction are likely to stress the personal factor, whereas political advocates focus on the distribution of power. All of these perspectives and strategies are required if any developmental change effort is to have a deep, enduring impact. We can begin in any of the three domains of change or with any of the four knowledge utilization strategies. The important thing is to start and to recognize that eventually we must draw on all of these strategies if we are to meet the distinctive challenges and exploit the potential of each of the six cultures.

Recent Modifications in the Developmental Culture

By the mid-1970s, a relatively sophisticated and unified set of concepts had been developed about ways to approach development effectively in all aspects of postsecondary life (Bergquist & Shoemaker, 1976). The culture did not stop maturing, however, at this point. During the past thirty years, the developmental culture has been at least partially reactivated and redirected through the work of various writers and practitioners who have influenced the views of academic leaders on both scholarship and faculty development.

Developmentalists since the 1980s have tended to focus on the assessment of prior learning, authentic assessment, student learning outcomes, and a view of nontraditional scholarship that includes teaching and learning. These new developmental initiatives have in turn been inhibited by the weight, influence, and attraction of the dominant collegial and managerial cultures, and by financial and political issues. In some instances, these initiatives have morphed into associations and partnerships with other aspects of organizational life. In other instances, they have become embedded into institutional practices or discarded as lacking financial viability or academic merit (Newman, Couturier, & Scurry, 2004). Obviously, there has not been much of a shift in the overall structure of the higher education organization during the past two decades—with a few notable exceptions that have been identified by George Kuh and his colleagues in their study of student success and DEEP (Documenting Effective Educational Practice) institutions (Kuh et al., 2005a).

Learner- and Learning-Centered Education

There has been a surge of activity over the past dozen years in learning-centered practices (Bates & Poole, 2003). This surge was prompted by prior learning assessment, authentic assessment, the learning paradigm, and learning outcomes. Under the leadership of its president, Sister Joel Read, Alverno College has been engaged in the scholarship of teaching since 1973, well before Boyer coined that term in 1990. Alverno College has been cited as a model of good practice when it comes to undergraduates learning what they should learn. Over the past fifteen years, Alverno has developed and disseminated to other higher education institutions in Canada and the United States learning theories that deal with domains of growth, learning, and action. It distinguishes itself through its ability-based curriculum and its assessment practices. External assessors evaluate the learning of student group projects based on the ability clusters of the courses they are taking and their own personal learning outcomes (Mentkowski, 2000). In many ways, the Alverno program offers an effective marriage of the managerial and developmental cultures. Perhaps that is one of the reasons why this formerly obscure liberal arts women's college has received so much attention (and funding) over the past two decades.

A focus on learning outcomes is another instructional approach advanced by the developmental culture over the past fifteen years. In institutions that require and enforce the assessment of learning outcomes, the focus has tended to be on the learning of students rather than the preparation and "resourcing" (to use a managerial culture term) of faculty for presentation of these learning materials. Faculty members need to be aware of the effects of their instruction. Learning outcomes are not formulaic; rather, they encourage professors to shift away from a focus on content toward a focus on how that content will affect the student after the course is completed (Stiehl & Lewchuck, 2002). We observe, once again, a powerful alliance between the developmental and managerial cultures.

The developmental culture has further matured as a result of the learning paradigm movement initiated at Palomar College in San Diego, California, during the mid-1990s. This way of thinking about teaching and learning was catalyzed by an article that Robert Barr and John Tagg wrote for *Change* magazine in 1995 ("From Teaching to Learning: A New Paradigm for Undergraduate Education"), and by a national conference held at Palomar College in 1997. The article and the conference helped arouse widespread interest in learning rather than teaching as the basis of the academic enterprise (Tagg, 2003). "In the Instruction Paradigm, the mission of the college is to provide instruction, to teach. The method and the product are one and the same. The means is the end. In the Learning Paradigm, the mission of the college is to produce learning. The method and the product are separate. The end governs the means" (Barr & Tagg, 1995, p. 4).

This learner-centered perspective represented a shift in the instructional thinking and practice of many developmentally oriented faculty members in North America. Faculty began to look at their teaching enterprise not as an act of passing something on to their students—from expert to initiate—but from the point of view of the outcomes of their teaching. Barr and Tagg wanted all instructors to see themselves first as teachers, and then as members of a disciplinary group. In keeping with the developmental culture, they emphasized that "faculty members partner with students in a collaborative, team-based environment" (Garner, Pepicello, & Swenson, 2005, p. 133). In the teaching paradigm, professors focus on the content that will be covered. In the learning paradigm (and the new developmental culture), instructors focus on what will be different because of their classes—the outcomes they expect in student learning: "In the Instruction Paradigm, teaching is judged on its own terms; in the Learning Paradigm, the power of an environment or approach is judged in terms of its impact on learning" (Barr & Tagg, 1995, p. 8). Outcomes can be measured by the degree to which students learn the prestated outcomes.

This new developmentalist emphasis on a learner-centered orientation in the classroom has been complemented by an ever broader emphasis on the learning-centered organization. Building on the work of Chris Argyris and Donald Schön (1974, 1978, 1996), and the work of their famous student Peter Senge (1990), organizational leaders in many sectors of twenty-first-century North American society have begun to emphasize the need for organizational learning—a focus not on avoiding mistakes (which is difficult if not impossible given the postmodern influences faced today) but on learning from the mistakes that one has made. Applied to higher education institutions, this model of the learning organization, according to Lick (2002), focuses on four premises: (1) we inevitably live in an ever-changing environment; (2) this ever-changing environment provides the opportunity for creative and transformative learning; (3) learning opportunities are readily available in this ever-changing environment (especially, we would add, in an academic environment); and (4) a true learning culture can be established in which "learning is valued and designed to bring all members of [the institution and] society to the fullest development of their powers" (Lick, 2002, p. 29).

Scholarship Reconsidered: Reflection-in-Action

The influence of Chris Argyris and Donald Schön (particularly the latter) on the developmental culture goes beyond just the notion of the learning organization. Schön (1983) claims that traditional research rests on the assumptions of *technical rationality*. Technical rationality is the view that "professional activity consists of instrumental problem solving made rigorous by the application of scientific theory and technique" (Schön, 1983, p. 21). From the perspective of technical rationality, we need increasingly specialized scientific knowledge to view the world instrumentally and to solve its problems. Professionals should always seek more refined ways to define and interpret themselves and their work. High-status professions in a technical-rational society create knowledge using research-based practices couched in this technical rationality. Lower-status professions then apply the learning gained from scientific inquiry. According to Schön, our academic institutions live in the midst of this three-hundred-year-old technical-rational viewpoint. From this perspective, the human condition can be improved by harnessing science and technology to achieve human ends. Positivists during the past century have grounded empirical knowledge in sensory experience so that we might rid society of mysticism, superstition, and pseudoscience. This was helpful a hundred years ago, but it leaves practical knowledge and inquiry based on practice as a second cousin to scientifically developed knowledge. Schön proposed that we move from technical rationality to *reflection-in-action*. We must develop a new epistemology of practice. A practitioner can indeed "do research" that is valid; however, this requires a restructuring of the way in which research is viewed and the way it is approached methodologically.

Schön was not alone in his criticism of traditional distinctions between research and practice; the relationship between research, practice, and scholarship was further reframed during the 1990s and aligned with the values and perspectives of the developmental culture. Ernest Boyer's *Scholarship Reconsidered* (1990) validated the developmental culture's emphasis on faculty development, instructional improvement, and instructional efficacy. As a result of his 1989 survey of faculty across America (sponsored by The Carnegie Foundation for the Advancement of Teaching), Boyer concluded that we must "break out of the tired old teaching versus research debate and define, in more creative ways, what it means to be a scholar" (1990, p. xii). Over time, much of American higher education "moved from an emphasis on the student to an emphasis on the professoriate, from emphasis on generalized education to [an emphasis on] specialized education, and from loyalty to the campus to loyalty to the profession" (p. 13). In essence, Boyer was describing the emerging dominance of the German research model and the collegial culture.

Speaking on behalf of the new developmental culture, Boyer suggested that the academy can broaden its view of scholarship (and, by implication, research and practice). He identified four types of scholarship: discovery, integration, application, and teaching. *Discovery* is what we would call traditional research. The scholarship of *integration* involves making connections between disciplines. The scholarship of *application* involves the possible consequences of the newly gained knowledge. Finally, the scholarship of *teaching* might be the knowledge examined and gained through the kind of reflection-in-action about which Schön writes. All four of these perspectives on scholarship may lead into other areas of discovery and knowledge creation. A fifth perspective—*the scholarship of engagement*—has been identified more recently (Rice, 2005) as an elaboration beyond the scholarship of application and a movement beyond the "outreach" (agricultural extension) activities of the land-grant colleges. We shall return to this fifth perspective when we describe service learning initiatives in Chapter Four as a bridge between the advocacy and developmental cultures.

Boyer envisioned a developmentally oriented academic world in which constructed, objective knowledge that is related to the teaching and learning enterprise can be rigorously researched. He welcomed such research into the purview of more traditional research and scholarship that would lead to and sustain, among other things, tenure. When Boyer wrote *Scholarship Reconsidered*, research was under the purview of the collegial culture. It was the stepping-stone to professional recognition and the entryway to tenure and the maintenance of one's career. Although Boyer was not attacking traditional research by suggesting that research could be something else, he was crossing a line where faculty members engage in the creation of knowledge. Boyer wanted faculty to employ clear goals and instructional priorities, to adopt rigorous classroom assessment practices, and to exercise critical reflective practice.

As a result of Boyer's alternative, developmental vision, faculty members now have the opportunity to expand their definition of scholarship: "While no single document has ever changed American higher education at its core, the Boyer report continues to influence faculty and academic administrators in rethinking criteria for tenure, promotion, and the scope of faculty development programs" (Quehl, Bergquist, & Subbiando, 1999, p. 40). In large part Boyer's vision has been sustained by one of his associates, Gene Rice, and by the leadership of the American Association of Higher Education (particularly Russ Edgerton) and the Faculty Roles and Rewards program that Rice conducted for many years. Boyer's work—and that of numerous researchers and authors who have sustained and expanded on his work (Glassick, Huber, & Maeroff, 1997; O'Meara & Rice, 2005; Huber & Hutchings, 2005)—validated the perspectives of the new developmentalists.

Even more important, Boyer's vision has given credibility to the developmental perspective in a framework and through use of language that is generally acceptable to those aligned with the collegial culture. Ernest Boyer was someone with academic status in the collegial culture who declared that the work that faculty members do with students in the classroom is identified and valued as scholarly activity. Credible researchers are providing both qualitative and quantitative evidence to suggest that a reprioritizing of faculty roles can enhance the primary educational mission of many colleges and universities. Boyer offered an appreciative view of (and, in turn, validation for) a new developmentalist perspective that is beginning to influence the work of many twenty-first-century academicians.

Boyer's view of scholarship clearly holds broad-based culture-bridging implications. He appeals to collegial faculty who want to expand their approaches to instruction while retaining many of the traditional faculty prerogatives. In describing how Boyer's new scholarship model can have a successful impact on a liberal arts college like St. Norbert's, his own college, Zahorski (2005) indicates that faculty remain in charge of the process and engage in extended and often heated debate (collegial culture), yet are encouraged to collaborate with colleagues, find common ground for discussion, and work toward compromise (developmental culture). Faculty members are also encouraged to relate their work more closely to their institution's mission (developmental and managerial cultures) and ensure that the reward systems of their institution are compatible with the new, expanded definition of scholarship (advocacy culture).

Faculty in the developmental culture find that Boyer's view tends to validate what they are doing in the classroom and that his perspective and values appeal to the new student cohorts, which include often older and more experienced adults who are jaded by the positivistic approach of the traditional (collegial) higher education institution. Both the developmentalist and nontraditional student is often disillusioned with traditional approaches to scholarship, research, and technology. Developmentalists, along with their virtual culture colleagues, are aligned with mature students in their understanding of the complexities inherent in our contemporary world. Students from nondominant cultures, and those aligned with the advocacy culture who have studied and perhaps even experienced the exploitative sides of Western culture, also know that traditional approaches deliver traditional answers. Hence, they are likely to support Boyer's critical perspective.

Putting It All Together: Classroom Research

We are seeing a growing emphasis in the developmental culture on institutional research that is much more focused and intimate. This research is being conducted by individual faculty members on the processes and outcomes of teaching and learning in the classroom. This so-called classroom research initiative is more important and challenging than many college and university leaders (and opinion leaders outside the academy) are inclined to believe. It is important and challenging precisely because it focuses attention on and calls into question several fundamental assumptions that are widely held in higher education, and particularly in the collegial culture.

The first assumption concerns the incompatibility between research and teaching. As Burton Clark (1997, p. 241) noted in describing this incompatibility thesis: "We repeatedly hear assertions that when university professors do research they avoid teaching, that the time they spend on one is time taken from the other, that deep interest in research entails low interest in teaching, and, notably, that when academics do research they abandon students." If one begins with this oppositional assumption then it becomes clear that research on the dynamics of a classroom and the nature of effective teaching and learning must be carried out not by those doing the teaching, but instead by an outside, objective, and nonteaching educational, psychological, or sociological researcher. This fundamental assumption has blocked effective research by teaching practitioners for many years and contributed to a chasm between the collegial and developmental cultures.

Those aligned with the new developmental culture are thirsty for additional, empirically supported information about the dynamic teaching-learning-developmental process. Conversely, collegially oriented professors are inclined either to believe that classroom research is inevitably second-rate or unfeasible (given the messy variables involved) or that classroom research can and should only be done by those who are "qualified" researchers. As Boyer has already noted, the oppositional nature of teaching and research is a fiction, and classroom research can put a final nail in this coffin. Teaching and research can complement one another, interweave with one another, and enable an academician to be both a better teacher and a better researcher.

The second assumption being challenged by classroom research concerns the exclusive formulation of classroom teaching and learning strategies by means of *replication* (doing what my favorite or most admired professor did), *intuition* (doing what "feels right"), *hard-earned experience* (doing what I have found to be effective as I have done more teaching), *appeasement* (doing what the students want or will tolerate rather than what I think they need), or *nihilistic retreat* (doing whatever will get me through the class period). Classroom research suggests that one can gain experience and improve one's own strategies and teaching practices through Schön's systematic, reflective inquiry. Although other developmental initiatives have encouraged faculty members to explore alternative teaching strategies and critically examine their own pet beliefs about teaching and learning, classroom research enables them to better understand what is actually occurring in their own classrooms—not in someone else's classroom or in a hypothetical classroom: "The assessment movement, and especially the phenomenon of classroom assessment, [has] sharpened higher education's focus on student learning and provided tools for faculty members seeking to investigate the impact of their course design and pedagogies on learning" (Huber, Hutchings, & Shulman, 2005, p. 35).

The third basic assumption is actually a set of two interdependent assumptions. The first concerns the critical time that must be devoted to any form of research in the classroom—that this is time taken away from the actual teaching and learning process. Furthermore, it is assumed that the only moment to do classroom research is when one is innovating. Traditionally, classroom innovation has been a very risky proposition. It has been assumed (especially by those in the collegial culture) that teaching is a nonspecifiable art form. Supposedly, there really is not anything new to learn about teaching because many great minds in many great institutions have been engaged in this subtle, artful process for many centuries. Classroom researchers call this third interwoven set of assumptions into question by showing that research practices can be incorporated into the daily life of the classroom without taking time away from the teaching-learning enterprise and that there is something new to learn about the classroom.

The developmentalist may agree with the collegial professor that teaching is an art form; however, through the use of classroom research practices, this art form can be better understood and improved. Similarly, although developmentalists have often been unsuccessful in the past in persuading faculty aligned with the collegial culture (or the advocacy culture) to try out new instructional practices, there is new hope when classroom research practices are engaged. Classroom research results frequently shatter enduring assumptions about the teaching-learning process. Considering the potential role of classroom research in challenging fundamental assumptions and enabling the new developmentalists to more effectively influence their collegial, advocacy, and even managerial colleagues, we will dwell on this emerging initiative and identify some of its sources, variations, and potential uses.

First, classroom research practices come directly out of the "heartland" of the developmental culture. Educational researchers like Feldman and Newcomb (1969) and psychologists like McKeachie (1964), Chickering (1969), and Sanford (1962) set the stage by conducting major research projects on the needs of students, the effectiveness of specific educational practices, and the developmental processes associated with teaching and learning. These major figures in the developmental culture, however, conducted these studies from outside the role of teacher. They operated exclusively as researchers, even though in many cases they were themselves gifted teachers and made use of their own research findings in designing courses, building curricula, and even creating new institutions. Classroom research moved a step further by directly involving teachers in the study of their own teaching and the resultant learning that occurs.

Nevitt Sanford and other more contemporary educator advocates for *action research* processes have always argued for the direct involvement of practitioners in research on their own work (Kember & McKay, 1996; Huber et al., 2005). As we noted earlier, Schön challenged the basic assumption about the opposition between research and practice—the fundamental assumption that underlies Burton Clark's incompatibility thesis. Schön suggests that all research is practice and that all effective practice inevitably involves the process of reflection that underlies all research (whether basic or applied). Other educators, who have generally focused on adult learners, such as Mezirow (1981, 1997) and Brookfield (1995, 2004), have similarly described the process of education and learning in terms of what Mezirow (1981) calls a *perspective transformation* that necessitates a reflection back on and a testing of one's own assumptions (hypotheses, if you will). With the recognition that this form of ongoing reflection was of great benefit to any professional—including a professional academician—many leaders in higher education (most notably Patricia Cross, 1990) began speaking and writing in favor of and preparing tools to be used in ongoing classroom research projects.

The world of classroom research has arrived and is now firmly established in North American higher education. It must successfully confront several significant challenges, however, if it is to remain viable and truly helpful to classroom instructors. First, the field is too dependent on psychological tools and concepts, yet, at the same time, classroom researchers are often relatively unaware of some of the most important concepts now being offered by psychologists. Unfortunately, many psychologists are still confined by Schön's technical rationality and early twentieth-century concepts of "scientism" (Magnusson, 1997). This has often led to the use of insensitive (usually quantitative) measures of complex teaching and learning processes. There is widespread failure to recognize the value of qualitative measures, such as interviews, participant observation, phenomenological analysis, and nontraditional quantitative measures, such as multiple regression analysis, factor analysis, and computer-based simulations of classroom dynamics. Some of the most valuable insights in contemporary psychology (on cognitive processes and the neurosciences) have not yet been brought to bear on the analysis of classroom dynamics, the construction of a curriculum, or the "semantic organization of a knowledge domain" (Magnusson, 1997, p. 197).

There is a second challenge. Although it is of great benefit to individual instructors to formulate a research question that relates specifically to their own classroom and their own instructional objectives, this individualistic approach can lead to a fragmented analysis of the overall teaching and learning processes of the academy. How do the processes operating in each classroom contribute to or distract from the institution's overall educational intentions and its definition of instructional quality? Classroom research is of greatest, sustained benefit when closely aligned with several of the other initiatives that have been championed by both the old and new developmental culture—namely, faculty development, institutional research, and in particular, the comprehensive assessment of student engagement and success (Kuh et al., 2005b). Classroom research has helped build a bridge between the developmental culture and the other cultures of the academy. It will only convey valuable insights into the teaching and learning process across this bridge, however, if aided by a sustained program of student assessment and faculty development that is closely tied to a comprehensive strategy of institutional research.

Living and Working in the Developmental Culture Today

The institutional values inherent in the developmental culture concern three distinct but interrelated aspects of institutional life: teaching and learning, personal and organizational maturation, and institutional mission. All three of these sets of values link the developmental culture more closely to the managerial than to the collegial culture. Proponents of the managerial culture are also particularly concerned with teaching and learning (as they relate to student learning outcomes), personal and organizational maturation (as this maturation influences institutional operations), and the mission and goals of the institution (as they inform and align with the institution's strategic plan). Yet as in all aspects of their culture, developmentalists attempt to address these values from a perspective that is compatible with, or at least not offensive to, faculty in the collegial culture.

Teaching and Learning

Those in the developmental culture generally believe that teaching and learning—rather than traditional research or scholarly pursuits—should be at the heart of the academic enterprise. They generally support an interdisciplinary, problem-solving, or theme-oriented approach to curriculum development as a result of their belief that the collegial culture's preoccupation with disciplines ill prepares students for a world of complex, systemic issues (Chickering et al., 1977). Faculty members who represent the developmental culture often identify themselves as teachers rather than as physicists, auto mechanics, or historians. They read higher education literature and research in other fields rather than sticking strictly to their own discipline, occupation, or institution.

Developmentalists are not parochial in their perspective on either the teaching-learning process or the dynamics of their own institution. Rather than focus on local and immediate issues, the developmentalists (like their virtual colleagues) have been inclined to read in the behavioral sciences (change theory, organizational theory and research, student development theory and research) and looked to those education-oriented philosophers and interdisciplinary scholars such as Dewey ([1916], 1944), Polanyi (1969), and Bateson (1972, 1979) who espoused experience-based learning, systemic thinking, and reorganization of human knowledge. More recently, there has been a call for a level and range of "pedagogical intelligence" (Huber & Hutchings, 2005, p. 118) that goes well beyond the behavioral sciences. This intelligence is required not just of faculty members and academic administrators who wish to enhance student success (Kuh et al., 2005a) but also of students—and perhaps all members of our contemporary society. It centers on systemic thinking, critical reflection on one's own assumptions, the capacity to rethink and reframe complex twenty-first-century issues, and (in a state of *flow*) the balancing of challenge and support (Csikszentmihalyi, 1975, 1990; Schön, 1983; Senge, 1990; Bergquist & Mura, 2005).

Personal and Organizational Maturation

The second set of developmental values, focusing on personal and organizational maturation, was borrowed during the 1960s from the literature on organizational development in corporate settings (Schein & Bennis, 1965). One of these values concerns the role that science plays in human endeavors. Developmentalists believe that a rational approach to understanding and planning for human interaction is imperative and inherently valuable. The spirit of inquiry that pervades the sciences is assumed to be appropriate and desirable in helping people and institutions mature. This long-standing hypothetical spirit is generally compatible with the collegial culture's skepticism about pat answers and programs, but it is incompatible with the managerial culture's emphasis on decisiveness and clarity. Conversely, the experimentalism of the developmental culture tends to be positively received by the managerial culture, with its emphasis on action and innovation, but is incompatible with the collegial culture's dislike of learning by doing rather than by deliberation or observation.

Another enduring developmental value involves choice and ownership. Representatives of the developmental culture inevitably seem to appreciate expanded choice and "consciousness" in the people with whom they work (Argyris, 1970). In addition, they respect the process of collaboration, whereby those with whom they work gain a clear sense of having participated directly in the decision to select a particular option. A developmentalist might suggest five different ways in which a course could be taught and then help faculty members collect pertinent information on which to base a rational choice among them. The choice is always in the hands of the faculty member rather than the developmental practitioner. In organizational settings, developmentalists strongly believe that decisions should be made by the people who possess the most information. These people are not necessarily located at the top of the organization's hierarchy (Beckhard, 1969).

Information is inherently valuable to individuals and organizations, according to the developmentalists. In accordance with a classic model offered by Kurt Lewin and his colleagues (best summarized by Lippitt, Watson, & Westley, 1958), developmentalists believe "unfreezing," as a precondition to real learning and change, will take place only with the introduction of new information that somehow calls into question an individual's or an organization's current self-perceptions. Developmentalists encourage direct, open, and clear feedback. They welcome (or at least purport to welcome) reactions, perceptions, and expectations of others about their own behavior. Information about one's own behavior, according to the developmentalists, is essential if one is to continue to mature and become more successful in organizational settings.

Most members of the developmental culture espouse two other values related to personal and organizational maturation. These are a commitment to inclusiveness and an emphasis on conflict resolution through rational means. Traditional authoritarian relationships between students and faculty are discouraged. Student involvement and rich dialogue between faculty and students into the nature of teaching, learning, and scholarship are encouraged. Huber and Hutchings' (2005) Carnegie Foundation study of teaching and learning embodies these values through the use of such phrases as "a teaching commons" and the "campus as commons." The developmentalists even move beyond the teaching-learning enterprise and join with some advocates when they suggest that students and staff should be free to question decisions made by faculty or administrators and to take part in the reformulation of plans, in the aforementioned spirit of inquiry, testing of hypotheses, and experimentation. Conflicts are regarded in the developmental culture as a symptom of unmet needs, lack of information, or inadequate planning. In this last enduring value, developmentalists often find the greatest incompatibility between their culture and the other cultures of most North American colleges and universities. Each of the other cultures espouses different ways of working with conflict and generally views the highly rationalistic model of the developmentalist as simplistic and minimally helpful in politically charged and complicated academic settings that demand quick and decisive decisions.

Institutional Mission

The third category of values associated with the developmental culture concerns institutional mission. A faculty member or administrator in the managerial culture often desires clarification of goals and more specific objectives as a basis for strategic planning and program evaluation. By contrast, the developmentalist frequently asks: What are we really doing in this college and university, and is it what we should be doing? Are our goals directly related to our essential mission (Kanter, 1984; Peters, 1988; Drucker, 1999)? Even more specifically, in recent years developmentalists have often centered their attention and questions on the core purpose of any educational institution—namely, the engagement and success of its students (Kuh et al., 2005a). At this point, the new developmentalist, now more a philosopher than a behavioral scientist, finds the greatest compatibility with those in the collegial culture. However, unlike the collegial faculty or those aligned with the tangible culture, developmentalists believe that the use of precedent does not enable a college or university to change in response to shifting societal needs and values, nor to enhance educational effectiveness on behalf of student success. Furthermore, the disciplinary goals espoused by many in the collegial culture (and in the tangible culture) leave a college or university fragmented and isolated. The teaching and campus commons envisioned by new developmentalists such as Huber and Hutchings (2005) is nowhere in sight.

Institutional Influence and Change

Finally, perhaps we should look, as we did in the previous two chapters, at the role played by developmental leaders in building a consensus-based model of quality improvement or in assisting the ongoing development of an institution of higher education. Faculty and academic administrators attracted to the developmental culture usually prefer a different mode of leadership than that found in the other cultures. Leadership here tends to be exerted in complex and nontraditional ways. Using Max Weber's analysis of power and authority (1947), we can postulate that the developmental leader tries to make use of "expert" power rather than the managerial culture's "rational-legal" power or authority derived from positioning the managerial hierarchy. Developmentalists also attempt to avoid the "charismatic" and paternalistic power that is so common in the collegial culture and choose instead a more collaborative or autonomous form of authority. In keeping with the broader analysis provided by Collins (2001) in his study *Good to Great*, developmental leaders are likely to be modest yet diligent in pursuing specific, and often long-term, goals. The leaders of colleges and universities who have been identified by Kuh and his associates (Kuh et al., 2005a) as being particularly effective tend to exemplify Collins's low-key leadership profile. Similarly, leaders identified by Bergquist and Armstrong (1986) serve as champions rather than initiators of successful new programs. The academic leaders identified by Lick (2002) as change sponsors also exemplify this developmental model of leadership.

Put another way, leadership is manifested indirectly in the developmental culture. Whereas leadership in the managerial culture is exerted through the authority of formal-line relationships, developmental leaders often serve in a staff role—influencing rather than controlling, suggesting rather than demanding, informing rather than directing. The political maneuvering of the collegial leader is replaced by the developmentalist's provision of service. Rather than attending faculty meetings on curricular change, these leaders conduct or attend (with colleagues) workshops on processes of curricular reform or alternative curricular designs. Instead of struggling through a departmental discussion of alternative tenure review systems, developmental leaders begin working with individual faculty members on career plans so that they can be prepared for either a positive or negative decision. Rather than operating through unions or other advocacy structures, developmentalists tend to work collaboratively (and perhaps naively) with all parties to a conflict.

This notion of indirect and collaborative leadership in the developmental culture is good news for many college and university leaders. Developmental leaders do not have to challenge the leadership of others in their institution. Developmental leadership can be exerted, instead, in more indirect ways—perhaps through a unique model of leadership known as *servant leadership*. This model was first articulated by Robert Greenleaf (1970, 1972, 1974, 1979, 1980) in his series of books on the servant-leader in higher education and remains a source of inspiration and even a guidebook for many developmental leaders.

Conclusions

Like leaders in the advocacy culture—to which we are about to turn—developmental leaders reside outside any formal role or lines of authority in the postsecondary institution. However, unlike advocacy leaders, developmental leaders do not seek to change the institution through collective force. They prefer to encourage increased collective awareness of the problems facing the institution and joint recognition of alternative solutions to these problems. In this way, the assumption of organizational rationality enters a developmentalist's strategy for effective institutional leadership. In order to redirect the attention of colleagues to the basic teaching and learning mission of the college or university, the developmental leader constantly asks: What is it we want to do in this organization? In this way, developmentalists direct attention away from the personal issues and power struggles that often preoccupy faculty and administrators in the other cultures.

Developmental leaders are frequently perceived by others as idealistic and ineffective in their abiding concern for teaching and learning and their use of service to gain influence. In recent years, however, proponents of the developmental perspective have begun to enter positions of formal leadership in American colleges and universities. Leaders in the field have become college presidents, deans, and directors of major programs in higher education. Will these men and women have to abandon or at least modify their developmental perspectives? Will they be able to influence their colleagues rooted in the managerial or collegial cultures? What about relationships between the emerging leaders of the developmental and advocacy cultures? Will they be able to collaborate on future plans for change in higher education as representatives of two cultures that have arisen in reaction to the inadequacies of the dominant cultures? Given the short history of the developmental culture, we will have to wait some time before we arrive at any adequate answers to these questions.

4

The Advocacy Culture

> *The advocacy culture:* A culture that finds meaning primarily in the establishment of equitable and egalitarian policies and procedures for the distribution of resources and benefits in the institution; that values confrontation and fair bargaining among constituencies, primarily management and faculty or staff, who have vested interests that are inherently in opposition; that holds assumptions about the ultimate role of power and the frequent need for outside mediation in a viable academic institution; and that conceives of the institution's enterprise as either the undesirable promulgation of existing (and often repressive) social attitudes and structures or the establishment of new and more liberating social attitudes and structures.

The advocacy culture emerged in response to the inability of the managerial culture to meet the personal and financial needs of faculty and staff. If administrators act as though they are responsible for the formulation of institutional policy, then faculty members will have to reestablish their influence through collective action. Although faculty unions and collective agreements about salary, job security, and working conditions have been present for many years in North American higher education, the movement toward faculty unionization and collective bargaining grew stronger during the 1970s—even in the four-year colleges and universities, which had been bastions of the collegial and managerial cultures. Unionization remains an important fact of life in many contemporary colleges and universities.

A faculty member in the advocacy culture believes that change takes place through confrontation and the effective use (or more often, withholding of the use) of prized resources. Collective bargaining negotiations have traditionally focused on compensation and personnel issues. Faculty members have also borrowed from their fellow teachers in elementary and secondary schools the notion that curricular and teaching-learning issues can be negotiated too. More recently, collective bargaining in higher education has focused on the nature of tenure and the part-time faculty member (Palmer, 1999). An entire culture, with its own philosophy of education, performance standards, and status criteria, has come into being.

Origins of the Advocacy Culture

Just as the community college provided a setting for the managerial culture to take root, so too did it prove to be fertile ground for the advocacy culture. The close connection between these two-year institutions and elementary and secondary education systems undoubtedly contributed to the early interest of community college faculty members in collective bargaining. Many of their colleagues in elementary and secondary school systems had already established collective bargaining agreements with their institutions.

Collective bargaining was much less welcome in the four-year institutions. Not until the late 1960s was collective bargaining established in any of these bastions of the collegial culture. In their early study of collective bargaining at four-year college and university campuses in the United States, Carr and Van Eyck (1973, p. 17) observed: "Faculty collective bargaining made its appearance at four-year institutions on a scattered, somewhat spotty basis. The starting point might be marked as September 1969, for on that date agreements took effect between the City University of New York (CUNY) and the two units into which its instructional staff had been divided for bargaining purposes." Although there was a union movement in the 1940s at the University of Alberta and the University of British Columbia, it was not until the early 1970s that collective bargaining was initiated in Canada in earnest. At that time faculty wanted to protect their jobs because there were higher demands by the public for professors and a decrease in student enrollments (Horn, 1999).

Collective Bargaining

Frank Kemerer and Victor Baldridge note that, as of 1975, one-eighth of the colleges and universities in the United States had faculty bargaining agents. At that time, "nearly 12 percent of all professional staff and over 20 percent of the full-time teaching faculty in American higher education [were] represented by unions" (Kemerer & Baldridge, 1975, p. 1). By 1979, faculty at 116 four-year institutions, representing at least 258 campuses, had approved collective bargaining (Johnstone, 1981). By 1986, over 208,000 faculty members were covered by collective bargaining agreements and were represented by collective bargaining agents at 458 institutions (Douglas, 1988). Of the 1,501 campuses in the public sector, 61 percent were unionized; approximately 5 percent of the 1,830 campuses in the private sector were unionized as of 1986 (Euben & Hustoles, 2001). These statistics suggest that by the mid-1980s the advocacy culture was strong in public institutions, whether two- or four-year, but not in private institutions.

Most faculty members in private institutions are restricted from entering bargaining units because of the *Yeshiva* U.S. Supreme Court ruling in 1980. This ruling claimed that Yeshiva University faculty members were in control of substantially enough decisions at that institution to be considered managers, not staff. This ruling has hindered many faculty members in private institutions from entering collective bargaining—though the *Yeshiva* ruling has been challenged in recent years and faculty members at private colleges in most other countries have no problem belonging to a union, even if they move into academic administrative positions (Gayle, Tewaire, & White, 2003). At the present time, most collective bargaining among faculty in private institutions in the United States is dictated by federal law, whereas the collective bargaining of faculty in public U.S. institutions tends to be dictated by state law (Cohen, 1998). Although differences between the legal status of collective bargaining in private and public institutions certainly influence the nature and power of collective bargaining, the more fundamental determining factor may be differing cultural preferences. Faculty members in private institutions may be more likely than faculty in public institutions to prefer the collegial or developmental models of decision making. They would rather play politics (collegial) than unionize, or would rather collaborate (developmental) than confront.

Although many faculty in higher education institutions are not unionized and many individual faculty members do not want to join unions, the overall support among faculty members for collective bargaining is impressive. As early as 1969, Ladd and Lipset (1973) found that nearly 60 percent of all faculty members in the United States gave general endorsement to the principle of collective bargaining. The total amount of support for collective bargaining as a reasonable approach to solving conflict in North American higher education appears to still be strong—perhaps because it involves much more than just formalized faculty unions. It involves the broader issue of what Robert Birnbaum (2004, p. 12) labels "procedural justice"—or "the perceived fairness of the processes through which organizational decisions are made."

This emphasis on perception rather than objective reality is particularly important in Birnbaum's (2004, p. 13) analysis (and in any assessment of organizational cultures): "Fairness of procedure has no objective criteria—it is what the members of the group believe it to be. Agreement on fairness comes from the processes of socialization through which group members come to share values and beliefs; new members of the group learn these values from the older members." We believe that this same analysis is applicable to the overall assessment of the advocacy culture's viability in all academic institutions, and more generally, to the viability of any organizational culture in twenty-first-century colleges and universities.

Thus, those who are associated with the advocacy culture are likely to look out for and be particularly sensitive to processes and procedures being used in their institutions that appear to be unjust or that do not square with their institution's espoused mission and values. They might not join collective bargaining units in their institution or join the picket lines—but they do grow angry and restless when they perceive injustice in any domain of the academy. In this volume, we have used the term *advocacy* rather than the term *collective bargaining* precisely because of this broader concern for and sensitivity to social justice and the broader base of support for this culture among many members of the academy.

Rise of the Advocacy Culture

What are the sources of the advocacy culture in addition to the perception of procedural injustice? What forces could have led to the eventual acceptance of this seemingly alien culture in a traditional academic setting? Why did collective bargaining appear at this particular point in the history of North American higher education? The key may reside in perceived threats to two of the three fundamental concerns expressed by the twentieth-century (modern) worker: job security, compensation, and organizational health (Bergquist, 1993). Perhaps academicians are not really that different from workers in other kinds of institutions. Although faculty during the 1970s were not very concerned about organizational health (with some horrific exceptions, such as the more recent mass shootings, there is usually not much need to worry about work-related injuries in the classroom), they were very concerned about compensation and somewhat concerned about job security.

Compensation was a big issue. Ladd and Lipset (1973) suggested that compensation was one of the major factors in faculty endorsing collective bargaining, and they pointed to the movement from post–World War II prosperity in higher education (responsive in part to the baby boom) to a period of financial retrenchment during the 1970s—a retrenchment that has continued in varying degrees ever since the halcyon days of the 1960s. Prior to the 1960s, faculty members did not expect to receive competitive salaries. Beginning in the nineteenth century, many faculty members found work outside the academy, often as clergy, to supplement their faculty salary. They could not complain about low salaries, because other recent graduates could readily take their jobs (Cohen, 1998). Other faculty members, in keeping with the elitism of the collegial culture, entered college and university teaching for the prestige, not the income, often coming from families of wealth.

By the mid-1960s, however, with burgeoning financial support for both public and private colleges and universities, faculty salaries suddenly became more attractive, and first-generation graduates were more inclined to look to college and university teaching as a well-paid profession. Only a few years later, the comparative salary levels tailed off and postsecondary teaching was no longer a road to financial well-being. "Faculty salaries reached their peak in 1972–73 and then tumbled with respect to the salaries of other occupational groups" (Gappa, Austin, & Trice, 2007, p. 53). Furthermore, "faculty found they could not receive pay increments sufficient to keep up with inflation.... The faculty might also have been demoralized by the variations in pay received by instructors in the different disciplines" (Cohen, 1998, pp. 211–212). The situation was ripe for collective bargaining to gain steam. The issue of job security was also beginning to arise during the 1970s—not so much because faculty members were afraid of losing their job (especially if they were tenured), but because it looked like their institutions were about to be "invaded" by part-time instructors, and eventually, non-tenure-track positions. Their fears were soon realized, as we will note in our discussion of the virtual culture and part-time faculty in Chapter Five.

Johnstone (1981) identified another reason: the bureaucratization of colleges and universities. We associate increased bureaucratization throughout this book with the spread of the managerial culture beyond the Catholic and community colleges. It may have also served as an impetus for a counterculture—namely, the advocacy culture. In the early 1970s, Ladd and Lipset (1973) pointed to growing organizational size and complexity as an additional factor in faculty endorsement of collective bargaining. The alienation that often seems to be associated with major growth in the size and complexity of any institution may be a related, contributing factor. In his very popular book *The Tipping Point*, Malcolm Gladwell (2000) suggested that 150 may be the maximum number of people that can operate effectively and coherently in a single group. People simply do not have the cognitive capacity to work with larger numbers of relationships and may, as a result, find larger organizational units to be confusing, at the very least, and often alienating as well.

Increasing academic specialization and professionalization that are associated, ironically, with both bureaucratization in the managerial culture and isolation in the collegial culture may be another source of energy for the advocacy culture (Johnstone, 1981). When faculty members are consumed by administrative "atrocities" and find that they have in common only their contempt for management rather than teaching, research, or scholarship, there is little reason to believe that any academic culture other than advocacy will find sufficient nourishment to thrive, or even survive.

Carr and Van Eyck (1973) identified still another reason for the rise in collective bargaining in the early 1970s: widespread faculty dissatisfaction with the governance systems employed by many higher education institutions. In this sense, the advocacy culture directly confronted the primary domain of the collegial culture. Carr and Van Eyck related the rise of collective bargaining directly to "the desire to improve working conditions other than compensation—in particular to alter [faculty roles] in institutional governance" (p. 57). Bureaucratized institutional structures may have contributed to this seemingly pervasive faculty concern about governance systems. The kind of governance that faculty members wish to have over the affairs of the organization has less to do with the administration of the organizational machinery and more to do with protection of the academic freedom that the collegial culture values so fiercely.

For both those aligned with the collegial culture and those aligned with the advocacy culture, there is a primary concern with what Gayle et al. (2003, p. 9) describe as "confidence building, over time, based on intensive, communication-rich interactions between permeable companies of co-equals." Unfortunately, many faculty members do not believe that the administrators of their institutions consistently act in a manner that builds this confidence. In many instances, an inherent conflict seems to exist between the administration's and the faculty's management of the academy—the "communities of difference" articulated by Tierney (1993). In arguing against faculty governance, according to Ernst Benjamin, leaders of our society often fail to recognize "that the effective management of the university requires, indeed thrives, on a constructive tension between faculty and administration" (Benjamin, 1997, n.p.). As we noted in Chapter Two, the higher education organization has grown to resemble a large corporation that requires management to make its decisions about cutting costs and dealing with efficiency, just as any large industrial organization might do. The turn to advocacy was inevitable (Nielsen & Polishook, 1985).

We seem to be returning once more to Birnbaum's (2004) focus on procedural justice, as many observers point to the desire of faculty members to retain their control of academic decision-making processes. On behalf of the advocacy culture, Benjamin (1997, n.p.) suggests that there is more to the academy and to faculty governance than just balanced books:

> When faculty bargain matters of academic policy, bargaining is rarely over substance but almost always limited to establishing and assuring the procedures for faculty participation and respect for faculty judgment in other venues....
>
> Consequently, despite the judicially created conflict between faculty bargaining and faculty governance, the legal right to bargain is the principal source of the faculty's collective power, in many public colleges and universities, to ensure continued and effective participation in shared governance.

If academic decisions are to consider the faculty's side, faculty must be involved. One way for faculty to have a say in academic decisions is for those in the collegial culture to bow to the advocacy culture. Faculty members often agree to enter a collective bargaining unit in order to protect the faculty governance model. Birnbaum (2004) addresses this concern directly when he writes about the potential end of shared governance models that involve both faculty and administration in ongoing decision-making processes in the academy.

Assuming something of an advocate role, Birnbaum (2004, p. 7) proposes that academic institutions are more effective when governance is shared: "Faculty involvement in shared governance may slow down the decision-making process, but it also assures more thorough discussion and provides the institution with a sense of order and stability." He expands on this point by noting the differences between academic institutions and market-driven institutions (including for-profit educational institutions). According to Birnbaum:

> [Academic institutions] . . . are not concerned with profit, but with performance of mission; because that mission cannot be clearly articulated, the means to achieve it is always a matter of contention rather than certainty . . . . The purpose of academic institutions is not to create products but to embody ideas. Academic governance cannot be rationalized for the same reason that it is not possible to rationalize the purposes for which academic institutions exist. [2004, p. 18]

Violating the Psychological Contract

At a much deeper level, the advocacy culture and collective bargaining are viable in part because with the dominance of the managerial culture over the collegial culture there has been a violation of the "psychological contract" between faculty members and their institutions. To understand the nature of this psychological contract and the role it plays (often implicitly) in the advocacy culture, we must pause for a moment and reflect on the shifting definition of what it means to be a human being in our society. We propose that in the modern world of the twentieth century, one of our primary definitions of humankind was economic in nature and that a psychological contract was established between employees and their organizations (Bergquist, 1993).

In higher education institutions, this contract involves the college or university's expectations of the individual employee and the employee's attempts to meet these expectations. It also includes expectations of the employee, and the employer's continuing willingness to satisfy those needs. Every member of an organization, in essence, establishes a tacit (unacknowledged, often unconscious) contract between himself or herself and the employing organization (Schein, 1980). The psychological contract usually has to do with the rewards that the employee expects from the organization and the resources, services, and attitudes that the employee will provide the organization in return.

The rewards that an employee expects range from seemingly rational and publicly acknowledged expectations about salary, benefits, and job security, to often unacknowledged expectations about career advancement, public recognition, and meaningful work, and even more highly irrational expectations about self-worth, personal security, and friendship. Employees also tacitly expect to provide a variety of services and display certain attitudes. Some of these services and attitudes are publicly established, such as schedules. Others are less public, such as a willingness to overlook the incompetence of managers or a willingness to work overtime without complaining. At a particularly deep level, the employee may be selling his soul to the company in exchange for personal self-esteem. Faustian agreements may be engaged in the deep recesses of many employee psyches. Usually psychological contracts are unacknowledged and not discussable in organizations. Everyone knows that they exist, but no one ever talks about them—in part because they are very personal and often unrealistic or unfair to either the employee or the organization.

We propose that much of the discontent inside many colleges and universities—and the rise of the advocacy culture and collective bargaining—can be traced to the breaking of psychological contracts between the academy and its employees. Major universities, for instance, that have a long history of stable employment may attract psychological contracts in which employees expect to have lifelong employment in exchange for faithful service, a passive acceptance of authority, and even the ineffectiveness of the institution's administration. Furthermore, the psychological contract for many faculty members in both colleges and universities undoubtedly includes the collegial culture's expectations about mutual respect, autonomy, and status. When these expectations are violated, then collective bargaining may be just around the corner (Bowen & Schuster, 1986; Cohen, 1998).

Multiple Faculty Perspectives on Advocacy

There may be yet another powerful and often unacknowledged dynamic operating. For at least some faculty members, advocacy may have gotten started in part to confront an internal enemy. This enemy is the established faculty power in many academic institutions. It is not just administrators that faculty accuse of being indifferent to their needs and interests; it is also fellow academics who have attained very powerful roles on campus that must somehow be confronted through collective, negotiating action. The war between the "Old Guard" and the "Young Rebels" that has for many years centered on issues associated with collective bargaining may reside at the heart or near the heart of this discontent (Carr & Van Eyck, 1973). Furthermore, this split between "Old Guard" and "Young Rebels" may even be greater today, with the increasing number of older faculty (Bland & Bergquist, 1997) as well as the recent increase in newly minted faculty as a result of the beginning groundswell of retirements.

The Old Guard may now be particularly interested in protection afforded by a union when it comes to retirement benefits, age discrimination, and new contractual arrangements for part-time faculty after formal retirement. The tension between old and new faculty may be further exacerbated when young faculty members identify themselves with an enterprising new president (or vice versa), rather than with department chairs or senior faculty members. In such situations, the decision to turn to collective bargaining is not necessarily the work of young faculty members. They might, however, attempt to influence or even gain control of the faculty's labor organization and the negotiations at the bargaining table once their more conservative colleagues have supplied many of the votes in favor of collective bargaining.

Though collective bargaining seems to have originated in the managerial culture, this Old Guard–Young Rebel conflict as a source of collective bargaining finds its origins in the collegial culture. Kemerer and Baldridge offered a keen insight over thirty years ago into the appeal of faculty unions to two different faculty groups: those who are "preservation-oriented" and those who consider themselves "deprived."

> The first are essentially high-status professors who, like their skilled counterparts in the industrial sector, have realized that their rights and privileges within the institution can no longer be safeguarded by tradition alone. The second—the "deprivation" group—are those who view collective bargaining as a means to gain power and benefits previously denied them. Like the semi- and unskilled workers in the industrial sector, they view collective bargaining as a means of enfranchisement. [1975, pp. 64–65]

Preservation-oriented faculty members tend to move toward collective bargaining from a collegial culture—often in an attempt to somehow secure the future of this culture. Faculty members who feel deprived generally have long ago abandoned the collegial culture in favor of a managerial (or antimanagerial) attitude that emphasizes personnel and fiscal concerns more than academic issues such as teaching, research, or scholarship.

Kezar, Carducci, and Contreras-McGavin (2006) seem to identify a third group of faculty who are attracted to and apply strategies of the advocacy culture. Making use of concepts introduced by Meyerson and Scully (Meyerson, 2001, 2003) in their study of social movement, Kezar and her associates (p. 82) describe the "tempered radicals who patiently and persistently advance an agenda of social change in their organizations or the society at large." These tempered radicals build a personalized and contextualized framework for change. They are likely to focus on congruence between what someone says and what that person does, rather than trying to bring about broader (and more abstract) organizational change. They are also more likely to attempt influence and change among a small group of people (depth) rather than try to influence or change a large group of people (breadth). Not surprisingly, many of these tempered radicals come from ethnic cultures that encourage community and collaboration and are influenced by the feminist epistemologies and change strategies of the late twentieth century. These women and men are advocates who speak softly and work collaboratively and congruently while effecting change that is likely to be sustained in their colleges and universities.

We believe there is also a fourth group not identified by either Kemerer and Baldridge or Kezar, Carducci, and Contreras-McGavin. We can call this group the *justice seekers*. This group resembles the *deprived* but is different in that its members defend anyone who has not been given consideration under certain egalitarian principles. This group is motivated by trying to see that justice is done. Like the tempered radicals, the justice-seeking advocates believe that community and interpersonal relationships must be preserved—and this can only take place if everyone is treated fairly and with compassion and understanding. Justice, in other words, is not just for those who are advocating justice.

These four groups are all driven to advocacy by the pressures of a dominant managerial culture. However, as we have seen, the bases for their reaction against the managerial culture are quite different. Kemerer and Baldridge concluded in 1975 (p. 65) that "collective bargaining has primarily fulfilled the second [deprivation] function." Even today, collective bargaining has not been very successful among many faculty members who are primarily concerned with academic issues, nor among many of those seeking justice through collaboration and community building; these individuals are often attracted instead to the developmental culture. Collective bargaining strategies have also failed to attract and hold the attention of many faculty members who work in elite institutions, embrace a traditional collegial culture, or are attracted to collective bargaining only because of its potential preservation function.

Academic Capital

Another contentious perspective has been brewing in the academy. This is the creation of *academic capital.* The academy acts and reacts in market-driven ways:

> For some time, we have seen the U.S. shifting from an industrial to a knowledge/information-based economy, leading colleges and universities to connect to new networks and types of businesses and industries. Some adjustments in academic programming to encompass the challenges of a shifting global economy obviously make sense. What makes less sense is to substantially restrict the academy to meeting short-term economic priorities—and what makes still less sense is to reduce the other significant roles that higher education has to play. [Rhoades & Slaughter, 2004, pp. 37–38]

Many administrative officers and some faculty are focusing more on the financial gain their department or institution might achieve by revising curricular offerings. These revisions are based on the use of institutional resources for purposes other than knowledge creation and dissemination. This has been made increasingly possible by hiring more part-time, nontenured faculty members, and "unbundling" (a managerial term) the role of faculty, especially in online environments:

> In those institutions where distance and online education are a major focus, this [unbundling] involves setting up what is essentially a "virtual assembly line" on which faculty members are but one group of many professional specialists involved in producing instructional materials.... Given the almost complete lack of professional protections and provisions for part-time and contingent faculty members and their inability to participate in academic governance—at least in the absence of a union—this shift in professional employment accords substantially greater

> influence to academic managers in all sorts of curricular matters. [Rhoades & Slaughter, 2004, pp. 44–45]

This academic capitalism mentality drives faculty members out of the stable collegial culture to look for ways to further protect their academy. They argue, as does Birnbaum (2004, p. 14), not for the expansion of academic capital but for the expansion of "social capital"—the rich interconnection and interdependency that exists among men and women who trust one another. Ironically, the most effective way to protect the academy from academic capitalism (but often at the expense of social capital) is through unionization—however contrary to the collegial culture joining a collective bargaining unit might be for these faculty members. Those members of the faculty who are from the justice-seeking group also join this drive in order to see equity achieved for the often-abused part-time (and untenured) faculty. Those associated with the tempered radical group are more cautious about the use of collective bargaining to address ills in their institution, for they are often quite sensitive to the loss of social capital and the collaborative spirit that comes with collective bargaining.

The Advocacy Society

Another factor contributing to the rise of advocacy was identified thirty years ago by Ladd and Lipset (1973). Legislation from the 1960s in the United States enabled faculty and other public officials to strike. "Though some unions were able to secure representation rights prior to the passage of such legislation," noted Ladd and Lipset (p. 4), "on the whole, full-fledged collective bargaining has occurred only after states have passed enabling legislation." This enabling legislation relates, in turn, to a broader societal movement—the creation of a litigious advocacy culture. This final historical reason for the growth and lingering influence of collective bargaining is found in militant egalitarian movements, which were often led not by faculty members but rather by students.

During the 1970s, faculty concerns often focused on the undesirable increase in student involvement in campus governance. The militant egalitarians were going to take over the campus (Ladd & Lipset, 1973; Carr & Van Eyck, 1973)! By the 1980s, an alternative perspective on faculty concerns prevailed. Faculty members began focusing not on student control but rather on administrative control and the rising influence of the managerial culture. Johnstone (1981), for instance, traced the issue of activism back to faculty concerns not about the threat of student participation in governance but about the lack of faculty participation in governance. From the perspective of the 1980s, Johnstone found that faculty members and students both wished to use more forceful and permanent methods to ensure their voice in the ongoing operations of the school. Advocacy-oriented faculty generally supported student efforts for more influence, along with increasing the influence of faculty members, and in particular, faculty union representation. The more conservative forces of the 1980s and the post–Persian Gulf patriotism of the 1990s may have helped academic leaders set aside (or at least contain) the antiauthoritarian and antistudent attitudes from the 1960s. However, we should not overlook the lingering effect of these experiences. Vietnam, the civil rights movement, the feminist movement, and the antiwar sentiments of the past few years in both the United States and Canada continue to play an important part in involving academicians in the advocacy culture.

The Advocate's Dilemma: To Develop or Not to Develop

The advocacy culture serves not only as a worthy opponent to those in the managerial culture but also as an alternative source of influence and power for faculty members who feel disenfranchised by the established collegial culture. Some tension seems to be present, however, about what the appropriate attitude of advocacy leaders should be toward the developmental culture. In some colleges and universities, collective bargaining units have demanded the inclusion of developmental resources in faculty contracts. They consider these resources to be part of the benefits package that should be available to faculty members for their own career advancement and job security. In other institutions, the administration has argued for faculty development, whereas the collective bargaining unit has fought against it. Developmental activities are seen either as an administrative ploy to retrain faculty in a new field or an implicit criticism of the existing levels of competence among faculty.

Developmentally oriented faculty members often find themselves caught between these two positions. They would like their faculty, curriculum, and student development activities to remain outside the negotiated contract, and they propose that development should be voluntary and a resource that potentially benefits all parties. In other instances, the developmental culture supports establishing joint union-management planning and cooperative programming in specific domains that do not represent problems for the vested interests of either party. In this way, the developmentalists wish to replicate the joint union-management "quality of work life" programs that have become popular in many corporate and public service organizations (Lawler, 1986, 1992).

The ambivalent feelings of many members of the advocacy culture about the developmental culture and the parallel ambivalence of those in the developmental culture about advocacy is quite understandable, considering that both claim to offer the most reasonable response to the stressful conditions of contemporary higher education. Both the advocacy and developmental cultures grew out of a reaction against a dominant force in higher education. Eventually, faculty members oriented to the advocacy and developmental cultures must come together to formulate common plans and integrate complementary assumptions about influence and change in higher education. Otherwise, both cultures will fail to provide needed corrections to the dominant collegial and managerial cultures.

Living and Working in the Advocacy Culture Today

Once again, we offer a general analysis of the values and perspectives associated with this academic culture. We focus in particular on two values that dominate the advocacy culture: equity and egalitarianism. These values are often antithetical to those held by representatives of the collegial and managerial cultures. The collegial tradition of individuality runs contrary to the collective bargaining tradition of egalitarianism. Collective bargaining agents favor policies and procedures that treat all faculty members alike. Such an approach tends to homogenize the distinctive features and differing levels of quality of faculty members. Although there is not strong evidence that collective bargaining has a leveling effect on faculty performance, the values of individuality (collegial) and egalitarianism (advocacy) seemingly come into immediate and inevitable conflict in the interaction between collegial and advocacy cultures, just as the values of entrepreneurship-based and differential compensation (managerial) conflict with an emphasis on equity and consistent compensation systems (advocacy). The developmental culture shares with the advocacy culture its commitment to both equity and egalitarianism, but the developmentalists support quite different strategies for realizing these values.

Academic Freedom

The issue of academic freedom is controversial both inside and outside the academy. It has become increasingly salient in recent years as colleges and universities in the United States and Canada have steadily begun to hire a greater proportion of non-tenure-track faculty. "Whereas tenure was the coin of the realm in the early twentieth century," note Gappa, Austin, and Trice (2007, p. 49), "now only 27 percent of all new faculty appointments, and 56 percent of new full-time faculty appointments are in tenure-track positions." Furthermore, "it is likely that the number of tenure-track faculty will continue to fall" (Guskin & Marcy, 2002, p. 10). Part-time faculty in Canadian universities have the same fate. They do not have the same pay or benefits as their full-time, tenured colleagues. There is a widely differentiated institutional treatment of these two faculty groups with the part-time faculty maintaining the teaching role, and their tenured colleagues pursuing research and development. Part-timers compensate for the fiscal shortfall of the institution and perpetuate a degradation of academic functions (Rajagopal & Farr, 1992).

Those faculty members who have not been placed in a tenure-track position cannot obtain the benefits that tenure confers—such as academic freedom and a guarantee of long-term employment (Gappa et al., 2007). Some believe that changes in faculty staffing have been exaggerated and have not hurt either academic freedom or student learning. Others contend that hiring more part-time and full-time non-tenure-track faculty diminishes educational quality and exploits those hired. They argue that the designation of part-time and non-tenure-track faculty has more to do with administrative control than with cost savings; they fear that the loss of academic freedom begins with a shift to part-time and non-tenure-track faculty:

> Many concerns have been voiced in response to the increased reliance on contingent faculty coupled with the declining opportunities for tenured positions. The lack of job security posed by term contracts, obstacles to academic freedom, and diminished opportunities for student learning are cited as some of the main concerns. Academic freedom, the right of faculty to freely express and publish their ideas without fear of reprisal, is a core value in higher education. The continued rise in the employment of

> contract faculty is a significant trend that is likely to have a lasting impact on higher education. [Holub, 2003, n.p.]

It can be argued, from the managerial point of view, that tenure is exclusively about the protection of jobs and security. It can also be argued, from the collegial point of view, that tenure is about protecting the right of individual faculty members to express a viewpoint that might offend the trustees or the organization's administration.

Academic freedom and tenure go together. Tenure protects faculty members from disciplinary action. Academic freedom is thus exercised. What then about the part-time faculty member who does not have tenure and probably does not have the protection of any association or union? According to the National Center for Education Statistics (NCES; 1999), 32 percent of full-time faculty members at public institutions in the United States were nontenured in 1998. This figure rose to 62 percent when part-time faculty members were included. The percentage of part-time and full-time faculty who cannot receive tenure has increased across the United States for more than twenty-five years. Non-tenure-track faculty made up only 45 percent of all faculty members in 1987. Non-tenure-track percentages for public universities differ considerably from those for public colleges. In 1998, 48 percent of faculty at four-year public universities in the United States and 81 percent of faculty in public two-year colleges were employed in non-tenure-track positions. The trend would indicate that the number of part-time faculty will overtake full-time faculty members in our higher education institutions. What then of academic freedom? What then of the inequity of institutional policies and procedures relating to full-time and part-time faculty members? "Regardless of their performance, the length of their employment, their qualifications for their positions, or the needs of their institutions, part-time faculty in most colleges and universities are employed under exploitive practices" (Gappa et al., 2007, p. 96).

From the perspective of full-time faculty in the collegial and developmental cultures, the exploitation of their part-time colleagues is, sadly, often not a major concern; however, the concepts of academic freedom and tenure are givens that are never negotiable in any setting. The issue is further exacerbated by the problem of required membership in a faculty union that has won collective bargaining rights. Thus, though the advocacy culture came about in reaction to the managerial culture, it shares with it the belief that anything involving educational programs and priorities is negotiable. Both the collegial and developmental cultures, by contrast, are founded on the belief that certain features of the academic enterprise are not negotiable. The developmental culture, in particular, views the compromise inherent in quasi-political negotiations as offensive and inappropriate in an academic institution.

Institutional Influence and Change

Collective bargaining affects both the formulation of organizational rules and the interpretation and adjudication of these rules through grievance and arbitration procedures. As a result, the power of formal managerial leadership in the institution is, in one sense, reduced. Upper-level academic administrators are prevented from making arbitrary decisions and must always keep in mind the welfare of faculty (at least as interpreted by leaders of the collective bargaining unit) when formulating institutional plans. It is generally agreed that faculty unions are now players in the formal governance processes of unionized colleges and universities—and this includes curriculum development and instructional processes as well as faculty welfare issues (Gappa et al., 2007).

The presence of collective bargaining on a college or university campus also complicates the role of midlevel academic administrators. Collective bargaining is particularly troublesome for the department chair or head. Usually the chair has been selected by colleagues inside the department and will return to a regular faculty position within several years. The position of department chair in most postsecondary institutions is not even full-time; chairs spend at least half of their time teaching and doing research. Yet department chairs do have to make personnel decisions, work with budgets, meet regularly with the dean, and supervise secretarial and clerical workers in the department. These are managerial functions in most organizations. Thus, the department chair often gets caught in the middle during collective bargaining. Even when managers (or heads) of academic departments have been selected by a dean rather than by department colleagues, they are caught in the middle, along with deans, assistant deans, budget officers, and others in middle management.

At one level, collective bargaining reduces the power of academic administrators of a college or university; on another level, it reinforces their authority. The managerial and advocacy cultures are interdependent. Gregory Bateson (1972) used the term *complementary schismogenesis* to describe this process. In 1936, Bateson, in his work *Naven*, coined the term schismogenesis to refer to escalating cycles in living systems that oscillate uncontrollably: "A process of differentiation in the norms of individual behavior resulting from cumulative interaction between individuals" (Bateson, 1936, p. 175). According to Bateson, in this mutually aggravating spiral, as one culture becomes stronger it aggravates the other, so its opposing culture becomes stronger as well. Because each culture needs the other to survive and to have an identity, these two cultures become inextricably linked. Conflict is inevitable and essential to both cultures while also strengthening both.

Up to this point, we have discussed primarily the impact of collective bargaining on managerial leadership. But the issue of faculty leadership is obviously important too. The advocacy culture tends to attract and foster a different type of faculty leadership than either the collegial or developmental culture.

Faculty members who assume leadership for collective bargaining units often share with those in the managerial culture a concern for formal structure and procedures. In contrast, faculty members oriented to the collegial culture often seem more disposed to work with ideas or with like-minded faculty members, not so much to achieve some objective as to share opinions. Developmental faculty members also appear more interested in the process of working with people than with accomplishing any specific task.

Faculty members who lead collective bargaining units share with managerial leaders a long-term commitment to their leadership positions. Whereas faculty in the collegial culture are supposed to be reticent about accepting formal leadership responsibilities (being in some sense "called" to these positions for a limited period of time by colleagues), the leaders of collective bargaining units are allowed to indicate their interest. Similarly, faculty members who are oriented to the developmental culture are not supposed to be drawn to leadership or the use of power and persuasion (at least as overtly expressed in formal administrative positions), whereas faculty members in unions are accustomed to using power and persuasion in confronting academic management.

Unfortunately, most of these faculty leaders have nowhere to go in the union hierarchy. Unlike unions in nonacademic organizations, there is no extensively staffed national organization to which academic union leaders can advance after successful performance at the local college or university union. Many faculty union leaders soon reach the frustrating point of either having to step down as head of the local union (and returning to teaching) or hindering the advancement of others who also wish to move into positions of union leadership. Some leaders of collective bargaining units therefore decide to make the difficult transition from union to management and join the ranks of academic administration.

Community Leadership: Service Learning

There is another way in which long-term faculty union leaders can shift attention away from the inevitably frustrating and often unsuccessful struggles between union and management. If they care deeply about the fundamental advocacy culture values of equity and egalitarianism, they can engage these concerns in their local community. This alternative route is being taken with increasing frequency by faculty members in contemporary colleges and universities. This route brings concerns for equity and egalitarianism in the community back to the academy, and opens the door for collaboration between those who are aligned with the advocacy culture and those who are aligned with the other cultures. This new route is a process called *service learning*, and through it faculty members begin to exert leadership not only on campus but also in their local community.

Service learning has been a part of North American higher education (in its role as a vehicle for social change) for many years—with John Dewey often identified as its godfather, the work of Jean Piaget, Kurt Lewin, and Donald Schön serving as its conceptual foundation (and linking the advocacy culture to the developmental culture), Antioch College its birthplace, and perhaps Alexander Astin (Astin & Astin, 2000) as its contemporary guardian (Jacoby, 2003a). Although there are many variations on the basic service learning process (Enos & Morton, 2003), an old definition still holds true: "Integration of the accomplishment of a task that meets human need with conscious educational growth. A service learning internship is designed to provide students responsibility to meet a public need and a significant learning experience within a public or private institution for a specified period of time, usually ten to fifteen weeks" (Duley, 1974, p. viii). The one fundamental principle that seems to have been added to this definition in recent years is a requirement for reflection and reciprocity (Jacoby,

2003a). With its emphasis on reflection and reciprocity, service learning moves advocacy beyond the reactivity and confrontation that typified the old-style academic advocacy of the twentieth century.

Through service learning a faculty advocate can directly engage in community action while also bringing along students, thereby not only inducing an advocacy spirit in those being taught but also expanding the human resources available to engage the community problem. Through a service learning project, a faculty member can help increase voter turnout in an underrepresented population. Rather than having to go door to door themselves, advocacy-oriented faculty members can be assisted by students taking their political science or sociology class. Similarly, faculty members in biology or chemistry can benefit from the services of students in their class who test water samples for mercury contaminants.

Service learning enables advocacy-oriented faculty members to fully engage not just their students (and their expertise, knowledge, and in particular, their energy and enthusiasm) but also the many other resources of their college or university on behalf of the community project in which they and their students are engaged. Furthermore, the legacy of community service in many postsecondary institutions, especially those that are publicly funded, can be brought to bear on and benefit from the service learning objectives. Bringle and Hatcher spoke directly to these two contributions on which the service learning instructor can rely when identifying the potential of service learning in contemporary colleges and universities:

> Universities [and colleges] have valuable resources (for example, students, faculty, staff, classrooms, libraries, technology, research expertise) that become accessible to the community when partnerships address community needs. They also have a tradition of serving their communities by strengthening the economic development of the region, addressing educational and health needs of the community, and contributing to the cultural life of the

> community. Emphasizing the value of community involvement and voluntary community service can also create a culture of service on a campus. [1996, pp. 221–222]

Service learning brings together not only the academy and the community but also differing cultures of the academy. Service learning allows for a remarkable confluence of learning by doing (the legacy of John Dewey and a value of the developmental culture) and action for change and improvement (the legacy of social activists and a value of the advocacy culture). In keeping with the developmental culture's values, service learning helps a college or university create a learning organization (Riemer & McKeown, 2003). Such an organization is much more likely to evolve if members frequently interact with colleagues from other institutions who think in different ways or at least face different problems. Furthermore, many studies have shown that learning by doing, and specifically, service learning "has a positive impact on personal, attitudinal, moral, social, and cognitive outcomes" (Bringle & Hatcher, 1996, p. 223). The fundamental principle of reflection and the concept of reflection while engaged in action are directly aligned with the developmental legacies of Kurt Lewin and Donald Schön.

Even more fundamentally, service learning embraces the developmental culture's emphasis on collaboration through service learning's fundamental principle of reciprocity. As Barbara Jacoby (2003a, p. 6) notes in her overview of the role played by partnerships in service learning, this initiative "is different from many educational endeavors in that it cannot happen within the confines of a classroom, a discipline, or even a campus.... As a program, a philosophy, and a pedagogy, service learning must be grounded in a network, or web, of authentic, democratic, reciprocal partnerships." Jacoby's words would certainly be music to the ears of developmentalists, and in this volume, we could easily have placed service learning in the developmental culture. We have chosen instead to align it with the advocacy culture because we believe that service learning will survive and perhaps even thrive over the long run not only because it provides a unique teaching-learning opportunity. We believe it will endure because it provides an exceptional opportunity for socially conscious faculty members (and students) who are aligned with the advocacy culture to find an effective outlet that is directly associated with their work in a higher education institution. Such concepts as civic renewal, social justice, civic responsibility, and social capital have been highlighted in a national commission (Jacoby, 2003b) and at several major conferences at the Wingspread Conference Center and the Aspen Institute (Hollander & Hartley, 2003) on service learning. These concepts greatly appeal to those aligned with the advocacy culture and the legacy of advocacy left by not only John Dewey but also more contemporary visionaries such as Robert Bellah (Bellah et al., 1985) and John Gardner (1993, 1995).

Service learning also serves as a bridge between the advocacy and collegial cultures. This initiative meets with the collegial culture's efforts to bring academy discipline to the "do-gooder" instincts of many students and to advance the role of the contemporary faculty member as an engaged scholar, building on the expanded notion of scholarship first presented by Ernest Boyer (Jacoby, 2003b). Rather than fighting against the desire of many students to actively engage in rather than just read about the world "out there," a service learning initiative enables the collegially oriented faculty member to provide direction and depth to this desire. A prime example is the whale preservation program (Chickering et al., 1977) offered for many years by the College of the Atlantic (COA) in Bar Harbor, Maine. Rather than just advocating for restrictions in the slaughtering of whales, students at COA learn about the biology of the whale, the physics and chemistry of the oceanic environment in which the whale lives, and the social and economic implications of whaling. Students thus acquire a liberal education while advocating for the preservation of the whale. Finally, to complete the cultural bridge, service learning often meets the managerial culture's interests in discovering new, low-cost ways to deliver education ("big bang for the buck") by awarding credit for student work in the community. Very few other initiatives of North American higher education in the late twentieth century provided as effective a means for bringing the differing cultures.

The New Advocacy

Another option is available to leaders of the advocacy culture. They do not have to turn away from the problems facing their own institution, but can instead reframe their vision and strategies in keeping with the shifting realities of twenty-first-century life. We propose that a new advocacy can be formulated based on the "essential elements" that have been identified by Gappa et al. (2007) as a road map for improvement in the academic working environment. This new advocacy includes a focus on (1) employment equity; (2) academic freedom and autonomy; (3) flexibility; (4) professional growth; and (5) collegiality. These essential elements, in turn, reflect the changing nature of faculty characteristics and needs, as well as the changing nature of the educational needs that must be addressed by educational institutions today. With more women and minorities now in faculty positions, there is a greater need for equity and flexibility. The new advocacy challenges the male-dominated world of both the traditional collegial and advocacy cultures. This male-dominated world was founded on the assumption that all faculty members would comply with the collegial culture's requirement—especially if they wanted to obtain tenure—and that academic work be assigned highest priority, with family and other responsibilities being secondary (Rice, 1986).

Although members of the new advocacy culture remain concerned with academic freedom and autonomy, they embrace the importance of professional growth, which serves as a link between the advocacy and developmental cultures. Furthermore, *collegiality* means something more than the gentle, or not-so-gentle, give-and-take of collegial culture politics. Rather, collegiality "is defined here as opportunities for faculty members to feel that they belong to a mutually respectful community of colleagues who value their unique contributions to their institutions and who are concerned about their overall well-being" (Gappa et al., 2007, p. 142). This deeper sense of collegiality is particularly poignant when it comes to the full participation of part-time, women, and minority faculty, in addition to European-American males and full-time faculty. We suggest that this "mutually respectful community of colleagues" should also include full appreciation of and respect for the various cultures of the academy.

The agenda that has been laid out by Gappa, Austin, and Trice is certainly challenging. It provides ample opportunities for those aligned with the advocacy culture to confront not only the often stultifying policies and procedures of the managerial culture but also the often inequitable and inflexible attitudes and actions of the collegial culture. This new road map for advocacy also confronts the often naive and narrow vision of the developmental culture regarding how to bring about significant, long-term improvement in the working environment of the academy. Furthermore, it provides an opportunity for those aligned with the advocacy culture to move away from a focus on confrontation and scarcity to a focus on collaboration and opportunity—the ingredients that are found in an organizational improvement strategy called *appreciative inquiry*, to which we will turn in the last chapter of this book.

Gappa, Austin, and Trice (2007) propose that this new approach to advocacy will only be successful when there is a culture of mutual respect—when an environment has been established "where every faculty member is respected" (p. 145). It is at this point that the advocacy and developmental cultures can benefit from one another. This agenda sets the stage for an even more ambitious and controversial option with regard to the role of advocates in the academy: performance funding. As in the case of the new advocacy, this final option requires collaboration between two of our six cultures—in this case, the advocacy and managerial cultures.

Performance Funding

We conclude this chapter by turning to an initiative that holds the promise of serving not only as a bridge between the advocacy and managerial cultures but also as a companion piece to Gappa, Austin, and Trice's new model of advocacy. This initiative goes by many names, but it is often referred to as performance funding. It is ironic that this new initiative in the advocacy culture may serve as a bridge between the advocacy and managerial cultures, while also expanding the gap between advocacy and collegial cultures. It all has to do with making postsecondary institutions more responsive to the needs of the sponsoring community. It involves reframing the advocacy culture's emphasis on equity and egalitarianism and returning to the use of government and other noneducational institutions to influence academic decisions about funding priorities.

"During the past decade," Alexander (2000, p. 411) has observed, "dramatic changes have emerged in the way governments interact with colleges and universities." We believe that the advocacy culture played a major role in bringing about this shift. As Alexander (2000, p. 411) puts it: "A new economic motivation is driving states to redefine relationships by pressuring institutions to become more accountable, more efficient, and more productive in the use of publicly generated revenues." Furthermore, "an increasing number of educational leaders are now exhibiting an awareness that the status quo is no longer a viable option for higher education." Those leaders who are aligned with the collegial culture may choose to ignore the growing disenchantment, and those aligned with the developmental culture may choose to respond to the disenchantment by seeking to create new programs. In contrast, leaders of the advocacy culture respond to the disenchantment by creating new models or borrowing models from other fields (common in the advocacy culture) that increase institutional accountability.

Although leaders of the managerial culture tend to stick with tried-and-true models of assessment (traditional cost-accounting procedures), those who are aligned with the advocacy culture are testing out radically different performance assessment models and building funding formulas based on these models. Furthermore, these advocates are often successful in getting approval for these performance funding initiatives. "The 1999 Almanac issue of the *Chronicle of Higher Education* reported that twenty-two states provide appropriations to individual public colleges partly based on their meeting of specific performance measures" (Robst, 2001, p. 730).

First, the new advocacy culture is embracing an outcome measure of quality. This criterion of quality moves beyond the output criteria of quality that are embraced by the managerial culture and suggests that the outputs of a postsecondary institution are only of value if they are responsive to the emerging needs of the society. Society will believe the education received in a specific program is relevant if its outcome will be of benefit to society.

Second, the advocacy culture is concerned not with performance in very selective and elitist settings, but rather with institutional performance that leads to expanded opportunities for the education of an entire population—"advancing the democratic concepts of massification and universality of higher education and [rejecting] the more traditionally restrictive practices grounded in meritocracy and exclusion" (Alexander, 2000, p. 413). From this advocacy-based perspective, human capital is substantially improved in a society not by focusing on those who are already receiving a high-quality education but rather on those for whom higher education has often been unavailable. From this perspective, we find a bridge between the advocacy culture and the developmental culture's emphasis on value-added measures of quality, and a bridge between the advocacy culture and the managerial culture's emphasis on the quantity of students being served and the quantity receiving credentials and degrees.

Third, the advocacy culture, unlike the managerial culture, is concerned not with measurement per se but rather with the effect that measurement might have on the actual work being done by an institution. Whereas the early years of accountability in postsecondary education emphasized the preparation of reports on institutional performance, the more recent emphasis on accountability comes with tangible rewards (and punishments) associated with actual institutional performance (Burke & Modarresi, 2000, p. 434): "Performance funding differs from these earlier efforts by allocating resources for achieved rather than promised results. It shifts somewhat the budget question from what states should do for their campuses toward what campuses do for their states."

Although performance funding shares three components with performance reporting, it moves beyond performance reporting with three additional components. The shared components are program goals, performance indicators, and success standards:

> Program goals—avowed or implied—include external accountability, institutional improvement, increased state funding, improved public perception of higher education, and meeting state needs. Performance indicators—such as retention/graduation rates and licensure test scores—identify the areas of anticipated achievements. Success standards use improved performance for each campus, comparisons with the results of state or national peers, or a combination of these criteria. [Burke & Modarresi, 2000, p. 434]

These three components are to be found in most accountability initiatives supported by the managerial culture. The next three are where "the rubber hits the road" and where the advocacy culture has real-world implications:

> Funding weights assign the same or different values to the indicators or allow some campus choice. Annual funding levels comprise a percentage of state operating support for campus operating budgets. Funding sources involve additional or reallocated resources or a combination of both approaches (with most programs calling for additional funding). [Burke & Modarresi, 2000, p. 434]

Conclusions

As is the case with many other cultures of advocacy in North American society (for example, health care, mental health care, and criminal justice), there is a strong emphasis in the new academic advocacy culture on bringing economic forces from outside the institution to bear on academic practices that the advocates wish to reform. Newman, Couturier, and Scurry (2004, p. 4), along with many other observers of the academy, have concluded: "[T]he demand for institutional accountability by political leaders has become a major issue. They recognize that higher education is ever more central to their goals of economic development and civic renewal, while at the same time more frustrating to deal with and more set in its ways." This political and economic focus involves either actual shifts or threatened shifts in the allocation of scarce governmental funds based on documented performance.

Important outcomes that are valued by members of the collegial or developmental cultures might not be easy to measure, and hence will be left out of the performance funding formula. Furthermore, members of the managerial culture might easily feel threatened by these funding formulas, because they, the managers, no longer determine or monitor the performance of subordinates. There are now overarching criteria of performance that determine the nature, scope, and size of the programs for which these managers are accountable. The stage is set for a new point of leverage and negotiation for members of the advocacy culture.

Admittedly, most performance funding programs involve considerable input and influence on the part of both administrators and faculty. In fact, the performance funding programs that are most stable (sense of achieving goals, stress on quality more than efficiency, sufficient time for planning and implementation, and so on) show more input from those working inside higher education, whereas those that are unstable are driven primarily by outside forces, including legislators, governors, business leaders, and community representatives. Furthermore, unstable programs fail to protect institutional diversity (Burke & Modarresi, 2000). Participants in unstable programs tend to feel that a cookie-cutter approach is being applied to their institution, without recognition of its distinct needs and students.

This concern about failure to recognize institutional diversity may become particularly important as performance funding moves into the independent, private college sector. The boards of private colleges and universities do not have to make decisions about the allocation of scarce tax dollars. However, they do have to decide about the extent to which funds are allocated to one academic program or another, and whether these scarce funds should be allocated to nonacademic programs such as athletics, administrative support staff, buildings, and so on. Clearly, the performance funding models of public institutions are relevant to private colleges and universities. We are likely to see widespread use of highly sophisticated funding formulas that are directly linked to institutional performance in all North American colleges and universities in the near future. Advocates may have finally gained a victory in North American higher education—but at what cost? The challenge for advocates is to use these external leverage points with great care while respecting the values and concerns of those who engage the performance funding process from the perspective of one or more of the other cultures.

5

The Virtual Culture

> *The virtual culture:* A culture that finds meaning by answering the knowledge generation and dissemination capacity of the postmodern world; that values the global perspective of open, shared, responsive educational systems; that holds assumptions about its ability to make sense of the fragmentation and ambiguity that exists in the postmodern world; and that conceives of the institution's enterprise as linking its educational resources to global and technological resources, thus broadening the global learning network.

Most colleges and universities are confronted with very difficult economic constraints, and because of this tight financial climate, higher levels of accountability and measures of educational outcomes are expected. Many contemporary postsecondary institutions are troubled and are looking for ways to address their financial, environmental, and managerial problems. At the same time, the general public is providing significantly less support for higher education as fewer tax dollars are available and many philanthropic sources are no longer as generous as they once were.

The environment in which our postsecondary institutions find themselves is turbulent in other ways too. There is extreme unpredictability with regard to governmental policies, student career interests, and student educational needs as well as competition from other educational institutions. Significant organizational change is necessary to respond to the turbulence—and this change will be complex and lengthy if it takes place in a bureaucratic educational setting. Many constituencies and stakeholders must be incorporated into this change effort. Although these inclusive processes help build commitment to the change effort, they also minimize the institution's flexibility and responsiveness to the external environment.

As a result of these challenges, there has been a major shift in the type of organizational cultures that dominate twenty-first-century higher education compared to those that dominated in the twentieth century. Although it remains prevalent, the traditional collegial culture is no longer as powerful as it once was. The managerial culture has grown stronger, as has the advocacy culture, which has grown in response to the strengthening managerial culture. The developmental culture remains marginal, though it potentially offers many solutions for today's colleges and universities, if it were to receive more attention and gain more credibility. And there are two new cultures: the virtual culture has emerged and the tangible culture has become more salient in recent years.

Origins of the Virtual Culture

We understand that the reader will have come across the term *virtual* before. It has a variety of meanings, some aligned with the meanings ascribed to it in this book and some not. Nonetheless, we decided to name this culture *virtual* because, compared to all the other terms we considered, it best typifies what we mean when we talk about the characteristics of this culture.

We have most often heard the term *virtual* used to describe concepts that relate directly to computer technology and the Internet. We have heard of virtual shopping, virtual travel, virtual learning, virtual communication—virtually everything, and most often these relate to technology. What is engaging to us about the term is that it represents some sort of connection or collaboration or initiative that exists somewhere but may not have a physical presence that can be plotted. Virtual is a term that connotes the nature of a relationship. Technology can assist in this, but is not what the culture "is."

A modern organization has a physical presence and an organizational chart that at first glance describes its presence, its purpose, and the roles of the individuals who perform their work functions within it. It is a somewhat closed system. The virtual organization has no such presence—or if it does, that presence is limited. The boundaries, structures, and patterns of influence in a virtual organization shift with the variables that influence it. It is a very open system.

Certainly children and adults in the United States and Canada are being influenced by the technologies they interact with on a daily basis. Just as the use of electricity changed almost everything about the way in which we live and work, so too does digital technology affect our interactions today (Brown, 2001). Digital technology is bound to affect the way individuals think, make decisions, and act. In the United States, three out of five children under the age of eighteen and more than three-quarters of children between the ages of twelve and seventeen go online. In Canada, 86 percent of children surveyed use the Internet. These children's parents believe their children use the Internet for "schoolwork (65 percent); search for information (31 percent); playing games (29 percent); instant messaging (28 percent); chat rooms (28 percent); e-mail (18 percent); meeting new friends (15 percent); personal Web page (6 percent); downloading music (6 percent)" (Industry Canada, 2003, n.p.). Postmodern pupils in the twenty-first century use the Internet to do their schoolwork in dozens of different ways. They relate to the Internet as a reference library, a virtual tutor, a virtual study group, and a virtual guidance counselor. They also use the Internet to store their schoolwork and Internet resources (Levin & Arafeh, 2002).

Virtual Education

The trend toward virtual education has extended to the college and university classroom (Palloff & Pratt, 2003). Using Everett Rogers's (2003) categorization of innovation diffusion, higher education has moved beyond the "early adopter" stage, with an "early majority" of faculty members and students now accepting online coursework, Internet-based education, and distance education as givens. Although many faculty members and some students have not yet participated in electronic courses, they know that this is an option and accept its inevitable presence. Online education now spans all age groups and most ethnic and racial groups (Palloff & Pratt, 2003); it appears to be a permanent reality on the higher education landscape.

Certainly the world has changed over the past generation. We communicate differently, we have different expectations of the academy, and we interact and organize information differently than we did when most of us were enrolled in college. The virtual culture connects with the postmodern world. It creates meaning by first having interactions with information that is generated throughout this world. It connects this information socially and creates knowledge in meaningful ways. Those who are aligned with the virtual culture realize that the knowledge generated by it is ambiguous and unfinished; knowledge is always changing, it is intangible and amorphous. The virtual culture differs from the four previously described cultures in that it originated primarily outside of, and exists independently of, the academy. One of the unique aspects of the virtual culture in the academy is that it connects directly with the virtual culture globally. The other academic cultures do not have this same direct connection. Hanna (Hanna & Associates, 2000) noted this aspect of the virtual culture when he described what he called the *entrepreneurial culture:*

> The entrepreneurial culture values the ability to change and to change quickly, to respond to market forces, to connect with and

> generate support from external audiences and constituencies, and to introduce new ideas, programs, delivery mechanisms, goals and purposes into the other four cultures described by Bergquist [1992], which are focused more internally within the institution. [p. 96]

We prefer the term *virtual* to *entrepreneurial* because the preceding activities may be temporary, exist outside of the organization, or indeed have no real "place." The term entrepreneurial connotes a business side or a culture that may be more in line with the managerial culture.

The global virtual culture affects the academy in two ways. First, the academy must interface with information-based technology (most notably, computers) and the ways this technology can be networked (for example, the Internet). Second, the virtual culture incorporates new ways of organizing, managing, and indeed, envisioning the purposes and activities of the academy. With regard to the first impact, it is important to reiterate that the virtual culture is much more than just the technology; rather, physical technologies are catalysts that generate new ways of thinking about the world and the organizations in which we work. The technology triggers a new way of doing things, which in turn triggers a new way of thinking about our world and our relationship to it. Digital technology is the latest tool for demonstrating the virtual reality that is emerging in our world. As we noted at the start of this book, we use the term *culture* to identify a particular set of assumptions and values. Although these assumptions and values may lead to certain behaviors, the measure of the culture is the measure of these assumptions. So, for example, just because someone uses the Internet to communicate with colleagues across the globe does not mean that person highly values the assumptions of the virtual culture.

New Technologies and New Challenges

The virtual culture, as it exists in the global context, was spawned at the dawning of the postmodern era. It affects everyone who has ever watched television, used a cell phone, or sat at a computer. When we think of the virtual world we think of digital technology. When we make a telephone call we are talking to someone, but that person is not there, not face-to-face with us. When we watch television there is another sort of reality created that we can observe. The news brings us into a war zone or hospital. We take a break during the commercials to fold the laundry, and when we return the scene may have changed to an interview with Madonna. We know that we are not there in person, but we feel we have been there in a sense—in a virtual sense.

Television is a linear type of instrument in that it delivers its images and sounds on a one-way channel. We take a step further when connecting to the Internet. We can link to whatever kind of information we want on the Internet. There is more information on the Internet today than there was in all the libraries of the world ten years ago. Now we have access to all of it, and the connection is relatively low cost. The information does not really exist except as zeros and ones on a chip somewhere, but we can duplicate it, manipulate it, and connect with all or part of it. There is an abundance of information at our fingertips with which we can connect virtually.

Virtual Culture in the Academy

Many factors have contributed to the creation and expansion of the virtual culture in the academy—and not all are about satisfying student needs and interests. At least 30 percent of students in a recent survey prefer educational delivery systems other than online education, with another 47 percent finding online education to be no more satisfying than face-to-face education (Palloff & Pratt, 2003). We must look elsewhere to identify the primary reasons for the flourishing of the virtual culture, and perhaps voice concern that this culture might falter if the quality of online instruction, and in turn, student satisfaction, do not improve.

Obviously the virtual culture has flourished in part because the computer has flourished. Increasingly, however, we must also consider the many other ways in which the digital revolution relates to the work of the academic institution. We must consider the virtuality that comes from the Internet and other ways in which the digital revolution connects the individual and the institution to the globe. Far beyond this we must look to the computer and Internet as they affect local, national, and global economies. We are entering an era of information and knowledge economies that accelerates the impact of the virtual culture on the academy.

In addition, we see an emerging virtual epistemology in the academy—the application of new sciences to the ways in which we conceptualize knowledge. What are the implications of that epistemology for those of us who work in the academy? Clearly, it challenges fundamental assumptions held about the role of technology and our relationship and interactions with technology. The modern view—the modernist episteme, or set of assumptions—is that technology is radically separate from us. Yet technology determines our identity in certain ways. The postmodern and virtual episteme suggest that technology exists in a social space with us and that we co-create our lives with technology. We are not passive recipients of technology (as in watching television); rather, we participate with it (as in video gaming with someone globally). In doing this, we co-create a reality (Wise, 1997). We will now look specifically at five elements that contribute to the creation and expansion of the virtual culture in higher education.

Computers as Tools

Although many forms of educational technology were expected to have a profound impact on postsecondary education during the twentieth century, computers and their ability to connect to each other clearly had a greater impact than any of the other candidates, including television, telephony, film, fax, and xerography. Computers and other forms of digital communication and digital processing have assumed an increasingly vital role in the instructional life of American and Canadian colleges and universities.

Computers currently serve at least six major functions in instructional settings. First, they are a vehicle for storing and processing information. As a vehicle for record keeping and test scoring, computers have been used for many years to track student activities and accomplishments. A second instructional function of computers is that they can be studied in their own right. Most students now acquire computer skills and at least rudimentary knowledge about computer systems programming. Computer literacy is now one goal of most general education programs and liberal arts sequences. The rapid growth of computer use in all areas of life and their decreasing size and cost clearly demonstrate that their use is fast becoming a prerequisite for study in other fields as well as a necessary skill for all educated persons. Computing science is an area of study in its own right.

In a third function, computers can be used to convey and test for comprehension of new instructional material. Computer-assisted instruction is widely used in such diverse fields as psychology, biology, accounting, auto mechanics, and carpentry. Computers can be of particular value to instructors in teaching writing, computation, and other basic skills—especially when combining text with other symbols, such as videos and graphics. Furthermore, computer labs can readily supplement repetitive, concrete training, feedback, and remedial work in the classroom with infinite patience and accuracy, freeing up the instructor to focus on higher, postformal levels of learning.

Fourth, computers enable faculty members to simulate complex physical or social systems. Engineering faculty use computers to simulate the construction of bridges, whereas ecologists use computers to model complex ecosystems and epidemiologists simulate the spread of infections through different urban populations. The computer can replicate many different kinds of environments, including the scientific laboratory. Computers fulfill a fifth function when faculty members use them to create high-quality graphics, art and animation in presentations, and lectures and reports. Standard classroom presentations come alive with the assistance of computers. Finally, computers are increasingly being used by students for scholarly and research activities. Various databases have been used extensively by many students over the past decade. Since faculty and students discovered the Internet during the mid-1990s, they now make full use of this tool to supplement or even in some cases replace library-based research. Computers nudge students from passive to active mastery when they are used as tools for scholarship and research.

The Internet: The New Information Base

During the 1980s, the microcomputer allowed academia to crunch numbers and perform text processing more efficiently. Today, the computer is a tool to communicate through many modalities—words, numbers, sounds, graphs, pictures, and videos. However, the real revolution is the exceptional capacity of any computer that is connected to the World Wide Web (by which we mean links between computers) and the Internet (by which we mean the ability of almost anyone to search the Web through the graphical interface known as a browser). The computer enables interaction to occur among and with these various modalities. Multimodal communication is simultaneous, instantaneous, interactive, and easily manipulated, depending on the application. It is to the Internet that we must turn in identifying the primary factors contributing to the creation and expansion of the virtual culture in our academies and our postmodern life.

The Internet is not organized, but it appears to be organized because of the software we use to navigate it. According to results from the Web Characterization Project's most recent survey (Online Computer Library System [OCLC], 2002), the public Web as of June 2002 contained 3,080,000 Web sites, or 35 percent of the Web as a whole. Public sites accounted for approximately 1.4 billion Web pages, with the average size of a public Web site 441 pages. When we use commercial search engines we are not searching the entire World Wide Web. When we discuss the public Web, we are referring to the part of it that is accessible through publicly available search engines. A specific search engine's abilities limit what we know about and can access from the Internet. Given various interpretations about the content of the public Web, we can conclude that it is now about the size of a major research library. Whether content is of the quality or usability of a research library is still in question (O'Neill, Lavoie, & Bennett, 2003).

There are a variety of ways to access some of the information available on the Web; however, the general public, students in higher education, and most probably many faculty, are not using the tools or have the skills to access these "deep" Web sites (Mardis, 2001; O'Neill et al., 2003; Price & Sherman, 2001). This increased access will occur if there is greater demand on search engines like Google, Yahoo, or AltaVista to incorporate and search for more complete sets of information or to organize the search process differently. It is likely, however, that the child who is using the Internet today will be fairly satisfied with the way search engines organize the information and likely grow up to look to it for primary sources of data—much as we, from a previous generation, settled for the resources contained in one library or even our favorite section of the library (usually devoted to our home discipline).

In sum, it appears that Internet information and the way it is presented has become the primary resource for the next generation—even though the Internet does not yet contain all the information held by a library. Furthermore, there is no quality control on the Internet, and our access to it is limited. Librarians and academics can argue that the Internet does not a library make, but we believe that youth will continue to use their "first language" (Internet) to access information (Prensky, 2001). Libraries and librarians are thus compelled to find ways to make their resources more accessible online. As Newman, Couturier, and Scurry (2004, p. 25) note: "Soon those institutions skilled in the use of technology to improve learning will be seen as more dynamic and effective than their less engaged competitors. The use of technology will become a source of prestige and competitive advantage."

The Knowledge Economy

The profound economic shift that has been occurring over the past twenty years is a third factor contributing to the creation and expansion of the virtual culture in higher education—and more generally, to the digital divide that exists in our colleges and universities, and our society (Palloff & Pratt, 2003). The ability to interact with information using a variety of modes at relatively little cost has resulted in the *virtualization* of information and caused our world to think in terms of a knowledge economy, instead of an industrial economy. Higher education is intimately involved in the processes of knowledge creation and dissemination; therefore, this new economy is worthy of our attention (O'Driscoll & Briki, 2006).

As the ability to link computers to the Internet has improved, more of the information in the world is being digitized. When information is digitized, it means that it is relatively free. It is also easily duplicated and universally available. Economists have begun to look at information as a raw resource available to the economy. Raw materials were essential in the industrial economy, and they are still required today. As the available information is interpreted and utilized it becomes the foundation for a knowledge economy. The digitization of information turns information and its resulting knowledge into the basis for global action in industry, politics, and education.

Digitization of information means that there are more immediate links with information and among those individuals accessing or contributing it. Information becomes more widely dispersed and less easily vetted or coordinated. Information is out there for anyone's contribution and for anyone to access. Knowledge, organized through different arrangements, becomes that which is valued and traded in the new economy. O'Driscoll and Briki (2006) tell us that the enterprise of tomorrow will be driven by an abundance of information rather than a scarcity of capital. Learning opportunities and access to dynamic workplace technologies will attract human capital. Talent will be migratory, and resources will not be owned by the enterprise. Consequently, two interrelated core competencies will be needed for success. First, students as well as faculty will need to develop *information literacy*—which is not only "the ability to know where information is kept" but also "the ability to ask questions and [know] the difference between ignorance and understanding" (Watts, 2005, p. 348). Second, faculty and students will have to be able to convene people, processes, and technologies that can rapidly respond to identified needs and engage appropriate information and understanding in seeking to meet these needs.

In the modern world prior to the PC and the Internet, we had more limited information, and it was channeled in particular ways. For example, the producer of a television program organized the content—we watched it or not, but it was aired the way it was produced. The lecture acts in the same way in higher education. The lecture, created and delivered by the professor, is one-way and linear. In the modern world, higher education institutions created systems that organized information into "courses" and courses into "programs" and programs into "credentials." Measures were created. In contrast, when we use computer tools in alliance with Internet tools, we can link all the knowledge that these networks (as well as the intranets of higher education) have in their storehouses, which continues to compound at an extraordinary rate, to create new economies in the world.

Loose Organizational Boundaries

A fourth factor contributing to the expansion of the virtual culture is the loosening of organizational boundaries. Faculty members and administrators today must let go of past conceptions about their role in the institution. Administrators and faculty members must form new partnerships with their college or university. For example, Langara College in British Columbia, Canada, offers some of its programs away from its institution. One program is given in Thailand and Laos, another involves tours of Western Europe. The classes begin on campus, but are soon followed by raft trips on the Mekong River or museum tours in Europe. Faculty members take on different roles as coordinators, chaperones, health service coordinators, and travel advisors while they are on these trips. The student-faculty relationship is altered. Students must come to understand the parameters of these new roles. It is a far cry from sitting at desks in a classroom. The leaders of Langara College, and its faculty union, support these initiatives because they believe it is best for the institution, the faculty, and the students. This arrangement is finite. Faculty members have taken on professional and lifestyle changes dictated by the situation, but that role ends when they return to campus. They revert back to their previous roles and assume their traditional duties.

The Internet also loosens organizational boundaries. As noted in the preceding section, today we have an oversupply of information that is accessed and manipulated by whoever participates in the network. But it is uncoordinated. This information lacks its own organizing system. It has no boundaries. The information is just out there. Everyone who participates in the Internet has equal access to the information that exists on the Internet. We are not sure which information bits are needed or not needed until a question is posed with reference to this vast storehouse.

Our difficulty with the unbounded Internet is that the vast array of information so much further stretches our capacity to contain the information and make it meaningful. We must be vigilant in developing and using our information literacy skills when we use the resources of the Internet. Which of the sites are valid and valuable? Which of them pertain to the topic of interest? Which of them is reliable? How does one decide? How does one make sense of the panoply of data and construct this information so that it becomes a reality? We need a reality to begin with—hence the lure of our sixth culture, the tangible culture. We need to have a very clear intention before entering the data maze in order to come out with something meaningful. The information itself does not offer an internal structure; we must provide that structure by way of our own clear intention and vision (Bergquist, 1993, 2004).

The knowledge economy became the business of higher education when interested faculty began to create links with this network in their work—thus further shattering organizational boundaries. Researchers and educators now have the ability to travel virtually via the Internet throughout the world to create new knowledge and disseminate knowledge in novel ways with unpredictable ends. They can participate with the world in this global knowledge economy. Their students have access to this network of information as well.

Virtual Epistemology

A final element has contributed to the creation and expansion of the virtual culture in higher education: the way in which we conceive of knowledge. Computer and Internet technology assist us as we transit to new ways of thinking. Empirical science—the basis of the modern way of thinking—is shifting its own weight toward the postmodern door. Science began to shove that door open by pushing against what science itself was based on—namely, the measurement of finite matter. On the other side of that door is a new way of thinking about science. Scientists have been finding that matter has little or no substance. If matter is in fact not solid, if the atom has more space or energy than anything else, then matter (and the atom) has more to do with space or energy than it does with matter. Matter and our earthly world have more to do with relationships than they do with substance. Finite matter cannot be measured except by the relationships between energy parts. In fact, relationships are what give the matter we perceive its tangibility. Although parts of our world do not appear to be organized—they look chaotic, unpredictable, and turbulent—these parts actually self-organize into a whole (Prigogine & Stengers, 1984).

The technology helps a change in thinking. Notwithstanding the shortcomings of the Internet, we can point to two Internet media that demonstrate this approach, albeit raw and unvetted. They indicate the beginnings of a new kind of episteme. A *blog* (from *Web log*) contains an individual's personal page of comments and selected links listed in reverse chronological order on which others can usually make annotations. A *wiki* is a Web page that anyone can edit or even discard completely. There are more blogs on the Internet now than there were Web pages a few years ago. Blogs have grown rapidly. There is a sense that one's ideas can be put out to the world and will have value. Of course, there are serious blogs and banal blogs, there are accurate blogs and blogs that are totally misleading. We see the emergence of a Web-based phenomenon that takes human thoughts and makes them public. Like philosopher cafés that encourage public discourse, the blog and wiki also encourage public discourse—but on a global rather than local basis.

Some individuals would say that such resources have no internal or external validation. Therefore, they cannot be used for serious research. There are examples, however, of wikis having created useful educational tools. Accuracy is still an issue, but there is promise in this technology for creating a collective knowledge base. For example, *Wikipedia* (*http://en.wikipedia.org*) is an online wiki-made encyclopedia that today, after four years, holds more than half a million articles. In both the case of blogs and wikis, the content is valid as viewed by the users-editors. It is a relative truth. Probably the more a site is used, the closer it is to the "true" truth—that is, scientific modern truth.

The relationship of the blog and the wiki to higher education, and specifically, to the virtual culture is intriguing. The blog is an expression of an individual's conscious thoughts and the wiki of individuals' collective consciousness. Both of these forms exist virtually. What is ultimately powerful about both of these media is that knowledge and meaning are created as they make connections between people and within groups that they allow and support. From an instructional point of view, a blog can be used as a discussion engine for a class; a wiki can be used by a group to present information on which they mutually build for some assigned topic or problem.

These five reasons for the presence of the virtual culture in the academy—computers and how they are networked, the Internet, the knowledge economy, the loosening of organizational boundaries, and the development of a virtual epistemology—align with Watson and Johnson's (1972) model of sustained change in organizations. As we noted in Chapter Three, Watson and Johnson proposed that leaders of an organization should consider three strategies when seeking to introduce organizational change: structural change, change in organizational processes, and change in organizational attitudes. Computers (the tools that connect us to one another and the Internet) can be viewed as the structural element of the change. The knowledge economy and loosened boundaries produce new organizational processes by which we engage each other and exchange goods, services, wealth, and power. And virtual epistemology, which prompts, supports, and in turn, influences postmodern thought, helps create an attitude that is aligned with these changes in structure and process.

The notion of being right is less important than the notion of applicable understanding. The faculty member, as part of an institution that exerts certain management needs, is responsible for grading student acquisition of knowledge as that knowledge pertains to the course in question. That same faculty member in the virtual culture can be seen as someone who continues to assist a learner who is interested in an area of study beyond the course, because virtual learning always seems to go beyond the managed course. Faculty members thus become lateral thinkers who are pressed to continue to understand their area of inquiry and must be able to bring students to an understanding of how to gain ongoing access to specific streams of learning. Often these faculty members see themselves as both coaches and co-learners with their students. These students at times have access to the same knowledge sets as their instructor. The virtual classroom has democratized the learning field. Any sense of power that faculty members have in this culture resides in their ability to link with the various knowledge bits, orient their students toward learning outcomes, and learn themselves.

Living and Working in the Virtual Culture Today

As you might recall from our discussion in the Introduction to this book, a culture is a container for the anxiety that individuals feel about their environment. As they confront the many challenges associated with the broadening use of the computer as an educational and administrative tool, as they encounter the virtuality of the knowledge economy, and as the new sciences reinforce a virtual epistemology, twenty-first-century faculty members seek to create a new culture that will help explain (and even assuage) the accompanying anxiety. Faculty members have created the virtual culture in company with other members of their society. They gave birth to this new culture much as members of the academy created the other five cultures in response to impending or anticipated threats. Like faculty members aligned with the other cultures, those aligned with the virtual culture believe (and feel) that their sense of self-worth and competency, as well as their traditional ways of being in and perceiving the world, are being challenged.

A Need for New Computer Skills

How does a faculty member respond to the use of computers, to the new economy, and to a virtual epistemology? To accommodate the use of the computer for learning purposes, innovators must devote considerable attention to designing or redesigning existing software to fit curricular goals. Faculty members must understand the program's capabilities, think about room design, and generate funds for the purchase of the program. All these tasks cut into the time an instructor could be spending on more professionally rewarding work such as research and publishing—activities that are still highly valued in the collegial culture. Technical problems always take time and money. Inevitable upgrades and adjustments increase costs associated with continuing use of almost any computer software and hardware.

In online education, faculty members need to respond. Instruction is no longer confined to the physical (and tangible) classroom. In the modern culture of the academy, criteria of educational quality are tangible. Tangible measures examine the capacity of a college or university to meet its students' learning needs as measured by the number of full-time faculty members, the number of volumes in its library, the number and quality of its audiovisual support systems, or the size and design of its facilities. However, in the virtual culture of the twenty-first-century college or university, all resources of the academy, whether people, materials, or equipment, can be employed for instructional use. Many resources from outside the institution can be used as well. The boundaries have been shattered. A digitally oriented institution is best served through effective resource management: locating and efficiently using existing on- and off-campus resources. In this way the virtual culture is aligned with and increases the value of the managerial perspective.

There is yet another point associated with the digital revolution that needs to be considered. The digital industry has created new technologies that threaten to make two foundational elements of the higher education institution obsolete—namely, the student cohort and the book. With regard to the student cohort, when initially viewed online education seems to be a highly isolating experience. We envision a student sitting alone with a laptop computer responding to questions offered by a faceless instructor that are also being addressed by unseen fellow students. Although video correspondence is on the horizon and videoconferencing is already a viable (though expensive) option, most virtual correspondence now consists of the written or spoken word. Even more fundamentally, virtual education seems to be inevitably based not on pedagogy or andragogy, but instead on *heutagogy*, or self-directed learning (Palloff & Pratt, 2003).

Although this is the usual impression of virtual education, and perhaps a big source of discontent among many students participating in online courses, it is certainly possible—Palloff and Pratt (2003) would say essential—for virtual education to be embedded in a student cohort, or what they call an *online learning community*. According to Palloff and Pratt, online education can evoke transformative learning if it is collaborative as well as reflective, conditions that are also emphasized in the much more tangible initiative known as service learning, which we described in Chapter Four. They suggest that online education should involve (1) active interaction among students about course content (as well as more personal matters); (2) collaborative learning involving discussions among students (rather than just between students and instructor); (3) efforts among students to arrive at agreement about the meaning inherent in specific issues being addressed in the course; (4) sharing of resources among students; and (5) support and encouragement among students, echoing an emphasis in the developmental culture on the balance between challenge and support. Certainly, if an online learning community can produce these conditions of collaboration, an in-person student cohort may not be missed.

What about loss of the second fundamental element—the book? Unfortunately, books are not easily transferred from bound text to computer screen. Transposing books as latent objects into digital form does not increase learning. When plain text is introduced, the strengths of the electronic medium—that is, interactive capability, ability to search for information in worldwide digital libraries, capacity to present information through sound, video, and animation—are not fully exploited. Siegal and Sousa (1994, p. 49) observe that "by its very nature as a static, passive medium, the printed . . . book is unable to fulfill its instructional goals. . . . [B]ooks are not being sufficiently improved because they cannot be improved sufficiently." So books will be missed if they are not retained and fully integrated into the virtual culture.

Librarians are aware that the digital revolution is on their doorstep—or has already entered their building. Librarians often take the lead in furthering the revolution. Their involvement is evident in the automation of print-based technologies and expansion into nonprint media, audiovisual materials such as records, cassettes, audio CDs, videotapes, and laser discs; microfiche and microform; CD-ROM and software collections. The accumulation of new technologies and nonprint media beg important questions that challenge some assumptions about higher education, the teaching and learning process, and the collegial culture itself. These questions take us far beyond the library. What is the appropriate role of the faculty member? How do colleges and universities with limited resources afford the initial costs and ongoing maintenance costs of high-powered, technologically driven instructional tools? Are consortia (such as the Online Computer Library Center) the answer, as they are with the sharing of printed materials? Will these new technologies force all but the wealthy and largest institutions to the margins of educational excellence? How deeply will these new technologies affect the dominant collegial culture of our institutions of higher learning?

Although books and other printed media continue to be the primary instructional materials for most colleges and universities, they are being supplemented (and replaced in part) by electronic media (Duderstadt, Atkins, & Van Houweling, 2002, p. 72):

"The library is no longer a place. It is a utility. It is becoming less a collection house and more a center for knowledge navigation, a facilitator of information retrieval and dissemination." Today's students have been dealing with and learning with digital technology all their lives. They are accustomed to and will expect their professors to optimize the use of multiple technologies, both synchronous and asynchronous.

Without question, the computer's impact on higher education around the world has exceeded that of any other technology to emerge over the past century. The computer revolution requires that faculty members gain new competencies and rethink their work. However, the use of the computer in the classroom in and of itself is not the key to a more innovative or effective teaching system. Rather, the success of any application has more to do with melding technology with student abilities, curricular goals, and teachers' willingness to move to the role of coach or mentor in guiding their students to solve problems (Hanna & Associates, 2000). As Duderstadt notes (Duderstadt et al., 2002):

> More specifically, faculty members of the twenty-first-century university will find it necessary to set aside their roles as teachers and instead become designers of learning experiences, processes, and environments. In the process, tomorrow's faculty members may have to discard the present style of solitary learning experiences, in which students tend to learn primarily on their own through reading, writing, and problem solving. Instead, they may be asked to develop collective learning experiences in which students work together and learn together, with the faculty member becoming more of a consultant or a coach than a teacher. [p. 65]

A Need for New Structures and Processes

The noted organizational and managerial visionary Rosabeth Moss Kanter (2001) claims that a new way of working is required in the digital age. That individuals need to act quickly in this environment is taken for granted. Kanter (2001, p. 16) indicates that the digital age requires us to interact as a community: "[O]f my most robust findings about the e-culture is that it centers around strong communities, online and off. The community-forming potential of the Web presents both the greatest opportunity and the greatest threat to organizations and their leaders." Kanter's findings are relevant to faculty in the virtual culture: they must help students achieve their educational goals by interacting with the information maze. A key faculty role is to assist students in translating this information into knowledge and then into meaningful understanding and applications toward the student's and institution's intentions. To do this, faculty members must be expert in the use of these digital tools. Furthermore, they must understand the information networks and how they function (Hanna & Associates, 2000).

There is an even greater challenge. Faculty members in the virtual culture must understand learning outcomes—in this instance, they are aligned with faculty in the managerial culture. Like their managerial colleagues, the virtualist must know how to arrange appropriate learning activities and assessment activities that match these desired outcomes. The similarities between virtualist and managerial faculty members end at this point. "Assessment of the instructional use of the Web should have less to do with how subjects automatically respond to content features and more to do with students' considered use of that content. The educational challenge is not to assess the way students respond to stimuli, but to assess learning" writes Hanna (Hanna & Associates, 2000, p. 313). This means focusing on how students think as well as what they think. It means focusing more on assessing the impact of teaching on learning and less on assessing student performance, such as grading students.

We are getting to the heart of the matter—the primary source of anxiety in the virtual culture. The greatest challenge of the digital revolution is that the professor must undergo some major changes. As lecturers, professors have control of the information transmitted; as coaches in a virtual culture, they must respond to queries that may not be within the realm of their expertise. Before the Internet, faculty held a distinct advantage, particularly if they were conducting their own scholarship or research. They had access to up-to-date information in their field that was not readily available in the textbooks or even in the primary sources that their students were reading—much as the medieval European of wealth and education had exclusive access to information contained in the Bible. Faculty members often informally communicated with colleagues or at least attended disciplinary conferences where they found out what was emerging in their field. The Internet now provides access to both faculty and students on the latest developments in almost any field of study. Faculty members are no longer automatically situated at the top of the knowledge (and power) pyramid. This can be quite threatening and anxiety-provoking—as it undoubtedly was for the literate scholar of the Middle Ages when printed material became more widely available.

A New Attitude

Digital technology, the new sciences, and our experience with premodern and modern societies have led us to a different way of knowing—a virtual epistemology. Previously, epistemology had to do with how we perceive knowing. The territory was viewed by the professor-mapmaker. The professor would then make the map of knowledge so students could go back to it when they wanted to. Virtual epistemology has to do with how we perceive perceiving. It has to do with knowledge being viewed and rearranged by the participant-observer into contextual personal meanings. Knowledge shifts with the circumstances and with the participants and their relationships to the knowledge and to each other. In this virtual epistemology, higher education and its professors become guides rather than holders of knowledge. Participants need to be vigilant about their own boundaries.

They need to avoid being swept away by the flow of information. The map is created jointly while the journey is under way, and the map becomes the reality. In other words, the map precedes the territory (Baudrillard, 1995)—it is made and remade by the existing perception.

A virtual epistemology is based on the assumption that we know in a virtual way—a way that has no substance but that carries real meaning in the moment. We know in a constructed way. Higher education's response is to find ways of arranging for the construction and reconstruction of new ways of knowing and be able to navigate back there during future explorations. If first-order change has to do with fixing the problem and second-order change has to do with remaking the system (or a part of it), then third-order change—postmodern, virtual epistemological change—has to do with making a system-maker that responds to changing demands and truths as they emerge. In first-order, premodern learning (collegial), we teach. In second-order, modern learning (managerial), the student learns. In third-order, postmodern learning (virtual) we help our students become better learners. They become reflective and critical thinkers: "[R]eflection—whether on the results of a collaborative activity, on the learning process, or on course content—is a hallmark of online learning" (Palloff & Pratt, 2003, p. 12). "Virtual students are or can be developed into critical thinkers. They recognize that the instructor acts as a facilitator of the online learning process and that in order to have the best online learning experience, they must take charge of that process themselves" (p. 7). In other words, virtual students become more aware of the *metacurriculum*—what lies behind the learning, the truths and falsehoods and the principles that might be applied to learning in the future.

Institutional Influence and Change

Up to this point, we have focused on the teaching and learning side of the virtual culture. We will now look at administrative matters: how the institution rearranges its structures and processes to accommodate the reality of a virtual culture. It is no longer possible to achieve the intentions of a postsecondary institution using only its existing (modern) structures and processes. As leaders of the virtual culture share conversations about their motives and sources of inspiration, they may effectively argue that postsecondary structures and processes must change.

Certain conditions must exist in order to change the structure and processes of institutions so that they can more fully align with the virtual culture. Initially, there must be some sort of impetus to begin this change. Perhaps there are financial pressures or restricted resources that cause the college or university to consider offering online courses. Perhaps exciting ideas about the virtual world can influence an organizational change initiative. Initially, there have to be rational data-based arguments for this improvement and innovation to occur. Then there has to be technical expertise so that computer languages and digital revolutions can be understood and communicated within the work of the organization.

The options that managers have to consider can be enhanced by a virtual viewpoint. Kezar, Carducci, and Contreras-McGavin (2006) note that in some cases, globalization has increased higher education's appetite for entrepreneurial expansion. Competition for students and for exposure, and stresses in the "market" of education and learning, as well as the need for more financial support, have prompted some higher education administrators to broaden their entrepreneurial mandate. Many successful administrators use the methods of the virtual culture. They develop global alliances with industry, while collaborative academic and research platforms broaden their scope of control in the education market. "In the frameworks of globalization, academic capitalism, and new managerialism, the scope of academic leadership is no longer limited by the boundaries of the institution, the state, the nation. Instead, higher education leadership is marked by participation in [a] global market without boundaries" (p. 150).

However compelling entrepreneurialism, globalization, and accountability are, the traditional and influential higher education community resists them. These concepts will continue to press on the cultures of higher education and will be increasingly important to understand in future planning (Kezar et al., 2006). The virtual culture uses technology as a tool to create the connections to new learning resources and relationships that it values. By their nature, strategies for the use of technology need to be responsive and flexible—capable of changing with the evolving technological systems (Gayle, Tewaire, & White, 2003).

Challenges of a Virtual World of Education

Although the new technologies of the virtual culture offer the benefits of flexibility and cost reduction, they also create many problems. Organizational structures and processes are fragmented and inconsistent because of the disruptive mixture of the modern and postmodern. Established policies and procedures need to adjust to differing policies and procedures when institutions partner with other institutions. Institutions that are aligned with the virtual culture have often embraced unique postmodern incentive programs, joint union-management problem-solving groups, and elaborate interinstitutional partnerships that are not particularly compatible with a uniform set of policies and procedures.

Incentive programs may motivate workers to test out new ways of doing their jobs, as might joint union-management problem-solving groups. Self-governing task forces often must create their own performance criteria, while managers often ask their employees to learn new skills that were not anticipated when the personnel manual was originally prepared. Adjustments must be made for work being done in partnership with other colleges and universities that embrace very different performance standards and codes of conduct. As universities grow outward in their alliances and partnerships and their traditional core activities become relatively less important, these core activities will have less influence and there will be less coordination (Tierney & Minor, 2004): "[T]here will be less influence at the center and less coordination at the margins. In turn, universities will need to embark on strategies for 'smart growth' so that they do not become further disjointed and ultimately ungovernable" (p. 72).

These colleges and universities and their members face turbulent and unpredictable changes in the near future that may make formal lists of desired knowledge, skills, and attitudes obsolete.

Part-Time Faculty

One of the challenges of a virtual culture in which traditional boundaries are shattered, and a changing variable for higher education organizations, is the role of part-time faculty.

> In the 1990s, more than 40 percent of faculty members in BC's [the province of British Columbia] college, university-college, institute, and agency system held temporary positions.
>
> These positions often provided minimal or no benefits, little preparation time or support, no professional development time, and much lower salary levels than those of regular faculty members.
>
> Faculty members could spend years in temporary positions and were often laid off every summer, only to be rehired at the last minute for the next fall term. They frequently put together the equivalent of a full-time position by working at more than one postsecondary institution. [College Institute Educators' Association, 2000]

Recent observers of contemporary higher education (Gappa, Austin, & Trice, 2007) have related these new challenges to Handy's (1994b) metaphor of the three-leaf shamrock that is emerging in contemporary societies. One of the leaves represents the professional core of the workplace. In higher education this means the full-time, tenure-track faculty members (and the collegial culture). The second leaf represents freelance professionals and technicians who are self-employed and hired on an ad hoc basis. The part-time faculty member who is on a renewal contract is identified with this second leaf. The third leaf, referring to the contingent, hourly workforce, is usually associated with manual and migrant labor but also those faculty members who are on fixed-term or temporary contracts. This third leaf is growing in size at many colleges and universities that are using this "marginalizing" strategy to achieve both flexibility of staffing and cost reductions (Gappa et al., 2007). As a colleague of ours who teaches part-time in four postsecondary institutions recently noted, part-time faculty members "are simply moving around from institution to institution harvesting the latest crop" of students. The virtual culture is clearly aligned with the second leaf, and increasingly, with the third leaf of Handy's shamrock.

The trend to hiring part-time faculty members in postsecondary institutions is clearly growing and is creating a bifurcation in the academy between those with full-time (usually tenure-track) positions and those representing the second and third leaves and the virtual culture (Gappa et al., 2007).

Handy indicated that the second and third leaves of his workplace shamrock are increasing proportionally to the first leaf. This is certainly the case in American higher education. One mid-1990s study reported that part-time faculty members constitute 35 percent of the teaching faculty (Leslie & Gappa, 1994). These percentages have dramatically increased over the past decade. By 2001 there were 618,000 full-time and 495,000 part-time faculty members in the United States. Whereas the total number of full-time faculty increased by 167 percent between 1970 and 2001, the number of part-time faculty increased by 475 percent during the same period. Only 55.5 percent of individuals involved in the higher education system were teaching full-time in 2001 (National Center for Education Statistics, 2003).

Why has this shift occurred? First, part-time faculty cost much less than full-time faculty. They are paid at a far lower rate than full-time faculty, and they are only paid for the time they are teaching. Furthermore, part-time faculty contracts do not require the school to assume any long-term financial obligations. Part-time faculty can be hired outside the tenure track, thereby yielding further financial flexibility and educational responsiveness—and long-term financial benefits—for the school. These benefits have been acknowledged in particular by leaders of highly entrepreneurial colleges and universities like the University of Phoenix (Garner, Pepicello, & Swenson, 2005), which are becoming increasingly prominent in North American higher education (Gappa et al., 2007). Part-time faculty members can readily be hired and fired. This enables the college or university to remain highly flexible and adaptive in its academic programs when meeting the unpredictable needs of students and the community. Part-time employees can also be kept out of the ongoing decision-making and problem-solving processes of the institution, which reduces the complexity of any change effort. Part-timers are particularly valued by members of the managerial culture because they are much easier to manage than full-time faculty. They usually have no collective representation when it comes to salaries and benefits, and they have minimal input on the scheduling of courses, departmental curricula, or overall school policy and procedures.

There are other reasons to move to part-time faculty as well. First, part-time faculty members come from many different sectors of society and blend academic and practical experiences. They can enrich and diversify the curriculum of a college or university, and can serve as successful role models for students. Second, the lower cost and more highly diverse experiences offered by part-time faculty members can yield more affordable education, more richly textured education, and greater interplay between the academic and nonacademic worlds. This in turn helps the institution achieve both quality and access (Bergquist, 1995). Third, students benefit from the enormous commitment of time, resources, and experience of part-time faculty members—many of whom are driven by the notion of stewardship; they desire to serve students and make contributions to their students' lives. Finally, the move to part-time faculty complements the other dramatic shifts associated with the emergence of the virtual culture. As Gappa, Austin, and Trice (2007, pp. 93–94) have noted: "[J]ust as other products and services in the economy have become available on an around-the-clock, seven-day-a-week basis, the demand has increased for high-quality college instruction delivered at any time and to any place." The extensive (or even exclusive) use of part-time faculty also enables institutions such as the University of Phoenix to "unbundle" the role of faculty member in preparing online courses. "Teams of experts—not all of whom are faculty—design online courses in a digital environment that makes the unbundling possible and perhaps even inevitable" (Rice, 2005, p. 309). Clearly a large cadre of part-time faculty can help a contemporary college or university fill today's students' expectations for 24/7 service coupled with cutting-edge online instructional materials.

But the significant use of part-time faculty can also present a serious threat to the institution's academic integrity. The burden of curriculum development, departmental administration, and governance falls on full-time faculty members when an institution makes extensive use of part-time faculty members. As a result, these full-timers carry a disproportionately high load for the ongoing maintenance of a department or program, while also meeting other requirements, such as teaching, advisement, student review, and so forth. The picture is also clouded for the part-time faculty member. Often part-timers have little hope of gaining tenure. They are the first to be cut if enrollment is low, they have reduced benefits if any benefits at all, their pay is quite low, and they are rarely involved in campus governance. There is no community with which part-time faculty members can further develop themselves as scholars or thoughtful practitioners. All too often there are no professional development activities for part-time faculty. Furthermore, part-time faculty members rarely have any collective representation from either a faculty union or faculty governance system. Frequently, they are treated with indifference by the staff of the college or university, and often are seen, as noted by Leslie and Gappa (1994), as second-class citizens in the academy. Exploitation of contemporary part-time faculty is all too common, leading to a potential collaboration between leaders of the virtual and advocacy cultures, and perhaps, to further reformulation of the new advocacy strategy that we described in Chapter Four.

The Invisible University

Ironically, colleges and universities in one region that have very different identities and ideological orientations may end up resembling each other when it comes to what students actually learn in the classroom because the part-time faculty members teaching in these diverse institutions are the same. We have, if you will, one invisible university in a given geographic region with multiple identities. Whether institutions refer to part-timers by that name or call them adjuncts, non-tenure-track faculty, or contract workers, it is time for educational institutions to engage in discussions about the significant issues that are raised by the invisible part-time faculty and that contribute to an invisible university. Because they influence the purposes and outcomes of university life, they form an important sector in the virtual culture and represent a major portion of the virtual community in many twenty-first-century colleges and universities.

Part-time faculty members have rich real-life experience and are often eager to engage in the intellectual community of the college or university. How do you ensure that they have adequate employment and benefits? The Five College Consortium in

Massachusetts has addressed this issue by jointly appointing faculty members (Gappa et al., 2007, p. 225). This is to be commended—but what about an even more ambitious venture? How about involving part-time faculty members in curriculum development and academic planning? Because they have many other responsibilities, part-time faculty could meet once or twice a year for an entire day in a pleasant retreat setting, together with their full-time colleagues, rather than attend weekly or monthly curriculum meetings on campus.

In some cases, job security and compensation are not the primary issues for the part-time faculty members. The extent to which part-time faculty present a problem or promise to an institution lies, in part, in the nature and number of those who are hired. The American Association of University Professors (AAUP; 2000) and Gappa and Leslie (1993) have identified four types of part-time faculty: (1) those who would prefer full-time positions and are seeking through their part-time teaching to procure a full-time position; (2) those who serve part-time by choice and have no full-time employment outside the home; (3) those who have employment elsewhere and teach because of the satisfaction intrinsic in teaching or because of their altruistic desire to help students; and (4) those who are preparing to retire from another career or are already retired. All four of these types of part-timers are likely to increase in numbers during the coming decade. We are likely to observe not only many part-time faculty members who hope for full-time tenure-track positions but also retirees from other careers, people who have decided to embrace a multitrack career, and people who are employed as independent consultants and teach to supplement their unpredictable incomes (and often to attract clients from among their students).

Many colleges and universities, especially those in major urban areas, recruit their part-time faculty from among a group of professionals who are already fully employed but want to shift out of their professions for a period of time to teach, and perhaps, meet their midlife "generativity" needs (Bergquist, Greenberg, &

Klaum, 1993). Corporations, for instance, can set up sabbaticals for their older and higher-level executives so they can renew themselves by teaching for a year in a local college or university. Professionals who are in the midst of a career shift may want to teach full-time for a year, and professionals who have recently retired might wish to teach for several years.

For those part-time faculty members who are looking for greater job security, compensation, and even health benefits, individual colleges and universities can provide joint faculty and administrative appointments. Although a full-time faculty position might not be open, part-time faculty can be hired into full-time administrative positions and be allowed to continue teaching part-time as part of their contractual obligations to the college or university. Greater job security can also be established if new partnerships are formed between the college or university and noneducational institutions. A part-time faculty member, for instance, might be employed jointly by a postsecondary institution and a corporation to provide technical training and education in the corporation and comparable training and education in the college or university.

Colleges and universities need not go it alone in providing new opportunities and resources for their part-time faculty. Programs for these often-overlooked faculty members can be conducted in collaboration with several neighboring institutions. Rather than allowing a hidden university to form in a community, several colleges and universities can intentionally create an interinstitutional "Academy for Community Faculty." Professional development activities offered in this academy for part-time faculty who work at several institutions can be linked to issues of job security and career development. Part-time faculty could even prepare themselves, through such an academy, for transition to full-time faculty status, if appropriate. Career ladders could be identified to help part-time faculty gain a more realistic sense of what is needed to move toward full-time positions.

Virtual Institutions

In the twenty-first-century world of higher education we are beginning to see entire institutions that are structured around the principle of virtuality. For instance, Western Governors University offers asynchronous, on-demand learning over its computer network. Students apply and are assessed and accepted online. They select self-paced courses that build mastery toward with their study plan (Rowley, Lujan, & Dolence, 1998). Virtual Online University is another such example. It offers content from kindergarten through college. Students can enter multiuser environments in which they can interact with other students and the instructor online. Market-driven institutions also exist. Some, like IBM's Global Campus and the Global Network Academy, provide resources to students and to corporate organizations that are in pursuit of learning. African Virtual University, originally a project of the World Bank, exemplifies a social-developmental use of technology for education.

> Since 1997, the African Virtual University (AVU) has worked to create a technology-enhanced learning network to increase access to quality higher education for those living in Sub-Saharan Africa. Its current priority is to provide programs in selected areas of specialization, such as computer science, information technology, business studies, engineering, health, and teacher training, that are critical to economic development in the region.

> The growth of new (information and communications) technologies makes possible the creation of virtual universities where quality professors, libraries, and laboratories can be shared by people and organizations in physically unconnected places. Virtual Universities have the advantage of requiring minimum capital investments and operating costs. Hence, mass tertiary education in the scientific and technology disciplines, where the investment

> cost is the highest and the human resource base is the weakest, becomes a real possibility for Sub-Saharan Africa. [African Virtual University, n.d.]

Interinstitutional Partnerships and Consortia

Interinstitutional partnerships exemplify the virtual culture in contemporary higher education in yet another way. These arrangements provide an alternative to the traditional models of higher education and set the stage for the creation of a new kind of institution, one that Kenneth Boulding (1973) identified many years ago as the "intersect" organization—an innovative hybrid of profit and nonprofit, public and private, and even big and small. Long before other types of organizations recognized the value of what Rosabeth Moss Kanter (1994) called *collaborative advantage*, colleges and universities around the world (in particular, liberal arts colleges in the United States) formed closely structured interinstitutional consortia, in which resources and expertise were shared to mutual advantage. The twenty-first century will bring a greater need for such consortia.

Virtual partnerships may be long-term or temporary (project-based). The long-term partnerships, or consortia, may be based on a set of clearly established agreements between the leaders of autonomous colleges and universities who wish act in cooperation with one another. Colleges and universities usually enter into this kind of arrangement when they find they have insufficient resources or expertise to accomplish a specific set of goals. There is little centralized management and as a result minimal centralized control. Instead, the power resides with the participating colleges and universities and in the cooperative agreements they have made.

Short-term partnerships are even more virtual in nature. They require only a brief interinstitutional commitment to collaborate. A short-term partnership is usually formed when members of one college or university receive a request for performance of a large or highly complex task. It does not have sufficient time, money, or expertise to complete this task without the assistance of another institution—unless it wants to take a big risk in rapidly expanding its own capacity (and size) to handle the project. A temporary partnership is formed, with several other colleges or universities invited to participate as partners in the consortium. This short-term partnership usually has a strong but short-lived central office that coordinates specific projects or focuses on specific problem areas. One of the colleges or universities provides the central coordinating role, while each of the other colleges or universities contributes specific expertise to the project or independently completes specific components of the project.

Today, even more ambitious and far-ranging partnerships, both short-term and long-term, are required to bring educational institutions together with each other and with other types of organizations (Bergquist, Betwee, & Meuel, 1995). One of the most notable of such partnerships was formed by colleges, universities, research institutions, and other environmentally oriented organizations located in the northern regions of the world. Constituted as the University of the Arctic, this partnership involves institutions from Canada, the United States (Alaska), Norway, Sweden, Finland, and Russia. Each one is devoted to the environmental challenges of the Arctic, as well as preservation of the distinctive cultures of people living in the Far North.

This virtual university offers a shared undergraduate program—Circumpolar Studies—(University of the Arctic, n.d.). The courses are delivered online to provide maximum accessibility to remote northern residents, but may be delivered additionally as regular classroom offerings by members of the University of the Arctic. Furthermore, there are studies on specific topics of particular relevance to the north that are roughly equivalent to a semester of schooling, where students can participate in classes at other institutions.

Conclusions

New collaborations, such as the University of the Arctic, enable higher education institutions to blend their own certificate- and degree-granting authority and expertise in postsecondary education with the facilities, marketing expertise, fiscal resources, technical and scientific equipment and expertise, and prestige of other institutions. We see these new types of collaborations in the service learning initiatives of many colleges and universities (Jacoby, 2003a, 2003b). Service learning programs bring together community agencies with colleges and universities to provide both rich learning experiences to students and valuable human services to the local community. Although service learning partnerships are often short-term, they can be transformative not only for those who are directly involved in the project but also for the institutions that are involved (Enos & Morton, 2003).

Many in the academy feel that the new virtual forms, nourished by the great potential of the Internet, may threaten the structures and roles of modern colleges and universities. They certainly will force the leaders of modern colleges and universities to identify that which is distinctive and central to their institutions and that which can best be done by constantly shifting and responding through various short- and long-term partnerships.

6

The Tangible Culture

The tangible culture: A culture that finds meaning in its roots, its community, and its spiritual grounding; that values the predictability of a value-based, face-to-face education in an owned physical location; that holds assumptions about the ability of old systems and technologies being able to instill the institution's values; and that conceives of the institution's enterprise as the honoring and reintegration of learning from a local perspective.

As academicians and members of a twenty-first-century society, we may be entering a postmodern era. Our sights as leaders in higher education, however, are set as much backward as they are forward. The foundations of our postsecondary education institutions were established in premodern societies and we still base our most precious academic values on tangible evidence of quality: a beautiful campus, a rich endowment, prestigious degrees, esteemed faculty members, low acceptance ratios for students, and a hard-earned reputation measured by accreditation and national ratings. Everything in higher education may seem to be in flux, yet we hold on to that which is tangible. Furthermore, the tangible seems universal and unchanging. Gayle, Tewaire, and White (2003) convey this almost mythic image of tangibility in their description of the typical academic institution:

> Consider for a few moments the traditional characteristics of a college or university. It has a residential student body and offers a combination of graduate and undergraduate programs, along with various professional schools for medicine and law, for example. Although we can categorize some schools as national, most are regional or local in scope. They have a recognizable geographic service area within which they are known and from which they draw their students. These institutions have full-time faculty who exercise control over such issues as curricular design and degree requirements. Classes are conceived in terms of seat-time, with face-to-face instruction. Faculty can earn tenure through a well-defined process, requiring excellence in teaching, demonstrated development of a professional research program, and published scholarship. In the interest of support from institutional stakeholders, community and university service is part of the role of any university professor. In addition to the human side of education are the physical and economic dimensions of college or university existence. A central library with extensive holdings of books and periodicals and a carefully landscaped campus have been standard components of the traditional university. [p. 84]

Although this image of the traditional academic institution is still sometimes accurate, it seems to convey more about the traditional values and aspirations of our academic institutions than about the realities of most twenty-first-century institutions. We look back with a distorted and often nostalgic perspective on a world that we assume was simpler, a world that was conducive to strong academic leadership, and specifically, to men and women who could decisively solve straightforward problems. It was a world in which faculty members, students, administrators, and other members of the academy found gratification in the work they performed and community in the people with whom they affiliated. These remarkable colleges and universities with which we are affiliated were founded in communities that had an identity, or at least homogeneity, in values, culture—and socioeconomic status.

The tangible culture as it is manifest in the twenty-first century is based on reflection and the search for a deeply rooted identity, a supportive and appreciative community, and a grounding in religious or spiritual rather than secular values. It is based on a parochial perspective, in contrast to the cosmopolitan perspective often held by those operating in the virtual culture. The tangible culture has regained prominence in academic institutions through a reemphasis on standards (often defined as "quality"), the revitalization of academic institutions that are closely aligned with a particular religious doctrine (often Evangelical in nature) or set of values (for example, environmental preservation or holistic health), and the efforts to balance "high tech" with "high touch," with, for example, residency-based education, tutorial programs, and community-based service learning projects.

Is our yearning for a simpler place and time in the life of the academy nothing more than an attempt to escape from the vagaries of contemporary life? Are these new initiatives short-lived reactions to the technological tide away from parochial education that takes place in a specific place and at a specific time? Given the pressures under which we live in our postmodern world, it is quite understandable that we might wish for a simpler place and time. Yet there remain realistic reasons for our search for the premodern world of tangibility, because the premodern still exists in our society. The world community is only moments away from the premodern. Most societies were still premodern less than a hundred years ago. The premodern world is the reality in many communities around the world, including in North America. A thin veneer of modernism covers the fundamental and deeply rooted premodernism in nearly all societies (Friedman, 1999). Organizations are still concerned with shared values and play a central role in the creation or maintenance of a vital and caring community. A successful academic institution of the twenty-first century will inevitably incorporate diverse elements from many times and places, including the premodern.

Origins and Foundations of the Tangible Culture

Early European universities such as the University of Paris (La Sorbonne), Oxford, and Cambridge were founded as far back in time as the thirteenth century, while American colleges and universities such as Harvard and Yale were founded during the seventeenth and early eighteenth centuries. French-language institutions such as the Collège des Jésuites and the Collège Marie-de-l'Incarnation in Quebec were also founded in the seventeenth century. Thus, the founding values and perspectives of academic institutions are based not in modern societies but in premodern ones.

The tangible culture is the founding culture of these institutions and it resides in our contemporary society at a much deeper and broader level than do any of the five academic cultures we have already described. Founding leaders and founding stories continue to guide an institution, even if these leaders and stories are based in a society and a culture that are no longer viable. Kezar, Carducci, and Contreras-McGavin (2006, p. 53) touch on these deep, unchanging roots in their analysis of academic leadership. They point out that "the core principles that guide an institutional mission [in an academic institution] are frequently the direct results of one key individual and his or her beliefs and values. In many instances these values are passed on for centuries without being questioned."

There is an important second point to be made about the power of the tangible culture. Under stress, there is a regression in any society to more fundamental (premodern) forms and functions. Because much of our world is in stress today—as it moves into a mixture of premodern, modern, and newly emerging postmodern forms—we can expect a resurgence of the values and perspectives of the tangible culture. There is also the dynamic we have already investigated in terms of both the developmental and advocacy cultures. Just as these two organizational cultures depend in many ways for their prominence and influence on the rise (and fall) of their opposite cultures (the collegial and managerial), so too the tangible culture depends on the virtual culture. The tangible culture is reemerging in higher education precisely because the technological advances and socioeconomic pressures that have made the virtual culture possible call for a response from the tangible culture.

Given these dynamic factors—which suggest a continuing (and perhaps growing) role for the tangible culture—it is important to know something about and more fully appreciate the perspectives and values inherent in this very old academic culture. Gayle et al. (2003, p. 42) suggest that leaders of an academic institution cannot ignore this culture. Effective academic leadership requires contextual intelligence that is "rooted in an understanding of the customs and traditions, historical and philosophical evolution, formal and informal political structures, the language, and the myths that mold [their institution].... Such intelligence includes an understanding of the assumptions, values, norms, and tangible signs (artifacts) of faculty members, staff, and administrators and their interacting behaviors."

In seeking to make sense of this richly textured culture, we will focus on five of its dimensions: the notion of worth, the symbolic representation of institutional values, the tangibility of space and residency, the process of teaching and learning, and the psychological covenant.

The Notion of Worth

Worth is defined in any traditional or premodern society primarily by land, physical facilities, and reputation (Bergquist, 1993). Although private possessions (property) are of minimal value in a hunter-gatherer society, there is a strong need for both land and shelter when a society moves to an economic base that depends on the cultivation or extraction of natural resources. People are no longer migratory; they are now establishing themselves on a permanent plot of land in permanent dwellings. Those who possess property and can successfully defend it against other people have status and power in their community. Members of such communities are beholden to the others for respecting (and even protecting) their personal property rights. This community of trust also is needed for the exchange of goods. What is required is both the trade of goods and the development (through reputation) of trust in one's trading partners. Thus, both property and reputation become the primary indices of worth in a traditional premodern society.

Premodern colleges and universities were not immune to these criteria of worth. The academy was part and parcel of the exchange and a particularly important asset when it came to establishing reputation. The son (and more rarely, the daughter) who graduated from one of the prestigious European universities added to the worth—that is, the reputation—of the family. Advanced education thus became part of the "capital" accrued by wealthy members of a society. Young men did not have to use their education to "get a job," for they were assured of employment in their family's business or in an established institution of their society such as the priesthood, medicine, law, or the military. Even today we see evidence of education at a prestigious university being coupled with reputation and property (land and buildings) to form the "old wealth" or "landed gentry" in many countries.

Just as worth or quality is associated with property and reputation among individuals and families in a traditional society, so property and reputation become central to the identification of worth in the academic institution. The same criteria apply: land, buildings, library holdings, beautiful grounds, degrees and reputation of faculty members, institutional prestige, and entrance qualifications for students. These are primarily input measures and are closely aligned with the criteria of quality espoused by the collegial culture; however, these criteria take on a slightly different meaning in the tangible culture. We see this today in the reticence with which leaders of very old and prestigious universities participate in any accreditation process. It is simply "beneath" them and their institutions to be open to review and inspection. "One knows when one is in the presence of highest quality, and it certainly does not take someone of lesser quality and class to assess this quality!"—so might the statement read if the leader of a prestigious institution stooped to even reply to the request for external review, and if this person chose to make a perfectly honest response!

There is another way in which these criteria are interpreted differently by the tangible and collegial cultures. Input measures are assumed important in the collegial culture because these measures have been shown to produce excellent results with regard to the education of students. A good library and well-educated faculty are important for the proper education of students in a traditional classroom. But in the tangible culture, the assumption that input criteria of quality translate automatically into quality outcomes is simply not relevant. Instead, property and reputation alone are equated with quality. What we possess is critical, not what we do with what we possess. The larger and more beautiful the campus, the higher the quality. The more prestigious the institution, the higher the quality. The more honored the faculty and students (in terms of family backgrounds and pedigrees), the higher the quality. Those who are aligned with the tangible culture may be guilty of falling into a confusing and self-referencing tautology ("a rose is a rose is a rose") when defining and identifying institutional quality: high quality is achieved by assembling together that which is of high quality. There is no reason in the tangible culture to move any further in an attempt to demonstrate worth.

Clearly, those students and faculty who are of highest quality deserve the finest amenities that a prestigious college or university can provide. They deserve an elaborate fitness center, luxurious offices, spacious student housing, and a rich variety of locations where food can be purchased and informal meetings can be held. These amenities have often been given more attention than educational quality in the marketing of academic institutions (Newman, Couturier, & Scurry, 2004). Administrators, faculty, and board members are not the only ones who get caught up in the appeal of the tangible culture. Current and prospective students and parents are equally enthralled with these seemingly incidental luxuries. In many ways the tangible culture is a potential distraction from the fundamental mission of an institution. The amenities, rather than the core mission, get marketed.

Symbolic Representations of Institutional Values

Values inherent in the tangible culture are rarely explicitly articulated but they are manifest in many visible ways. At their best, colleges and universities create a culture of celebration "where collective, rather than only individual, victories are publicly valued and where service to colleagues, the institution, and the community becomes much more than stripes toward the achievement of tenure and promotion or a means of developing and more effectively positioning the institution in the market" (Gayle et al., 2003, p. 7). A state university has a coat of arms and display cases that contain memorabilia and honors conferred on the institution. Upon graduation, seniors at a liberal arts college bestow a plaque with their own class motto to hang on a wall in the dining hall. Respected faculty members at a century-old university sit at the high table. Symbols and ceremonies are still important.

To some extent a culture of celebration is created (and the tangible culture reigns supreme) at least once each year—at graduation ceremonies. Degrees are conferred at elaborately choreographed events, where elegant declarations written on parchment are delivered to worthy graduates and doctoral hoods are placed over the heads of advanced-level graduates. In most colleges and universities, faculty members and administrators march (actually "process") in specific order to the stage, usually accompanied by a traditional piece of musical heraldry (Elgar's *Pomp and Circumstances* is a twentieth-century creation). A senior faculty member often leads this procession, carrying the institution's flag, walking stick, or mace. The president frequently wears a special medallion bestowed by the board of trustees. Honorary degrees are awarded and graduates throw off their caps at the end of the ceremony. These are very old, richly textured traditions that are common in some ways to most academic institutions in the world and distinctive in other ways to each one.

Symbols represent important statements about the values and heritage of an institution. These symbols are not "secular" in nature, nor are they of democratic origin—even though the academic institution may be secular and publicly supported. Rather, these symbols are deeply embedded in religious traditions and in socioeconomic class structures. We continue to be drawn to the trappings of the tangible culture, though we are inclined to ignore their origins and underlying meanings, for these trappings are products of theology and hierarchy. They represent the bestowing of the "haves" with further prestige and reputation and the conferring of valued property (hood and diploma) on the graduate. Tierney and Minor (2004) suggest that these ceremonies also convey something about and reinforce the distribution of power in the institution while contributing to a tangible sense of community.

The Tangibility of Space and Residency

An even more powerful and stabilizing form of symbolism prevails in the tangible culture. This is the symbolism represented in the architecture of the buildings and campus that make up the physical structure of the academy. The values of an academic institution are often dramatically represented through, made manifest in, and reinforced by the architecture, physical layout, and even the interior design of a campus and its buildings: "One can tell a great deal about the culture of an organization by observing the image projected by major buildings, the extent to which they are maintained, and the arrangements of offices and furniture in them" (Gayle et al., 2003, p. 46).

The central courtyard (for example, the Harvard "yard") provides boundaries and serves as a sanctuary for both students and faculty. The buildings at Oxford, Cambridge, and many other traditional colleges and universities are grouped in a quadrangle, with only one entrance. In this way, the rector, resident faculty member, or residence hall director can keep track of the comings and goings of all students, and in particular, their arrival back in their residences by a specific parietal hour. The open areas away from the quadrangles are often assigned to play and intramural athletics. Students are to have disciplined minds and moral character (hence the closed-in spaces of the quadrangle), but are to be free of spirit though still establishing character when engaging their bodies (hence the open spaces of the playing field).

The Oxbridge and residential North American campuses were designed as both refuges and heavily bounded containers in another way, too. These institutions were usually built in the countryside—many miles from the temptation and depravity of the city. Furthermore, all students were usually required to reside at the institution and found it logistically difficult to return home except on long weekends. This emphasis on the location of residential institutions outside the city was particularly strong in the United States, with its Jeffersonian ideal of the countryside rather than the city as the best place for the education of future citizens and leaders of the republic (Egbert, n.d.).

Temporal boundaries such as curfew and class schedules complemented the spatial boundaries—the quadrangles and location of the institution in the country—at the Oxbridge and residential

North American institutions. In loco parentis was alive and well as a vehicle for tangible, localized control. The Oxbridge student is the "property" of his parents. His parents, in turn, have assigned the care of this property to the faculty and administration of the institution. The rights of the student are minimal, because this young man is considered property until he has "come of age." Furthermore, the primary purpose of the education received by the Oxbridge student is the temporary warehousing of the property, and optimally, the refinement of this property. This educative process of refinement ("polishing") has traditionally been defined by the Oxbridge administration and faculty in alignment with the values of the student's parents, who typically come from the same homogeneous socioeconomic class as the institution's leaders.

The architectural configuration of the Oxbridge universities clearly represents a set of distinctive values when it comes to protecting students and a set of assumptions about their inability to monitor their own behavior. Although these values directly align with those espoused by the collegial culture, there are, once again, several important differences. First, not all of the traditional institutions with a strong emphasis on tangible symbols represent the same values or hold the same assumptions as the collegial culture. Old, prestigious institutions in France, Germany, and other European nations tend to spread their buildings out, and each building has multiple entrances. Their students do not reside on campus; instead, the main campus is usually located in a major metropolitan area such as Paris or Frankfurt. Students reside in private housing near the university. As commuters, these students in many ways closely resemble the commuting students in much less prestigious American and Canadian state-supported universities and community colleges.

Using a term created by Robert Sommer (1969), the European universities and North American commuter institutions are *sociofugal* in design. Their architecture and campus plan brings people (students and faculty members) in for only a short period of time and directs them back outward to the surrounding city once the teaching, learning, or research function is performed. These institutions operate like a "centrifugal" machine that pushes objects outward. Their buildings and campus layouts tend to open outward, to suggest temporality. British universities and North American residential institutions, by contrast, are *sociopetal.* They draw both students and faculty inward and keep them there, as in the case of "centripetal" machines that draw objects closer together. The buildings in these sociopetal institutions and the location of these institutions in the countryside suggest and encourage containment, the administration and faculty's holding of trust and responsibility, and protection and enclosure.

Although many of the commuter-based North American institutions have sought to build in some architectural sense of community with university centers, student union buildings, and community plazas, these institutions remain sociofugal in orientation. Students and faculty may linger for a while at the student union, have a cup of coffee at a small lounge located in the building that also contains their classroom, and attend a football game at their university's stadium on Saturday. However, they are not going to "live and breath" their college or university as do residential students and they certainly are going to learn as much or more from their life away from campus as from their life on campus.

Another important architectural feature distinguishes the British universities and North American residential institutions from their European and North American commuter counterparts. Buildings on a British or North American residential campus are often of uniform design and intentionally placed to foster community and collectivity. It is a quite different situation in the European and North American commuter institutions. Each building in these institutions tends to be designed independently. Many are specifically designed to meet the unique needs of the discipline or department housed in the building. By assigning priority in the architectural plan to the special needs of one group of people, these sociofugal institutions encourage individuality and specialization of functions (disciplines, professional certifications, specific administrative services)—reinforcing the collegial culture.

Despite differences between the sociopetal and sociofugal colleges and universities of Britain and Europe, they were all initially aligned with the tangible culture—and may still be. The collegial culture may be dominant in both the British and European universities, yet we discover quite different values and assumptions when we identify the symbolic messages that seem to be conveyed by the tangible culture in the British and European universities. We can also look to differences in the architecture of the North American residential and North American commuter institutions in order to discover a comparable disparity in their inherent values and assumptions.

Disparities in the design of buildings and campuses in North American institutions, however, do not seem to suggest two variants on the tangible culture with a single underlying and unifying collegial culture, as appears to be the case in British and European universities. Rather, disparities in North American campus designs suggest a great difference between two types of North American institutions—a difference that is not easily resolved. The collegial culture is dominant in residential colleges and universities, which are designed on the basis of sociopetal assumptions and values, whereas the managerial culture is dominant in the commuter colleges and universities, which are designed on the basis of sociofugal assumptions and values.

A second important distinction may be drawn between the tangible and collegial cultures with regard to the Oxbridge architecture. The architecture of Oxford and Cambridge is distinctive. In many cases, the architects, such as Christopher Wren, who designed the buildings were innovative. They used Oxford and Cambridge as testing grounds for new ideas about how to design and lay out multiple structures. By contrast, those who embrace the collegial culture today are often quite conservative in their preferences for architecture and other symbols of their campus. They want their buildings and their ceremonies to look "just like" those of their older and ultimately more prestigious counterparts in Great Britain and on the European continent. They emulate rather than invent. Those who align with the tangible culture may actually show some disdain for those who espouse the collegial culture. They might, with some justification, equate the collegial culture's inclination to borrow from the traditional symbols of the tangible culture in an effort to gain prestige as nothing more than a variant on the attempts of the nouveau riche to emulate those with old wealth.

There is more to our analysis of the tangible culture's use of architectural symbols. The architectural designs of many academic institutions offer powerful statements about values and perspectives not only through the layout of the buildings (the horizontal dimension of architectural design) but also through the construction of lofty buildings (the vertical dimension of architectural design). Most campus designs include a centrally located tower, a church steeple (if it is a religious institution), a clock tower, a bell tower, a campanile, or an imposing administrative building. The structure's verticality suggests something about the institution's values. In their analysis of the symbolic use of architecture and furniture in domestic settings, Ruesch and Kees (1969) observed that vertical structures inevitably make a strong, tangible statement about what is valued in a building or residence. Flags are hoisted high on poles, corporate leaders build skyscrapers, and priestly architects build cathedrals with tall steeples. It is certainly no accident that Holder Tower on the Princeton University campus was modeled on the crossing tower at Canterbury Cathedral and that other North American universities have similarly replicated British and Continental cathedrals. Towers of this sort represent sacred (not secular) values. The tangible culture, with its origins in premodern European culture, does not distinguish between the sacred and secular when it comes to the mission of academic institutions.

The vertical structures in academic institutions hold additional symbolic value. They inevitably represent and convey authority and power. The bell in the tower rings at the start of each hour or even on the quarter hour, reinforcing the notion that education is measured by time spent in the classroom or library. One must comply with a specific schedule set by officials who are often housed in this tower. Much as the church bells in a Swiss town tell everyone what "reality" is and who is in charge (a Protestant God), so the bells of the college or university define temporal reality and remind everyone of where the ultimate authority resides. Although this authority might be tempered by the melodic strains of a carillon, such as the one in the imposing tower located at the heart of the University of California campus in Berkeley, the authority is still clear and pervasive.

The occupants of these tall structures typically look out over the campus. Their height, like the single entrance to the Oxbridge quadrangle, suggests overview and omniscience. This use of architecture to symbolize an overview or monitoring function was insightfully analyzed by Michel Foucault (1965) with specific regard to Jeremy Bentham's Penopticon. Foucault cited Bentham as a social reformer who envisioned a building (the Penopticon) that would allow observers from a much higher point, such as a tower, to look into rooms without being seen by those occupying the rooms. The occupants could be students in a university, patients in an asylum, or workers in a factory. The occupants would behave appropriately because they would never know when they were being watched. Bentham mused that there need never be an observer in the tower, for occupants of rooms in the Penopticon would have internalized control—the internal eye. Foucault (1979) draws an analogy between Bentham's Penopticon and the removal of external control (chains) from the inmates in French asylums during the nineteenth century. In the latter case, the chains could be removed because the reformers were able to exert even greater control over the patients through the introduction of the "internal chains" of shame and covert surveillance.

One might draw an analogy to the single-entrance quadrangles at the Oxbridge institutions or the towers located at the center of many campuses. The tower serves a symbolic function similar to that served by both Bentham's Penopticon and the French reformers' internalized control. In all three cases, there is the opportunity for and threat of surveillance. Furthermore, the primary assumption in all three cases is identical: the intentions or competence of the people being observed are not to be trusted. We install internal chains because we do not believe that the student, inmate, or worker is capable of monitoring and controlling his or her own behavior. One might even consider the honor systems and honor codes that were adopted in many residential North American colleges and universities during the mid-twentieth century as examples of internal chains. Rather than using formal authorities to monitor compliance with policies on plagiarism, cheating, or substance abuse, institutions with honors systems asked students to report on one another if the code was abused. Although students in such systems were asked explicitly to monitor their own behavior and even to report their own abuses of the code, these systems typically only had teeth when other students reported (usually anonymously) on the abuse. Furthermore, it is interesting to note that fellow students, as members of an honors court, usually managed the review of abuses and meted out the punishment.

Thus, in this revision of Bentham's Penopticon, observers are no longer just located in the tower, they are now located in the same cell as the student, patient, or worker. We see this revised strategy for the internalization of the chains played out not only in academic honors systems but also in mental institutions and corporations. The community treatment programs in many mental institutions enable (and encourage) mental patients to confront and treat one another, as dramatically portrayed in the film *One Flew Over the Cuckoo's Nest*. We also witness this revised version of the internal chains strategy being deployed in corporations that have shifted responsibility for managerial decision making and performance monitoring to their workers (Lawler, 1986, 1992). We will see this same value being played out in other aspects of the tangible culture. Perhaps this is one of the reasons why the tangible culture is experiencing a resurgence in academic institutions. We are less trusting of the intentions and competencies of many members of our academic communities to monitor and control their own behavior in the complex, unpredictable, and turbulent world of the twenty-first century.

Pedagogy

Among educators who are aligned with the tangible culture, teaching and learning take place in a particular time and at a particular place. Students are required to come to class and attendance records are kept. In many residential North American colleges and universities during much of the twentieth century, attendance was even required for a certain period of time at the institution's library ("study hall"). Much as in the case of the single entrance to the quadrangles at Oxford and Cambridge, it was, and in many cases still is, assumed that students as property cannot monitor or manage their own educational enterprise. They are to be passive receptacles into which knowledge and manners are poured in certain discrete quantities that can be observed and measured.

This notion of pedagogical passivity must not be mistaken for the kind of passivity to be found in the managerial culture or the operations of many large universities where knowledge is poured into the heads of students sitting in large lecture halls. Rather, tangibility implies intimacy. A faculty member who is aligned with and enmeshed in the tangible culture wants to directly engage a student, to witness the learning and development firsthand. This is why the tangible culture often encourages tutorial programs, teaching and learning inside the residency hall, and other preceptor-based methods of teaching. Faculty members aligned with the collegial culture often prefer the classroom, where they can demonstrate their own expertise in a specific discipline through lecturing. Faculty members aligned with the tangible culture, by contrast, prefer to work more closely and carefully with each student, monitoring progress (in all realms of life) of the student "property" that is entrusted to them, and serving (as do the dorm proctors and other residential directors) as quasi parents in loco. They look to such processes as mentoring, peer advisement, study halls, and informal gatherings in which students and faculty candidly discuss immediate issues that arise among students who are living together. They collectively focus on fundamental social values and the nature of cooperation and citizenship (Zeller, 2005).

The tangible culture also offers a distinctive perspective on the assessment of pedagogical quality. The issue of tacitly defined quality is embedded not only in the assessment of an institution's worth but also in the assessment of a student's worth. Usually, no one is dismissed from an elitist, "high-quality" college or university, because it is assumed that if you are attending such an institution then you are, also, by (tautological) definition, a high-quality student: "We don't think of you as 'failing' or 'flunking out'; rather you are making slower progress through the program than are other students and if you apply yourself you will graduate—eventually." In this kind of setting there are no formal mechanisms for quality control other than the tangible evidence of attendance, attention, and assignment completion. The tangible culture measures education in terms of time spent (tangible) rather than amount learned (intangible). Self-paced instruction that is formally instituted would never make sense in the tangible culture; rather, students end up pacing themselves by completing or failing to complete course requirements.

This emphasis on stable pedagogical time and space was vividly illustrated in an interaction that recently took place during an international conference that one of us attended. The attention of those attending this conference turned to the emerging role of innovative colleges and universities that were attracting mature learners—such as the University of Phoenix—and are increasingly aligned with the virtual culture. Several of those in attendance at this conference, who were leaders of major universities throughout the world, dismissed these new institutions with disdain. They explicitly indicated that they found no value in institutions providing education to students at the time and place of the students' choosing. They labeled them "convenience" colleges and universities, and viewed them not only as a threat to their own universities but even as a threat to the integrity of the entire higher education system in their country. The label *convenience* is both an accurate description of the virtual culture (which we described in Chapter Five) and a diminution of the virtual culture and these thriving institutions. The death of traditional universities may not be imminent, but the cavalier dismissal of a rapidly growing sector of higher education throughout the world indicates attitudes that could eventually bring about the demise of these traditional institutions.

The Psychological Covenant

Although the psychological contract plays such an important role in the advocacy culture (see Chapter Four), its flaws are inherent in the highly secularized, economically driven world of contemporary colleges and universities that are heavily saturated with the managerial culture. First, a contract can be broken by either party. Thus, there is no tangible, enduring commitment to the ultimate welfare of the employee (on the part of the organization) or the ultimate welfare of the organization (on the part of the employee). Everyone is in it for themselves. This leads to the dissolution of community in existing organizations and the absence of community in newly formed organizations. No commitment holds everything together, especially during difficult times. There is no glue. Academic institutions must move away from the secular and economically driven notions of work to a model of work that is both secular and sacred. Such a model would embrace and more fully explore the notion of a psychological covenant rather than a psychological contract.

The psychological covenant is not readily broken. It involves a deep commitment on the part of both the employee and the organization. In the case of a traditional college or university, this commitment is made between and among faculty and academic administrators, at least implicitly, at the start of the school year (the convocation) and again at the end of the school year (the graduation ceremony). Neither party can break a covenant without the other party's permission. Thus, men and women in a covenant-based organization must work through their problems rather than simply give up and part company, much as is the case in a covenant-based marriage.

Second, covenants, as opposed to economics-based contracts, are based on sacrifice, as in the Old Testament covenant between Abraham and Jehovah. Both parties are willing to give up a part of their selves in order for the relationship to work. It is not a matter of money or of either short-term or long-term personal gain. It is a matter of commitment and honor—two very important values in the tangible culture. This notion of sacrifice flies directly in the face of individualistic concerns and speaks to the value placed in a community-oriented tangible culture on collective responsibility rather than an exclusive emphasis on individual rights. The individualistic, rights-oriented emphasis may be directly aligned with the advocacy culture (and indirectly with the managerial and collegial cultures) and with a more masculine way of knowing and valuing things. By contrast, the collective emphasis is more closely aligned with the tangible culture, and indirectly with the developmental culture, and with a more feminine way of knowing (Gilligan, 1982; Belenky et al., 1986).

Enduring Contributions of the Tangible Culture

We are generally critical of the tangible culture and its often outmoded, patronizing, and elitist attitudes toward the processes of education and the students being served by these processes; however, we also greatly appreciate the inherent wisdom in this oldest culture of the academy. The tangible world is of great relevance to contemporary higher education institutions because it holds at least partial answers to the emerging challenges of postmodern education. The tangible culture can help us set the agenda for our colleges and universities with regard to reemerging values. It provides us with important insights about the long-standing and deeply embedded dynamics of the academic enterprise.

Virtually all transformations in social systems begin with the bashing of the previous, dominant era: "Let me show you the modern way in which we build houses" (or grow peas or serve members of a church). Many of the contemporary advocates for new paradigm thinking similarly begin with an analysis of modern world failure. This is quite understandable; however, in the long run it is foolish to leave behind the rich traditions of the past and knowledge gained from years of practical experience. Colleges and universities situated in an emerging postmodern world are likely to be successful, in part, if they borrow from both the premodern and modern worlds. Leaders of the twenty-first century academy can learn from the tangible culture while also inventing new forms and formulating new virtual perspectives that are neither premodern nor modern.

Tangible Culture in the Twentieth Century

During the twentieth century we were told that large-scale initiatives were good and deemed successful if they led to something big. This became a new—and very important—criterion of tangible quality in all sectors of society. Academic institutions were not immune to this emphasis on size. Large colleges and universities represented the pinnacle of modernism in most societies. We know that we have become modern the first time a high-rise building is constructed on our campus, and when men and women are being trained in our colleges and universities to fill technical and managerial positions in large corporations. The leaders of modern academic institutions and corporations speak a common language. Their institutions look alike and operate similarly. The languages of nations may differ, but the language of modern colleges, universities, and corporations is universal. Instead of the distinctive vernacular (ritual, stories, customs) of premodern communities, many of us have lived through our tenure as academicians with the universality of modernism. In this world, the managerial culture and tangible culture come together and form a powerful alliance.

Corporate leaders have considered their companies, and themselves as managers, to be successful if they are among the Fortune 500. Modern academic leaders have often defined their institutions in a similar manner. First and foremost, leaders of the modern academy were measured for success in terms of the number of students enrolled in their institution, the size of the faculty and library, and the number of professional staff that they have hired. In many cases, it was even more important to assess (and publicize) the size of the institution's endowment as well as the size and number of buildings and size (and beauty) of a college or university campus. Although the premodern era concentrated on the process of growth itself as the vital element of the organization, emphasis in modern colleges and universities has been placed on the outcome of growth. The desired outcome is large size. Typically, not much thought is given to the compatibility of organizational culture or the real financial savings associated with large bureaucracies (Bergquist, 1993).

As we examine the characteristics of the modern tangible culture in higher education, we find the potentials and problems associated with "bigness" emerging in many different forms. Largely in response to their growing size and complexity, modern colleges and universities have tended to emphasize structures and procedures that are drawn up and reinforced in a systematic manner and are uniform throughout the organization. The design of these colleges and universities is based on mechanistic models of efficiency rather than agricultural or biological models of continuity as in the premodern era. A critical issue arises, however, that nurtures the seeds of destruction for this mechanistic, modern model of organizational structure and growth and leads the way to a new, postmodern assumption about structure and growth. This issue is the need for integrative functions that compensate for the increasing differentiation in a rapidly growing, bureaucratic organization.

During the premodern era, when colleges and universities were relatively undifferentiated, every member of the academic community knew how to do virtually every job and was frequently involved in all aspects of the organization. As a result, no one had to rely on anyone else to provide specialized services. By contrast, during the modern era, any one person in an academic institution can perform only a small percentage of the total number of tasks that must be accomplished to meet the institution's needs and maintain its stability. This interdependence of the modern era, according to the early modernist Durkheim ([1893], 1933), can create a feeling of solidarity among members of an institution, or even an entire community, but it also can create a feeling of isolation, fragmentation, or even alienation. The specialization of functions and language creates a feeling of isolation when members of the institution can not readily communicate about their work with each other. Guilds, associations, and academic disciplines are created to bring people together—but only among those who do similar work.

Durkheim (1933) uses the metaphor of the husband and wife to explain this paradoxical aspect of the division of labor. During the modern era in Western societies, husbands and wives began to do quite different jobs. Men went off to work. Wives stayed home to perform domestic chores. The husband depended on the wife for a clean home and the wife depended on the husband for a paycheck. Although this differentiation made husbands and wives more dependent on each other, it also created a gap between them as they increasingly began to live very different lives. Similarly, as colleges and universities grew larger and more complex in the modern world, greater attention was given to those activities that enhance coordination and cooperation among the differentiated functions of the organization. In this way, the feeling of solidarity of which Durkheim spoke almost a century ago was amplified. The solidarity, however, came with some considerable costs.

The first cost is uniformity (leading to rigidity) and the loss of distinctive institutional identity. Much of the emphasis in modern management theory on uniform policies and procedures and on the critical role of supervision and delegation exemplifies this emphasis on solidarity. One of the key features of the modern era in higher education is the remarkable uniformity in the ways in which colleges and universities operate, whether these institutions are for-profit or nonprofit, secular or sacred. Jencks and Riesman (1968) pointed to this homogenization in American higher education many years ago, and more recently, Peter Drucker (1999) has pointed to this broad managerial uniformity as an organizational outcome that can be found in virtually all sectors of modern society. "The larger [higher education] institutions became," concludes Cohen (1998, p. 385), "the more they began to look like business corporations. Presidents were being selected less because of their scholarly accomplishments, more for their ability to manage large-scale enterprises."

The second cost is efficiency. In general, as an organization grows older it tends to devote an increasingly large proportion of its resources to indirect integrative services that create and sustain solidarity. The even more powerful, and influential, variable, however, is size. The larger the organization, the greater the proportion of resources of any kind that must be devoted to integrative, solidarity-producing services (Bergquist, 1993). There is a strong trend in virtually all colleges and universities to devote increasingly greater proportions of their total resources to integrative services as these colleges and universities grow older or bigger. Very young and very small colleges and universities devote a relatively small percentage of their resources to integrative services, whereas very large and very old colleges and universities devote a large percentage of their resources to them.

In his description of the "mass higher education era" in American higher education, which, he notes, ran from 1945 to 1975, Cohen (1998, p. 245) observes that "greater size led to complexity in management, as each institution added administrators in greater proportion than it did students and faculty. Complying with state and federal regulations, managing financial aid and affirmative action, and providing assurances that the institution was accountable in everything from student admissions to pollution control demanded that additional offices be opened." Cohen suggests that it has been very difficult—even "elusive"—to find the optimum institutional size: "Every college [has] to have some faculty and administrators, some buildings and books. The cost per student in each of these areas decreased [during the mass higher education era] as the number of students increased, hence up to a point growth seemed to suggest efficiency. However, as institutions grew they often found certain costs going up" (p. 256).

Cohen points, in particular, to the expansion of several integrative functions—the increased cost of internal coordination and overlapping managerial functions. As in the case of many corporations, the only answer to reduced efficiency and greater cost is to increase student tuition and devote even greater energy and resources to marketing and advertising. In many instances this has meant expansion in the geographic area from which students are recruited, often resulting in greater competition between colleges and universities that are supposed to be cooperating under statewide planning guidelines. Cohen concludes that there seemed to be no way during the mass higher education era to calculate the most efficient size for an institution. Unfortunately, there is not much that can be done, even today, about this problem of size and complexity. Once an organization gets bigger and integrative services begin to expand, it is very hard to move backwards in time or downsize the organization. Even if the organization is reduced in size, the proportion of integrative services is likely to remain rather large.

In essence, it seems that the tangible culture was quite powerful during much of the twentieth century. Its influence was manifest implicitly in the primary objective of colleges and universities to grow larger. Whereas premodern colleges and universities, dominated by the Oxbridge model, concentrated on continuity and tradition, which usually required very gradual growth, modern community colleges and universities, dominated by the German research and American land-grant models, emphasized rapid growth. As modern colleges and universities expanded in size and added more units and levels of organizational structure to accommodate their growth, they became more difficult to control. The premodern culture of the Oxbridge-based college provides integration through its customs, dress, ritual, and stories of great triumphs (and defeats); this premodern glue was often disparaged in modern twentieth-century academic institutions.

The premodern tangible culture did not offer sufficient integration for very large colleges and universities. They needed modern, managerial bonds to hold them together. As colleges and universities grew more complex in the modern world, increasing attention was given to those activities that enhanced coordination and cooperation among the differentiated functions of the organization. As colleges and universities grew larger, they required clearer boundaries so leaders could maintain control and emerging organizational anxiety could be assuaged. Financial monitoring and auditing functions were added. Personnel offices ensured uniformity of hiring practices as well as coordinated training efforts. Newsletters proliferated, as did office managers, purchasing agents, and departmental administrators. These offices, roles, and management functions were devoted to the integrative functions of the organization. As an academic institution grew larger and older, an increasingly large proportion of the resources of the organization were devoted to these integrative and anxiety-reducing functions. As a result, large modern colleges and universities were likely to be ineffective, and still in the twenty-first century, they are likely to be both large and inefficient.

Tangible Images and Myths

The tangible culture has strengths in its amassing of tangible objects and buildings—items that have inherent nondepreciatory value. This culture cherishes tangibles that continue to gain value for the institution. They include book and media collections, buildings, grounds, and flora. Physical plants are enhanced through donations and endowments. Land was one of the dominant forms of capital in the premodern era and remains important in the tangible culture. James Harrington (1611–1677), considered the father of the English political philosophy out of which grew Locke, Hume, Burke, and *The Federalist Papers*, indicated in his book *Oceania* ([1656], 1883) that "power follows property." It was the shift in property from the great nobles to the country squires, he argued, that explained the English Revolution that occurred in the 1640s, the overthrow of absolute government, and its replacement by the parliamentary government of the new property owners, the local gentry.

As we already mentioned, two other primary assets are less tangible but no less important to the tangible culture: ancestry and reputation. The tangible culture relies on its reputation as a means of creating value and worth. The academic institution's reputation and the reputation of individuals in it are the currency it uses to attract new students, faculty, and administrators. Individuals in the tangible culture will find Harvard appealing not primarily because of the learning that will result in its attendance but because of its worldwide reputation. Students will pay high tuition in exchange for that honored reputation. While faculty members in the collegial culture want their students to identify with a particular school of thought, faculty members in the tangible culture want their students to identify with specific individuals. Faculty members in the tangible culture are not as concerned about their salaries or working conditions as they are about keeping their place in the institution. One of the most honored traditions in the tangible culture is the "dollar-a-year" professor—an individual who has been so successful in a career or inherited such a large amount of money that he or she does not need any income from the academic appointment or donates the entire salary back to the institution. Faculty members in the tangible culture want to gain the respect of others on an individual basis; they want to ensure their place in the annals of their institution. The reputation of its faculty thus becomes another source of currency in the institution.

Living and Working in the Tangible Culture Today

Colleges and universities with a strong tangible culture usually have implicit intentions and boundaries. Faculty members and administrative staff simply do what their predecessors have always done. One would never have asked a professor in the old days—or today for that matter—what his intentions were or should be. A professor is simply in the business of teaching or doing research. That is his whole life. There is tangible value inherent in what he has always done and always wanted to do or was expected to do by his family. A professor who is aligned with the tangible culture would be confused or bemused if asked about his intentions, as would an artisan if asked about personal aspirations or the gratification she finds in the work she does. The professor would simply invite the inquirer into the classroom or laboratory. If the inquirer probed further, the professor would be likely to declare the need for academic freedom and the inappropriate nature of any inquirer who probes into purposes or outcomes: "Good teaching can never be captured by a number" or "Research for research's sake" would be the message.

To understand this tangible disdain for explicit intentions, C. Wright Mills (quoted by Best, 1973, p. 11) observed that "the craftsman has an image of the completed product, and even [if] he does not make it all, he sees the place of his part in the whole, and thus understands the meaning of his exertion in terms of that whole. The satisfaction he has in the result infuses the means of achieving it, and in this way his work is not only meaningful to him but also partakes of the consummatory satisfaction he has in the product." Mills's description of the craftsman certainly seems to apply just as appropriately to college professors or the dedicated registrars or academic deans who live in and thrive in a tangible culture.

Belief in Their Craft and a Face-to-Face Reality

Faculty members in the tangible culture believe in the craft of teaching, research, and scholarship. They value the face-to-face nature of interactions, the written word, and the location of icons throughout their campus that represent the institution and its historical roots. Heraldry and tradition are honored in the tangible culture. Faculty members are expected to attend graduation in full regalia. There are traditional annual events that must be conducted appropriately. These reinforce the distinctive values of their institution and the fundamental principles on which it was founded.

Although the premodern era primarily helps us set the agenda, with regard to reemerging values it also can provide us with some important insights about the human enterprise. We cannot re-create the simpler premodern structures and processes, as many small-is-beautiful and back-to-basics neoconservatives and neoliberals would have us do. We can, however, learn from the accumulated wisdom of this long era in the development of world civilizations and recognize the value inherent in a premodern, tangible culture operating in our academic institutions. New lessons can be learned from very old sages and forgotten or repressed societies, much as Rianne Eisler (1987) suggests we do in returning to the lessons about partnership and cooperation we can learn from the pre-Christian cultures of Old Europe.

Institutional Influence and Change

The emphasis of the premodern world and the tangible culture on land and reputation is reinforced by laws about property. There is not only the divine right of kings for those of noble ancestry but also the rights of a common man to own property and pass on property to his descendents. Although many non-Western societies, as well as those of most Native American cultures, have embraced the notion that property (land, home, livestock) belongs to the entire group or tribe, the gods, or nature, our ancestors in the Western world created a society in which personal acquisition was allowed and even highly valued. Western notions of leadership and assumptions in the tangible culture about institutional influence were founded on this principle of property.

Among those in the premodern era who could not acquire land or own a small business built on reputation, there was nothing much to hope for except a life of security in a highly paternalistic setting. Douglas McGregor (1960) provided a vivid and highly influential description of this world of work when he described the Theory X model of management and leadership. According to this model, people inherently dislike work and will do almost anything to avoid it. They must be motivated by external inducements and controlled by managers in the workplace in order to continue to work toward the organization's goals. Those individuals who are less driven by their emotions and can self-motivate must assume all the management responsibilities. McGregor proposed more than forty years ago that this Theory X style of leadership, which was dominant in premodern times, was no longer appropriate in modern institutions. The positive side of Theory X is that an employer, viewed as a kind of head of a family, is expected to take care of his or her employees much as this person takes care of other family members—spouse, children, elderly parents, extended family. We still find evidence of this orientation in many organizations, including independent colleges and universities.

When academic leaders come home after a long and difficult day shifting gears between five different projects and meeting with four different constituencies, each with its own agenda and perspectives on the world in which we live and work, they often become nostalgic. A harried leader seeks out the reassurance of tangible evidence of success in his institution: a major building is finally about to be erected. Another leader recalls a recent graduation ceremony when she was able to witness the "moving on" of young men and women she mentored. Yet another academic leader takes great pride in an orderly admissions process she helped design and now manages. Academic leaders tend to revert, in other words, to a premodern emphasis on tangible property.

As we already noted, premodern societies also emphasize reputation. A good reputation is not easily acquired or easily regained once lost. In its own way, reputation stands as the cornerstone of a tangible culture, even though in some ways reputation is not tangible. We find that the complex and difficult interplay between premodern values and twenty-first-century realities continues throughout the world of the academy. The premodern world and the various enterprises of premodern societies are typified by powerful and often implicit intentions and boundaries (Bergquist, 1993). Premodern people simply do their thing on a day-to-day basis, without much concern for long-term planning, acquisitions of other businesses, or formal clarification of roles or responsibilities among organizational members.

Conclusions

In the premodern world of higher education, emphasis is placed on the maintenance of traditions and the process of gradual growth, rather than on size per se. Tradition and gradual growth provide glue for the formation of a premodern tangible culture. Tradition inherent in very slow growth offers an antidote to the anxiety induced by institutional change. If there is to be change it must be gradual and it certainly must not challenge the status quo—the traditions of this community. Much as premodern societies celebrate the growth of crops or livestock, and the gradual and organically based growth of family and family-based products, they also celebrate the maturation of their sons and daughters through the pedagogical processes of formal (and informal) education. Kenneth Boulding (1968, p. 64) made an important distinction in this regard. He distinguished between simple growth and structural growth. Simple growth has to do with the "growth or decline of a single variable or quantity by accretion or depletion." By contrast, structural growth involves not just a greater or lesser amount of a single variable or quantity but also the addition of new elements or operations to the existing organization.

Premodern growth is of the first type. Premodern colleges and universities grew by gradually adding more of the same—more acres to the campus, more buildings and classrooms, more members of the faculty. These were all tangible signs of institutional maturation. The modern college or university, by contrast, usually defines growth not only in terms of greater size (simple growth) but also greater complexity (structural growth). As the modern college and university grow larger, they also change form, thereby often making growth that much more stressful and difficult.

The virtual culture, which tends to have few boundaries in either location or specific actions, needs clear intentions to keep it on track in what it sees as unpredictable variables. This emphasis on the institution's intentions is shared by the tangible culture. Where the virtual culture would co-create and re-create intentions, and then use these intentions to keep the institution (and program) on track in the tumultuous future, the tangible culture would use past intentions to remind us of our true mission. Both the tangible and virtual cultures are required for academic leaders to steer a course through the turbulent world of twenty-first-century colleges and universities. The concepts and strategies we offer in the next, and final, chapter of the book may help engage and bring together these two cultures, as well as the other four cultures of the academy.

7

Bridging the Gap

Appreciation and Irony in the Academy

Now that we have explored the profound differences that exist between the six cultures of the academy with regard to their history, assumptions, perspectives, values, and models of leadership and institutional influence, it would be quite easy to conclude that the gulf between them is too great to cross. However, we have already pointed to several ways in which a bridge between the cultures might be built. In this final chapter, we turn to other methods that can be used to build bridges. We focus on strategies that are most effective in addressing the varying concerns of the six academic cultures. Specifically, we focus on two perspectives: the appreciative perspective and the ironic perspective.

The Appreciative Perspective in the Academy

Although we have ventured into all six cultures and suggested several ways in which they might be bridged, there are still lingering questions about the feasibility of this bridging task and our ultimate task: to improve the life of those who work and learn in the academy and the institution as a single, learning-oriented entity. How can we help the many men, women, and institutions still struggling with difficult challenges in a manner that builds on the strengths and values of our six cultures? A new strategy for institutional improvement has entered the academic arena in recent years. It does not fit with any of the models or strategies already described. This new strategy has been labeled *appreciative inquiry*. In its broader application, as it is being used in this book, this strategy might better be called an *appreciative perspective* or an *appreciative approach* to institutional improvement (Bergquist, 2004).

Appreciative Inquiry and Perspective

First formulated by David Cooperrider in the 1980s, appreciative inquiry has been defined as "a collaborative and highly participative, systemwide approach to seeking, identifying, and enhancing the 'life-giving forces' that are present when a system is performing optimally in human, economic, and organizational terms" (Watkins & Mohr, 2001, p. 14). A definition offered by Coghlan and her associates (Coghlan, Preskill, & Catsambas, 2003, p. 5) also reflects a focus on strengths, vision, hope, and the future: "Appreciative inquiry is a process that inquires into, identifies, and further develops the best of what is in organizations in order to create a better future." The word *appreciative* comes from the verb *appreciate*, or value with gratitude. By itself, having an appreciative approach is positive, but appreciative inquiry is not simply "an exercise in optimism, a rhetoric of hope" (Srivastva, Cooperrider, & Associates, 1990, p. 13). What gives appreciative inquiry its strength is that it is a method of inquiry involving exploration, questioning, and discovery.

Change models that exist outside the appreciative perspective tend to be deficit-focused—that is, they focus on what is wrong, the problem or issue that has to be resolved, the barriers in the way of action. Methods to improve organizations usually focus on what is absent or not working well: What is not there that needs to be there? What is not working that needs to be fixed? What barriers stand in our way? Yet it is possible to take an approach that is not deficit-based. Organizations have their own history. That history does not include what they have not yet done. When we ask an organization to do something other than what it is doing, we are asking it to create a script—a map of unknown, uncharted territory. It is difficult when working with an altogether "foreign map" to gain commitment and foster excitement among those about to take the journey. It is preferable to begin instead with a map of our past history, for this map shows known paths to success and greatness.

An appreciative perspective incorporates aspects of organizational life that most strategies of institutional improvement dismiss. Although most modern improvement strategies rely exclusively on either change in structure or change in processes, appreciative inquiry (and more broadly, an appreciative perspective) begins with attitude and then seeks to create processes and structures that align with and enhance an appreciative attitude (Watson & Johnson, 1972; Bergquist, 2004). An appreciative perspective focuses on the successes of an organization in order to build a preferred future for it. It focuses on what members of the organization have done best, that of which they are most proud, what they most value, what they most want to keep of the organization's existing state—and they build from there. An appreciative perspective is based on the organizational reality as its members know it in the present as they envision and build toward the best possible future.

Critics of the appreciative approach ask: What about the problems? You cannot ignore them, they say. You can focus on the positive, but the negative has to be dealt with as well. This criticism is often justified, because there is an underlying naiveté in the work of many practitioners of appreciative inquiry, much as there is naiveté among those in the developmental culture. Several credible answers to this criticism, however, are offered by those who have been involved in the work of appreciation for many years: "We are not urging members of an organization to deny or ignore problems. Rather, if you want to transform a situation, a relationship, an organization, or community, we suggest that you focus on strengths rather than deficits. This is much more effective than focusing on problems" (Whitney & Trosten-Bloom, 2003, p. 18).

It is possible, however, to approach even the problems from an appreciative inquiry mindset. Our greatest problems sometimes remind us of what it is that we value most deeply. We might ask: What has dealing with this problem told us about what we value about our institution and our work in it? Thus, an appreciative perspective provides us with guidance in solving a problem. We can use past successes to direct our future attempts at solving problems. An appreciative perspective provides energy and motivation. Knowing that we have been successful in the past provides us with the incentive to persevere and be courageous. Past success also speaks to the issue of accountability. If we have been able to solve similar problems in the past, then we should be able to solve this one: "There is no excuse!" is much harder to say than "It can't be done!"

The forces that make up the traditional organization—such as its formal authority, goals, structure, bottom line, and control—can be aligned with the organization's more subtle forces, such as vision, mindfulness, integrity, communication, heart, and courage (Daft & Lengel, 2000). The more subtle forces can alter the organization in profound ways if the stronger forces are relaxed. Leaders are rarely willing to relax the stronger forces sufficiently to enable the more subtle forces to work effectively. This is certainly the case with academic cultures. Each of the six cultures has much to contribute to any institutional improvement initiative—such as quality improvement—provided the subtle, positive forces of this culture are allowed to emerge and be engaged in the improvement process.

An Appreciative Perspective on Academic Life

An appreciative perspective elicits the inner strengths of individual members of the academy. Appreciative inquiry, in particular, invites those of us in the academy to tell another person a very real and personal story related to the topic under inquiry: "Tell me the best example you have in your experience of this kind of situation." In traditional academic change models it is possible that individuals will offer a story of their inner forces at work, but it is unlikely that each person will do this; the individual is brought face-to-face with the strong forces of the academy. If people do, it is unlikely that their personal stories—their subtle forces—will influence the entire institution. We all have stories to tell about our college or university. In fact, our stories about the institution are part of the institution's story. That narrative guides us in our decisions about how we act and react to individuals and with events in our working lives. Appreciative inquiry asks us to redefine the narrative, eradicating the focus on what is wrong, and enhancing aspects that are right. "Organizations do not exist separate from our images of them. They are made and imagined in conversation. They are carried and conveyed in the stories we tell" (Whitney & Cooperrider, 2006, n.p.).

As members of the academy share their stories, they let their egos down and allow others to hear how their deeper and subtler selves have been involved in their work lives. As the common elements of the stories are gathered, the collective inner strengths of the group become manifest. This allows them to recognize their institution's core strengths and utilize these core strengths as they create visions and plans for the future. This, in turn, allows them to see multiple ways of perceiving organizational success. The group develops a "beginner's mind" and is more amenable to new ideas. Members of the group see relationships that were not apparent prior to engagement in the appreciative process.

In essence, the models and processes of appreciation are very postmodern. They are based on a social constructivist assumption: the reality that exists in a given moment or situation is created by the individual and organization in that moment or situation. "Organizations can be characterized as a series of concurrent and sequential conversations between people. These conversations (oral and written) may lead to the purchase or distribution of goods or to the initiation of machine-based production processes. However, the goods and machines are parts of the organization, whereas conversations are the essence of the organization" (Whitney & Cooperrider, 2006). An appreciative perspective enables members of an organization to be intentional in their choice of conversations and in the stories they construct about their organization—its strengths, hopes, and future. Our colleges and universities certainly need to have such conversations and tell such stories as they confront the daunting challenges of the twenty-first century.

The Ironic Perspective: Paradox and Polarity

In writing about the postmodern condition, one of us (Bergquist, 1993) speculated that there are three ways to interpret this condition. First, postmodernism may be seen as a transitional phase that is setting the stage for another, longer-term societal condition. Second, postmodernism might itself be that longer-term societal condition. Third, all of this categorization of societal forms may be nothing more than semantics. Perhaps nothing of substance has really changed in our society—in which case we are living in essentially the same kind of community as has existed for many years, or even centuries.

In typical postmodern fashion, Bergquist drew no conclusions in 1993 about which of these three scenarios seemed most viable. We are now in a much better place to speculate about postmodernism and what the next societal condition might look like. We propose that at the other end of postmodernism there resides a new societal condition—the *ironic condition.* Much as a philosopher, Jean-François Lyotard, helped define the postmodern era in a book entitled *The Postmodern Condition* (Lyotard, 1984), so another contemporary philosopher, Richard Rorty (1989), is pointing to a new era of irony with a parallel emphasis on contingency.

The ironist, according to Rorty (1989, p. xv), is the "sort of person who faces up to the contingency of his or her most central beliefs and desires." By *contingency* Rorty is referring to the contextual and transitory nature of all belief systems—a stance adopted by the postmodernists and constructivists. The ironist "is someone sufficiently historicist and nominalist to have abandoned the idea that those central beliefs and desires refer back to something beyond the reach of time and chance" (Rorty, 1989, p. xv). Although he begins his description of the ironic perspective by pointing to the subjectivity (contingency) of all belief systems, he moves well beyond the postmodernists by suggesting that irony is a "process of coming to see other human beings as 'one of us' rather than as 'them.'" He offers a utopian vision based in irony that would depend on human solidarity and the capacity of all people to be sensitive to the circumstances—and in particular the pain and suffering—of "other, unfamiliar sorts of people." "Such increased sensitivity," writes Rorty (1989, p. xvi), "makes it more difficult to marginalize people different from ourselves by thinking, 'They do not feel it as *we* would,' or 'There must always be suffering, so why not let *them* suffer.'"

Rorty substitutes this utopian thought, in its continually evolving form, for the modern notion of enduring truth:

> A historicist and nominalist culture of the sort I envisage would settle . . . for narratives which connect the present with the past, on the one hand, and with utopian futures, on the other. More importantly, it would regard the realization of utopias, and the envisaging of still further utopias, as an endless process—an endless, proliferating realization of Freedom, rather than a convergence toward an already existing Truth. [Rorty, 1989, p. xvi]

In this final chapter, we build on Rorty's utopian proposal. Along with Rorty, we propose that a new condition of irony is one in which we will not just recognize and appreciate multiple perspectives, multiple truths, and multiple narratives. It is a condition in which we willingly embrace these multiple realities and allow these realities to enter into our own consciousness—despite the ironic fact that these realities might contradict one another. We embrace these multiple realities (and accompanying truths) by fully appreciating and empathizing with the emotional experiences, especially anxiety and suffering, of those who live with these alternative realities and truths.

As for engaging the six cultures of the academy, we will begin, as ironists, not just to understand and appreciate the values and perspectives of each culture but to wholeheartedly claim each of these cultures as being part and parcel of our own working perspective on academic life. Although the specifics of this new ironic condition are yet to be fully worked out by us (or other writers about irony) it seems that such a perspective relates directly to two "p" words: *paradox* and *polarity*. In speculating about the world of higher education beyond postmodernism and in bringing this book to a close, we turn to a preliminary exploration of these concepts as they apply to engaging the six cultures of the academy.

Appreciating the Realities of Our Academy

Cultures do not change readily. Cultures in the academic institution are even more resistant to change than in other sectors of society. There are several reasons why this resistance is so great in academic cultures. First, at the same time that faculty create and teach new knowledge, institutions of higher education exist to maintain some stability, to convey lessons already learned. This stability resists change. Second, because faculty often self-regulate professionally, there is a degree of arrogance in their work. They are the experts and already know what is "right." This is a reason for the widespread lack of support for professional development and resistance to accountability and outside performance reviews.

Third, as we noted at the start of this book, great anxiety is induced by the work in which members of twenty-first-century postsecondary institutions are engaged. New knowledge is constantly being generated or encountered, and at an increasingly rapid rate. This causes anxiety. The performance of students is being measured and evaluated, often based on traditional standards. This is anxiety-producing given the volatile job market in which these evaluated students must enter the workplace or already work. Faculty peers and administrators are increasingly likely to scrutinize faculty work in the classroom and laboratory. Faculty members are encouraged, through classroom research initiatives and new instructional accountability measures, to assess the effects of their work with their students. This adds more anxiety.

The anxiety does not stop with the student or faculty member. College administrators are increasingly under the gun to produce economic and educational outcomes. They are anxious about obtaining these results and know that administrative tenure is nonexistent in a world where high-level academic administrators rarely remain in office for more than five years. There is also the matter of diffuse criteria of quality. It is difficult to make the case that one program (or one culture) is better than another or that institutional improvement has occurred, because the criteria of success and achievement are themselves embedded in the strategy (and the underlying culture) that guided the improvement initiative.

Because of this lack of clarity about criteria of quality, external stakeholders such as trustees, funding sources, and the taxpaying public are unpredictable in their acceptance of specific success criteria. As a result, they are also often unpredictable in their support for institutional improvement initiatives. At times these external stakeholders will accept criteria of quality offered by people inside the academy. At other times, they will look to outside sources, such as accrediting agencies, governmental agencies, or educational critics.

All of this adds fuel to the fire of anxiety in most academic institutions. What does this mean when it comes to engaging the six cultures of the academy? As we noted early on, where there is a high level of anxiety in an organization, cultures become strong. Where there are strong cultures and high levels of anxiety, there is greater resistance to and less tolerance for change. Although this book may contain material that helps faculty and managers change their institutions, the likelihood is that academic institutions will change slowly, and they will change for reasons that we may be unable to predict. For the most part, we are left working in our institutions alongside individuals from our own and other cultures. Our greatest need—a need greater than a vast overhaul of our whole organization—is to get to work, avoid interruptions, interact with our colleagues in an amicable and productive manner—in short, to make what we already have work to the best of our ability and to our institution's best ends. This is the appreciative approach.

We believe that college leaders must understand the need each culture has for the other cultures, and in particular the need each culture has for the one with which it is most markedly in conflict. Believing that one culture is most important sets up a duality between the cultures (you said, I said; you value, I value) that blocks progress. Understanding the cultural interplay that is paradoxical, and therefore not resolvable, leads to an integrated understanding of the organization (we say, we value). We maintain that this ironic understanding of the cultures develops a capacity for transformative growth. This ironic understanding also maintains the uniqueness of the cultural tapestry—without loss of cultural integrity.

The six cultures have arisen in response to trends that have occurred over the history of higher education and in response to the other cultures. The developmental culture arose to find a way to temper the collegial approach—to bring others besides faculty into the governance of the organization, and to bring disciplines together in their discovery and application of learning. We could say that the developmental culture exists in part as a counterpoint to the collegial culture. This is true for the managerial and advocacy cultures as well. The advocacy culture grew in resistance to the technical management of higher education institutions by the managerial culture. Those aligned with the advocacy culture took exception to some of the approaches of the managerial culture and created their own assumptions partly in opposition to managerial approaches. The tangible culture always existed, but it became more obvious with the emergence of the virtual culture.

In this chapter, we assume an ironic perspective, focusing on how the polarization that exists between cultures can be seen as a way to move forward organizationally rather than remain locked in conflict. Through this analysis we can move away from the belief that our personal assumptions—and the assumptions of the cultures with which we are most closely aligned—should prevail in the academy. Through this analysis we can also gain a deeper understanding of the interrelatedness of the cultures.

From an ironic perspective, we can predict that once leaders of the academy understand the dynamics of conflict between the six cultures, they can be more intentional about working with these conflicts—more aware of how the conflicts exist, how opposition might be dealt with, and where that might lead. We all want to see the academy operate as harmoniously and effectively as possible. We want the higher education organization to be resilient enough to withstand the next fifty years—the postmodern and perhaps ironic challenges that it will face, the market shifts that it will confront—so that the next generation of teachers, scholars, researchers, administrators, and learners can lead the academy forward.

Paradox

According to Lewis and Dehler (2000), "[P]aradox denotes contradictory yet interrelated elements—elements that seem logical in isolation but absurd and irrational when appearing simultaneously." All organizations have paradoxical situations within them: teamwork and individuation, cooperative action and political conflict, stability and change. We welcome paradox when it helps us understand things (Lewis & Dehler, 2000, p. 710). But paradox can be a point of tension in organizations. Left unchecked, paradox can be deflating for the individual and destructive for the organization. However, paradox can also be used as a strategy for exploring contradictions and complexity between groups so that these groups can work more effectively together.

Charles Handy (1994a) offers an inverse donut to portray the nature and dynamics of paradox. The center of the donut is fixed—perhaps like a job description. The outside of the donut is open to be filled in—like the latitude one might have in one's work to go beyond the job description. To keep their lives in balance, people need to do enough in the open area to keep the job interesting but not so much that they are overextended or worn thin. To understand paradox people must learn to develop "a deeper understanding of three elements: the nature of underlying contradictions, the defenses and paralysis that paradoxical tensions often fuel, and their management via paradoxical thinking" (Lewis & Dehler, 2000, pp. 710–711).

To make sense of the world it is natural for each culture to dichotomize it into frames of reference (light and dark, good and evil). Each defines what is in and what is out of these frames. All create these frames so that they can produce understandings about the workplace and their culture's place in it. In the workplace, through the six cultures, those who work in the academy create ways of thinking about their purposes, their work, and their students. These frames become the bases of their belief systems. They help them contain the anxiety that they would otherwise feel as they go about their work. But during their workday they are exposed to individuals who have different frames. These interactions set up paradoxical tensions.

Paradoxical tensions are cognitively and socially constructed, and produce the simultaneity of conflicting truths while obscuring the relatedness of the contradictions. The problem with paradoxes is that they attack what we value and at the same time point out where we are weak. As cultures work, they may define and reinforce these constructs until individuals working in those cultures believe that their culture is organizationally superordinate. They are therefore most likely to defend their position and entrench the views of their own culture. Splitting (creation of subgroups), repression, projection, reaction formation, and ambivalence are ways that defenses against paradox are created. Reinforcing cycles are produced wherein there is paralysis and defensiveness. Cultural groups can become stuck in these "paralyzing and often vicious cycles via greater cognitive and behavioral complexity" (Lewis, 2000, p. 761). These reinforcing cycles are initially comforting, but eventually they exacerbate the tensions.

Ironists suggest that faculty members and administrators can learn from these tensions or can be paralyzed by them; they can use these tensions to reexamine their positions or they can become defensive about their positions. Paradox can hamper the organization or encourage organizational development. By studying paradox much can be understood about the complexity, diversity, and ambiguity of organizational life. Contradictions in the life of the organization demonstrate that change is not a linear and planned process. If faculty members and administrators explore the tensions they can tap the potential energy, insights, and power of the paradox that enables dramatic change. They can ask what the paradox is, and how they might grow to understand the nature of the underlying tensions in the conflict that a paradox might bring to the surface, and the reinforcing cycles that are enacted when faced with these paradoxes. Lewis (2000, p. 763) offers an optimistic, ironic perspective on paradox: "Managing paradox means capturing its enlightening potential. The goal is to journey beyond reinforcing cycles, dramatically rethinking past perceptions and practices."

Unlike continua, dilemmas, or either-or choices, paradoxical tensions signify two sides of the same coin. Just as a coin must have two sides to maintain its dimensionality, so too must cultures have opposition inside the academic organization. In other words, one view is not better than the other, but the ability to read both—indeed, the reading of all views related to this cultural map—is required to maximize this rich cultural diversity. Academic leaders who want to maximize the attributes of all aspects of their institutions will develop both cultural literacy and the ability to read conflicts and manage culturally polarized issues.

Polarity

Managing polarity is one way to work with the paradoxes between academic cultures, as well as the paradox-filled problems that twenty-first-century colleges and universities face. In his book *Polarity Management*, Barry Johnson (1996) says that polarities cannot be "fixed." They can be understood and managed rather than allowed to run their course—and they do have a fixed course. Johnson believes that if we manage polarities we will have a more productive, healthy workplace and achieve our goals more easily. In addition, we will create a different kind of resistance dynamic with our colleagues.

Many issues in the academy can be solved when addressed with the proper resources. Then the group can move on to other matters. If someone has a flat tire or his statistical analysis requires a computer, these are troublesome, but they are solvable puzzles that can be fixed by changing the tire or securing the use of a computer. Other interactions are insolvable and persist no matter what resources are thrown at the problem. Polarities exist where two individuals or groups are in conflict at the level of principle. A respondent to the flat tire may say, "You shouldn't drive your car; the bus is more socially and environmentally responsible." This would move the issue of the flat tire from simple transportation (a resource problem) to values related to transportation (the common good versus individualism, individual versus group decision making, taxes and economies).

Johnson (1996) challenges us to consider whether some of the issues that exist in our organization are actually polarities that cannot be resolved. Johnson suggests that two questions need to be answered to determine if the issue is actually a polarity. First, is the issue ongoing? A dilemma that persists after the application of solutions is a polarity. Second, are the dilemmas interdependent—that is, does one side need to exist for the other to exist? Thus, a polarity is an ongoing issue or struggle in which opposing views are interdependent.

Barry Johnson (1996) uses the metaphor of breathing in and breathing out to help understand the dynamics of polarity. A person may like breathing in, but at a certain time will need to breathe out. As much as breathing in might be desired and valued, breathing out is required in order to breathe in once again. In a similar manner, an organization must act on both sides of a polarity to reap the benefits of what it prefers. Planning and acting can be used as an example of an organizational polarity. An organization must have a plan, and then it can act on the plan. Based on the results, it can plan again. Planning without acting or acting without planning is inappropriate. The organization must keep both perspectives in mind. Leaders who are aware of these as polarities know when such shifts should take place and how they can be managed. Groups they lead are not left with only negative aspects of the leaders' personal points of view—waiting for something better while "holding their breath."

Polarities and the Academy

Many polarities emerge in a higher education institution. McNaught (2003) defines issues in higher education that would pose themselves as polarities during the implementation of information technology at a higher education institution in Australia. These polarities are as follows:

- Top-down versus bottom-up
- Management versus scholarship
- Systems versus services
- Controlled versus devolved
- Focus versus variety
- Mass change versus growing individuals
- Competition versus collaboration

McNaught argues that "changing 'versus' to 'and' allows a new perspective to be added to university implementation of policies and practice" (2003, p. 76). She suggests that these polarities come into play in what she describes as a zone of effective change:

> The zone of effective change is not a fixed entity. It represents a situation where the organization's policies are in balance and support each other. For example, if a university adopts a mainly "top-down" approach, there is a risk that individual academics will not have sufficient flexibility to develop their own creative work. Conversely, if the university adopts an extreme laissez-faire approach, limited financial growth may result and the infrastructure for research decline. It is all a question of balance. [p. 76]

McNaught lays out a map of the zone of effective change and suggests that organizations can rate how they are accommodating the balance between the different polarities that they are trying to manage in a strategic initiative.

Though colleges and universities are assumed, by definition, to hold a unified vision and mission, this rarely is the case. Thus, the concept of a strong, integrated institutional culture that is advocated by some writers about the academy—such as Tierney

(1988) and Toma, Dubrow, and Hartley (2005)—may fly in the face of a powerful reality: dynamic academic institutions always embrace polarities. There are competing views. When a radical change initiative is raised at the college or university—such as the implementation of information technology—all sides emerge with their histories and arguments. Taking an "either-or" attitude is less productive than taking the best of all sides—taking an "also-and" attitude (McNaught, 2002, p. 2). "Remove all oppositional 'versus' thinking and replace it with ways to consider how to gain maximum benefit by embracing both ends of poles. The zone of effective change can only be formed by the inclusion and balancing of both ends of each dimension" (p. 6).

Flow of Polarities

Johnson (1996) proposes that there is a usual flow to the focus on polarities. Every point of view has an upside and a downside. The traditional mindset would examine the "problem" from the positive side (upside) of our point of view and from the negative side (downside) of the other point of view. Johnson has opposing groups lay these points out on a two-by-two grid with the upsides of each view on the top of the grid and the downsides of each on the bottom two quadrants. He purports that the flow of activity in a polarity moves up from the downside in a sideways figure-eight pattern on this two-by-two grid.

Traditionally, people argue for the upsides of their point of view and against the downsides of the other point of view. Arguments and solutions can be typified as crusading and tradition-bearing. *Crusading* is trying to make things better by moving away from the downside of one pole to the upside of the other. *Tradition bearing* is defending the upside of the status quo while pointing out the need to avoid the downside of the opposite point of view. For example, a tradition-bearing collegial culture would argue for maintaining the positive sides of its culture for fear of slipping onto the negative side of the developmental culture. A crusading developmental culture would want to move away from the downside of the collegial culture toward the advantages of the developmental. Both tradition-bearing and crusading approaches can only hold their own point of view. They cannot hold both views at the same time, nor shift quickly from one view to the other. The arguments and solutions become cyclical. One point of view balances off the other point of view. This maintains the problem's insolvability.

Polarities cannot be resolved, but they can be managed. The ironic management process begins with the ability to either shift from one point of view to the other or hold both points of view at the same time. Individuals must keep both the upside of their position and the upside of the other's position in mind at the same time. Typically, in a polarity management situation, two groups with opposing views come together to map out the upside and the downside of both sides. Focusing on the upside of both, they then engage in a dialogue about both upsides to see what might come about as a result. At a minimum, they will increase their understanding and ability to explain the reasons why each group acts the way it does, rather than merely react from their blind side. Optimally, the two sides will be able to discover a shared understanding of their vision or mission—their intentions may become clearer. What remains, given their differences, is how to work together toward that shared intention.

The intuitive reaction to paradox is to resist it or hide it. To confront it does not give the initial relief that we may seek. It does not deescalate the conflict. It does, however, allow us to examine it. "Researchers suggest three often interrelated means of managing paradox: acceptance, confrontation, and transcendence" (Lewis, 2000, p. 764). In confronting the paradox, one can construct a more accommodating understanding and relationship. Opening up to the paradox might require understanding the opposing forces in more detail. As individuals or groups are relieved from the paralysis they face, they are also challenged to look at their own reinforcing cycles and reexamine their own values. Participants in paradoxical analyses can move from "You are wrong" to "I don't get it" (Lewis & Dehler, 2000, p. 719). This latter statement allows for further dialogue about the situation and perceptions at hand. It allows for both perceptions to be possible and valid at the same time and for both groups to employ the strengths of each side. In sum, transcendence can emerge from an appreciation of paradox—this appears to be a central theme in any ironic perspective.

Culture and Polarity

At the beginning of this book we pointed to Schein's (1992) definition of a culture. He proposed that culture is made up of a set of assumptions that were taught to individuals as they adapted to internal and external variables. Thus, individuals in cultures hold similar values and assumptions. They cluster around these values and assumptions and use them—their culture—to protect themselves against or ease the anxiety they might otherwise feel. As a group develops anxieties or fears about situations in their environment, its members develop ways of dealing with these anxieties and fears. When these ways are engrained and feel "usual," they become part of that group's culture. These assumptions create meaning in the group's environment. Group members use these assumptions to gain a sense of order—a social pattern—on which they can rely in their job and in their working relationships. Language is developed that reinforces these assumptions and ways of acting. Heroes and myths emerge over time. A narrative is developed about the culture and the way things are done in it.

Everyone's anxiety (and indeed, each group's anxiety) is contained by the culture that they adopt. Any other set of assumptions—another way of perceiving, thinking, and feeling about internal or external circumstances—comes to be seen as foreign. It is important for a given cultural group to resist these other ways because, now that the original anxiety has been quelled or contained by the adopted culture, there is a desire to maintain cognitive and emotional stability. There is a desire to preserve one's own culture. A natural response is to resist other ways of perceiving, thinking, and feeling so that comfort and stability are maintained.

From an ironic perspective, we suggest that positive cultural change may take place if each culture acknowledges that both sides of the polarity exist in the organization, and if there is a will to honor, utilize, and balance the resources of both sides. The informed leader of a postsecondary institution will recognize the polarities that develop and find ways to manage these, so that members of the academy will work more in a dialogical frame than in a confrontational frame.

Polarity Theory Applied to the Six Cultures

We will now examine some polarities that might emerge between specific academic cultures. There are a variety of ways that any two cultures might interact with positive, negative, or neutral effect. As they interact, tensions and conflicts arise based on the fact that each culture values different things. Unsolvable problems exist because there are two groups and each resists the other with different sets of assumptions about the structure, process, or attitude of the organization. Each group views the world from its own perspective and finds it difficult or even impossible to see or accept the other side's view.

There may be unsolvable problems between any two groups in our academic organizations. However, in the next part of this chapter we look at academic organizations through the lenses of pairs of the six cultures. For each pair of cultures we devise a major area of conflict. In doing this we are not saying that this is an actual conflict or the only one that may exist. Rather, we are using these hypothetical conflicts to illustrate a particular model for managing intergroup differences in a constructive manner. Like the individual shadow (Broom & Klein, 1999) that serves as a counterpoint to the dominant traits of the individual psyche, a culture that resists one's own culture—the shadow culture—creates a blind spot about which we develop a repertoire of denial. Yet to remain vital, one culture needs the other resisting culture. There is a way to grow beyond the blind spots and the denial by examining the interactions that make up the resistance. Being clearer about patterns allows leaders in organizations to make more informed and positive choices about future interactions.

Polarity in the Collegial and Developmental Cultures. Those aligned with the collegial culture want to create and disseminate knowledge, especially in their own discipline area. Value is placed on research and scholarship: faculty members should be allowed to conduct research and scholarship independent of institutional or societal exigencies. Academic freedom must be granted in order for individual collegial faculty members to study what they find compelling, interesting, and germane to the advancement of their area of study and discipline. To sustain this academic freedom, faculty members must govern themselves and their institutions. Collegial faculty members value academic stability in departmental units and therefore value departmental self-governance. They assume that their colleagues have the right to work in their own departments in the manner best suited to their particular area of study or discipline. More than anything, these faculty members desire autonomy in their work and in the governance of their institution. They fear not being able to extend knowledge of the world to their students and disciplinary colleagues—especially knowledge of their own field.

Even more fundamentally, those aligned with the collegial culture fear ignorance or not knowing. They are interested in acquiring more knowledge. They value the development of knowledge in their specific discipline and wish to find ways in which to create and disseminate new knowledge in their discipline. Collegial faculty value the ability to study whatever they deem appropriate to further knowledge in their area. Thus, they must have autonomy—the ability to act on their own behalf, to self-regulate. They expect a reasoned approach to their work and expect the institution to give them the academic latitude to achieve their aims.

In the developmental culture there is an underlying resistance to one basic tenet of the collegial culture. Those aligned with this culture do not believe that their discipline can be autonomous. Developmentalists value their collegial colleagues, but believe that it is in collaborating between areas, and sharing information and instituting ideas, that progress is made. Those aligned with this culture will collaborate with any individual or culture if they feel the idea or program will nurture professional and personal growth.

The developmental culture fears impotence or not acting on knowledge that is already available. Developmentalists desire collaboration—being together with others from throughout the institution. They greatly value innovative space. They want to engage knowledge that their colleagues have developed and possess. They believe that collaboration between disciplines will consolidate the knowledge and therefore increase its value. Application of this collaborative effort will increase the desire to find more knowledge. Developmentalists do not understand why one would simply sit on knowledge; they believe knowledge should be engaged, shared, and used by everyone. They will share ideas and research with anyone if a new idea might offer greater value for the institution and all of its participants.

A fundamental question might arise between these two cultures: How will knowledge be addressed? This question has two parts. First, will knowledge be focused (on a disciplinary area) or integrative (bringing areas together)? Second, how will groups work: in departmental silos or across disciplines and in groups? Those who are aligned with the collegial culture typically would not feel comfortable moving outside their own discipline area. They do not have the background, expertise, or even permission to attempt research or projects in someone else's domain. Collegial faculty would not usually be in favor of applied projects that deal with soft data such as personal and professional improvement. Conversely, members of the developmental culture would not want to deal with facts and figures that do not lead anywhere. Discovering data is the first step toward doing something meaningful with that data. Clearly, the central issue that exists between these two cultures is their relationship to knowledge.

The collegial culture highly values *autonomy in one's work*; the developmental culture highly values *collaboration between areas*. An advantage of the collegial culture's autonomy is that those associated with it work in an area of expertise, developing new knowledge, and relying on what is provable. They work with others who also have expertise in their areas of study, but not outside that area. They believe that the academy is based on the premise that institutions should not regulate academic inquiry. Faculty members need reasonable autonomy. In order to have academic freedom, a faculty member must be able to assist in the governance of the institution.

Developmentalists would counter these advantages by saying that expertise is not the whole picture. A wide range of possibilities is being excluded if one only looks in one's own area of expertise. New knowledge is only useful if it can be integrated and applied to improving the personal or professional lives of all individuals in the academy. Developmentalists would say that the institution comprises groups, not just individual faculty members; therefore, all groups need some say in the institution's governance. Academic freedom can still exist in that context; it is just more broadly defined.

Developmentalists would say that innovation and collaboration are valued. Innovation occurs through collaborating about new ideas in untried waters. To innovate, there must be collaboration. (We are all equals in the institution—faculty, administrators, students, and staff.) Those aligned with the collegial culture would counter the advantages to collaboration by stating that innovation does not prove anything. They would say that collaboration expends resources that could be used toward activities that could illuminate the facts; collaboration is gray and fluffy; collaborative work often results in thinking and analysis that is watered down and has lost academic rigor. They believe that although employees are all equals on a personal level, faculty members are hired for their expertise, and that should be recognized in the institution. If not, faculty work will average out to the lowest common denominator.

Polarity in the Managerial and Advocacy Cultures. One abiding value in the managerial culture concerns the act of setting and attaining goals individually and for the institution—particularly goals that can be measured against the success of students completing their courses of study. The managerial culture sees access as a key way to achieve institutional goals. Academic managers define access as allowing able students to enter programs that are best suited for them and assisting them in achieving their goals. Managerial faculty will go out of their way to help a student who is showing motivation to succeed. Nothing could be worse for the managerial culture than to lose control of these aims. A managerial culture is concerned with FTE counts and a balanced budget so that the institution can produce graduates.

Those aligned with the managerial culture fear loss of control over the institution, the curriculum, or the faculty. Individuals who adhere to the values of this culture believe that access to the institution means giving able students the means by which they can achieve their credentials. Completion and production are measures of success. Control is exerted through the ability and authority of administrators to set standards for their own work as well as the work of faculty and students. Performance based on these standards can be measured. Everyone is accountable to these standards. People in this culture do not want to waste time. They want to be successful, and they honor and reward success.

Those aligned with the advocacy culture believe in access, but define it differently from their managerial colleagues. Access has to do with allowing able students, as well as those who have been disadvantaged, into courses and programs. What counts for them is not the number of graduates but rather the number of traditionally underserved students who graduate. Faculty members in the advocacy culture see this as a basic right. Human rights are upheld in the institution not only for students but also for faculty members, who may need support against the rigid rules of management. Advocates would like their institution to view access as based on equitability. They fear being controlled by managers or an institution that does not value individual rights. This culture does not want to see the institution controlled by policies and procedures that take away the prima facie rights of each individual.

We see the central issue for these two cultures as a concern about access and control. Who is in control of access? How is access controlled? The two cultures may agree that an overriding issue is access, but they define it differently. The managerial culture defines access as student success rate: access is the number of students who have been successful (graduated, FTEs). The advocacy culture sees access as a measure of how the institution has equalized the ability of all students to attend and learn. The advocacy culture also considers the rights of faculty members, with little regard for managerial objectives. Those aligned with the managerial culture consider the curriculum to be something that faculty teach (curriculum leads faculty); those aligned with the advocacy culture consider the faculty to be individuals who teach their curriculum. From the advocacy perspective, faculty members lead the curriculum and require the authority and resources to implement this curriculum in a successful manner. There is a connection between the collegial and the advocacy cultures when it comes to this last point: collegial faculty members will move toward the advocacy culture if their autonomy is not honored.

There are advantages associated with *access as successful achievement* (as viewed by the managerial culture); the best and greatest number of students are being offered an education so they can move on to other things in their lives. In this way, graduation rates are maximized. The curriculum is predetermined and knowable; it drives teaching and learning. Faculty members must offer their best to the curriculum and their departments for the sake of student success. The system is fair because everyone is given the same chances.

The advocacy culture would counter by saying that helping able students does not recognize the potential of all students. The system is unfair, they would say, because not everyone has had the same prior advantages. Faculty members have to be concerned with the curriculum and the student. The advocacy culture would say that there are advantages to seeing access as a right. Everyone has rights and everyone has potential. That potential must be honored. Rights mean that all students are given an equitable chance to learn. Everyone is given equitable support for their legitimate needs. Some students must be given alternate services. The principle of everyone's rights to equitable support for success is more important than supporting only those who show initial promise—even if it means that fewer students will graduate. Faculty members have rights too, and these rights must be recognized in practice.

Members of the managerial culture would say that the disadvantage of treating access as a right is that it uses resources. They do not want to accept everyone because that might limit the ability of the system to assist able students. In fact, they assert that we do not know that all students gain something unless they complete their courses—that is the only measure. Faculty members are educated to teach in their area, not to counsel students. If money is spent on faculty support for students, it will take away from the primary task for which faculty members are being paid, which is teaching the curriculum.

Polarity in the Virtual and Tangible Cultures. Those aligned with the virtual culture are interested in connecting with the vast resources that are available globally, usually through technological means and sometimes through partnerships with other groups or agencies. These connections create a new picture of a dynamic, shifting world. Meaning is created through connecting and understanding this shifting view. Nothing could be worse for the virtual culture than to be cut off from these other resources and connections and only be able to participate in the local view. Those aligned with this culture fear isolation—being cut off from global contact. They find and create meaning in the global knowledge economy.

Members of the virtual culture fear that orderliness will cut them off from this kind of contact. They desire virtual contact or making meaning together outside the restrictive boundaries of a single academic institution. Virtualists believe that reality is co-constructed and shifts with the experiences of the individuals involved. Their "academy" is the virtual world—not the specific institution with which they happen to be affiliated. The institution's involvement with global networks in the creation of reality enhances the academy's ability to deal with a chaotic world. As the world expands, nothing could be worse than sitting idly by, looking only at the world from within the confines of a single institution.

Those aligned with the tangible culture fully realize that the world is changing and that the virtual world is a part of the emerging worldview; however, they view tangibility—the ability to connect with physical places, objects, and people—as the only real way to identify with the academy. The tangible culture holds primacy of place over the pressure exerted by virtual space. Whatever our disciplines or views of the world, we cannot doubt the authenticity of the physical world and the campus that embodies this world. Students, faculty, and administrators connect on campus through face-to-face contact and in real time.

Traditionalists fear being cut off from the physical campus. They find meaning through being with others in the academy.

At a more fundamental level, members of the tangible culture fear that chaos will cut them off from direct contact with the academy. They wish to make, or identify existing, meaning through their direct affiliation with a specific academy. Individuals in this culture need contact on a personal and face-to-face basis. The campus and the individuals who work there are real and understandable, regardless of the chaos that might exist in the world. There is a visceral identification with the campus by those aligned with the tangible culture. Meaning resides in this local community, not in the external and extended world.

When we compare these two cultural views, we find that a central issue concerns contact with reality. The question they both answer in their own culture is this: What is real and how do we get in contact with it? Reality in the virtual culture is found in the meaning that can be discerned from the disorder of the postmodern situation; in contrast, the reality of the tangible culture is found in the meaning inherent in the institution—its facilities, its traditions, and its community. Several cogent arguments can be made for the creation of *learning space* by the virtual culture. This space allows for postmodern variety and scope. Serendipitous events and novel learning can occur. This approach to learning is open and flexible, allowing nimbleness, since it is not constructed in a fixed way. Members of the tangible culture would say that the disadvantage of a virtual learning space is that it is uncoordinated. With no plan, how does one know when something is achieved? Flexibility is good until one heads in the opposite direction.

Members of the tangible culture offer yet another insight. They would say that the advantages of a specific *place of learning* include support, community, and the predictability of concrete objects and relationships. They can rely on individuals and things that are present. They can unite in the quest for learning regardless of discipline by being together in a physical location that is rich with precedence and history. They say we learn when we are "at home" with members of our academic family. The virtual culture would counter these arguments by saying that a predictable approach does not prepare the institution, its employees, or its students for change. Just because something is concrete and enduring does not mean it is inherently valuable. Furthermore, a tangible place of learning requires a physical location that is costly and cumbersome.

Summary of Cultural Polarities

We have presented sets of polarities—that is, central issues and irresolvable problems—that are likely to exist in academic institutions between pairs of cultures. The polarities we presented had to do with our relationship to knowledge, access to control and control of access, and definition of reality and how we connect with it. Notwithstanding the logic of these examples and arguments, it must be remembered that each institution will have its own polarities. The six cultures all exist and interact in twenty-first-century postsecondary institutions. They vary from institution to institution in intensity and power. They also vary in the size of the constituencies attracted to each culture. Each institution has its own history and narrative. We cannot lay out the details of each institution's possible polarities. We did, however, lay down a framework for how the polarity model might work in the context of a broad range of issues.

We have shown that three cultural pairs tend to be enmeshed in ironic, or polarity-based, relationships with their opposing cultures. Each pair has a conflict that cannot be resolved—which helps, in turn, provide each one of them with meaning, purpose, and as a result, greater strength. The stronger one of the cultures is in each pairing, the stronger the other will be in opposition. We have suggested that a greater appreciation of all six academic cultures will increase one's understanding of one's own institution. This deeper, ironic appreciation enables employees of the academy to work more effectively with their entire institution—rather than only with those constituencies that align with their own, favored, cultural perspective.

Conclusions

The six cultures that we have identified in this book are markedly different. They "live" together on each campus. Each one vies for students, resources, space, a place to govern, and a way of approaching learning and teaching. Their aspirations are different. Yet they live with each other in the same institution with all of these differences. Perhaps these cultural differences are what make the higher education institution so vibrant and challenging to learn in, work in, administer, and lead. The fact that the six cultures exist together is a testament to the value that the academy places on diversity of thought. It would be either naive or unwise to think that conflicts would never emerge among these cultures.

From an ironic perspective, the first step in any organizational change process should involve changing contending points of reference. Members of the organization should first change the ways in which they view paradox before attempting to somehow resolve the paradoxes they confront. They must view and understand their organizations from the points of view of those with whom they are most likely to disagree before they attempt to overcome these disagreements. Given the strength of the six academic cultures we have identified and analyzed in this book and the contentious relationships between them, taking an ironic perspective seems to be most appropriate.

New ways of thinking and new strategies for institutional improvement are required to meet the challenges that our higher education institutions face in the postmodern world of the twenty-first century, besides the additional challenges they may soon face in a world filled with irony. There is a much bigger and broader implication for each of us as leaders in the academy. Our colleges and universities can play invaluable roles in addressing the overall postmodern and ironic challenges that confront North American and global societies. We all must serve as wise, brave, and visionary stewards of these institutions. And to provide this stewardship, we must all come to fully appreciate and engage the strengths of each of the six cultures of the academy.

Appendix I

Academic Cultures Inventory

This Academic Cultures Inventory documents an individual's opinion of how other members of his or her higher education institution perceive that institution's cultures. Complete the twelve statements based on what you believe members of the organization *now* think, feel or believe about the organization.

Place a check in the boxes beside *two* items for each statement. The items are randomly arranged.

Most people in this institution think that this institution exists

☐ **1** To generate, interpret, and disseminate knowledge.

☐ **2** To serve and represent the history and values of under served populations in our society.

☐ **3** To honor historical roots and fundamental values in the community and society.

☐ **4** To encourage the potential of all of its employees and students.

☐ **5** To inculcate specific knowledge, skills, and attitudes in students.

☐ **6** To link its educational resources to emerging technologies and global information bases.

Note: Additional information on the Academic Cultures Inventory, including a variety of forms relating to groups and whole organizations, is available at *http://www.sixcultures.com*.

Most people in this institution think that this institution exists

☐ **7** To enhance its diversity and its members' fundamental rights.

☐ **8** To prepare students for successful careers and responsible citizenship.

☐ **9** To develop knowledge that is supported by faculty-based planning and governance.

☐ **10** As a vehicle for the application of any field of research to the betterment of any of the institution's participants.

☐ **11** To contribute to the interinstitutional and global learning network.

☐ **12** To create meaning and personal identification through the campus and institutional traditions.

Most people in this institution believe that

☐ **13** Performance at all levels can be measured in an accurate and fair manner.

☐ **14** Knowledge should be shared and used by everyone in the institution.

☐ **15** The hard work and dedication of its employees can make the chaos in our world orderly.

☐ **16** The disadvantaged should be given additional and appropriate educational support.

☐ **17** It is myopic to view only this institution's perspective when the world is expanding exponentially.

☐ **18** A reasonable institution will give them the academic latitude to achieve their aims.

Most people in this institution believe that

☐ **19** Meaning resides within the institution's traditions being enacted, and in the work performed toward its mission.

☐ **20** Everyone has an equal right to achieve their life goals through a postsecondary education.

☐ **21** Knowledge should be shared and used by everyone in the institution.

☐ **22** For future societal leadership, students need to develop specific values and qualities of character.

☐ **23** Institutional size and productivity are primary measures of success in this institution.

☐ **24** The whole world should be the "campus" for this institution.

Most people in this institution believe that

☐ **25** All faculty have the right to study whatever they need to in order to expand knowledge in their area of expertise.

☐ **26** Collaboration between disciplines will consolidate knowledge and increase the benefits to the people the institution serves.

☐ **27** Institutional access allows able students to achieve career-advancing credentials.

☐ **28** All members of this institution are best served on a personal and face-to-face basis.

☐ **29** Open access to all eligible students results in equitable services and diversity of perspectives.

☐ **30** Reality is co-constructed and varies from individual to individual, so alternative perspectives must be appreciated.

Most people in this institution value

☐ **31** Fair bargaining between management and employees in this institution.

☐ **32** The development and dissemination of knowledge in their specific discipline.

- ☐ **33** Its involvement with global networks of knowledge creation in spite of the challenges of our complex, chaotic world.
- ☐ **34** Systematic institutional research and student-oriented curricular planning.
- ☐ **35** The identification and appreciation of its distinct traditions and founding principles.
- ☐ **36** Accountability to this institution's formal authority through standards, supervision, and outcomes.

Most people in this institution tend to trust in

- ☐ **37** The inherent desire of everyone in this institution to further their own learning and the learning of others.
- ☐ **38** The ability of traditional systems and educational methods to instill this institution's distinct values and perspectives.
- ☐ **39** The dominance of rationality in the institution.
- ☐ **40** The capacity of this institution's leaders to define and measure its goals clearly and objectively.
- ☐ **41** The ability of their leaders to make sense of the fragmentation and ambiguity that exists in our world.
- ☐ **42** The development of procedures to support the equitable distribution of resources and benefits to people in this institution.

Most people in this institution value

- ☐ **43** Financial responsibility.
- ☐ **44** Personal openness and service to others.
- ☐ **45** Faculty research and scholarship.
- ☐ **46** Constructive confrontation among constituencies of this institution with interests that are inherently in opposition.

☐ **47** The predictability of value-based, face-to-face education offered in this institution.

☐ **48** An openness to the recruitment of teachers and learners who work both inside and outside this institution.

Most people in this institution find meaning primarily in

☐ **49** This institution's unique history and mission.

☐ **50** The expansion of the knowledge generation and dissemination capacity of all employees of this institution.

☐ **51** The honoring of cultural, social, and economic diversity in this institution.

☐ **52** The academic disciplines represented by the faculty in this institution.

☐ **53** The organization, implementation, and evaluation of work that is directed toward specified institutional goals and purposes.

☐ **54** The creation of programs and activities that further the growth of all members of this collegiate community.

Most people in this institution are particularly interested in

☐ **55** Collaboration—working together with other people in this institution.

☐ **56** The preservation of individual rights for all members of this institution—being a site of justice and mutual respect.

☐ **57** The accessibility of this institution to all motivated citizens—being able to serve many learners.

☐ **58** Ways they can keep up with the latest technological innovations as they access resources outside this institution.

☐ **59** Autonomy—being able to work in this institution without extensive outside interference.

☐ **60** Meaningful, trustworthy relationships with fellow workers—being a site of character and continuity.

Most people in this institution do not want

- ☐ **61** This to become a second-rate institution.
- ☐ **62** This institution to become a site of indifference or alienation.
- ☐ **63** Administrative anarchy or ineffectiveness in this institution.
- ☐ **64** To restrict what it means to be a part of this institution.
- ☐ **65** Stagnation of ideas in this institution.
- ☐ **66** Arbitrary authority to reign supreme.

People in this institution most fear

- ☐ **67** Being controlled by the administration of this institution.
- ☐ **68** A lack of clear lines of authority and control inside this institution.
- ☐ **69** That its leaders will lack knowledge about the disciplines in the institution, and that they will fail to support them.
- ☐ **70** Being cut off from contact with people outside this institution.
- ☐ **71** Being cut off from contact with other people inside this institution.
- ☐ **72** The inability or unwillingness of its leaders to enact strategies for institutional improvement that are proven elsewhere.

Appendix II

Marking Key for the Academic Cultures Inventory

This marking key will allow you to identify the specific cultures that you responded to in the Academic Cultures Inventory. To sort out the randomly arranged items so that you can determine a pattern to your responses, follow these directions.

Circle all of the item numbers that you selected when you took the inventory. Add the circled items in each column to determine the raw score for each culture. The highest number demonstrates your perception of the institutional culture that most people would agree has the strongest ranking. The lowest number demonstrates your perception of the weakest culture. With which culture do you believe you are most aligned?

Collegial

1

9

18

22

25

32

39

45

52

59

61

69

Managerial

5

8

13

23

27

36

40

43

53

57

63

68

Developmental

4

10

14

21

26

34

37

44

54

55

65

72

Advocacy

2

7

16

20

29

31

42

46

51

56

66

67

Virtual

6

11

17

24

30

33

41

48

50

58

64

70

Tangible

3

12

15

19

28

35

38

47

49

60

62

71

References

Adams, H. (1976). *The academic tribes*. New York: Liveright.

African Virtual University. (n.d.). *About AVU*. Retrieved May 21, 2007, from http://www.avu-lc.udsm.ac.tz/about.html.

Alexander, F. K. (2000, July-August). The changing face of accountability. *Journal of Higher Education, 71*(4), 411–432.

Alveson, M. (2002). *Understanding organizational culture*. Thousand Oaks, CA: Sage.

American Association of University Professors. (2000). *AAUP Policy Documents and Reports* (9th ed.). Washington, DC: American Association of University Professors.

Argyris, C. (1970). *Intervention theory and method*. Reading, MA: Addison-Wesley.

Argyris, C., & Schön, D. (1974). *Theory in practice: Increasing professional effectiveness*. San Francisco: Jossey-Bass.

Argyris, C., & Schön, D. (1978). *Organizational learning*. Reading, MA: Addison-Wesley.

Argyris, C., & Schön, D. (1996). *Organizational learning II: Theory, method, and practice*. Reading, MA: Addison-Wesley.

Astin, A. W., & Astin, H. S. (Eds.). (2000). *Leadership reconsidered: Engaging higher education in social change*. Battle Creek, MI: Kellogg Foundation.

Barr, R. B., & Tagg, J. (1995, November-December). From teaching to learning: A new paradigm for undergraduate education. *Change, 27* (6), 12, 14.

Bates, A. M., & Poole, G. (2003). *Effective teaching with technology in higher education*. San Francisco: Jossey-Bass.

Bateson, G. (1936). *Naven*. Stanford, CA: Stanford University Press.

Bateson, G. (1972). *Steps to an ecology of mind*. New York: Ballantine Books.

Bateson, G. (1979). *Mind and nature: A necessary unity*. New York: Dutton.

Baudrillard, J. O. (1995). *Simulacra and simulation*. Glasser, S. (Trans.). Ann Arbor: University of Michigan Press.

Beckhard, R. (1969). *Organization development: Strategies and models*. Reading, MA: Addison-Wesley.

Belenky, M. F., Clinchy, B. M., Goldberger, N. R., & Tarule, J. (1986). *Women's ways of knowing*. New York: Basic Books.

Bellah, R., Madsen, R., Sullivan, W. M., Swidler, A., & Tipton, S. M. (1985). *Habits of the heart: Individualism and commitment in American life*. Berkeley: University of California Press.

Ben-David, J. (1972). *American higher education*. New York: McGraw-Hill.

Benjamin, E. (1997, April 14). *Faculty and management rights in higher education collective bargaining: A faculty perspective*. Presentation at the 25th annual meeting of the Center for the Study of Collective Bargaining in Higher Education and the Profession. Retrieved May 17, 2007, from http://www.aaup.org/AAUP/issuesed/tenure/benjamincollbarg.htm.

Bergquist, W. H. (1992). *The four cultures of the academy: Insights and strategies for improving leadership in collegiate organizations*. San Francisco: Jossey-Bass.

Bergquist, W. H. (1993). *The postmodern organization: Mastering the art of irreversible change*. San Francisco: Jossey-Bass.

Bergquist, W. H. (1995). *Quality through access, access with quality: The new imperative for higher education*. San Francisco: Jossey-Bass.

Bergquist, W. H. (2004). *Creating the appreciative organization*. Sacramento: Pacific Soundings Press.

Bergquist, W. H., & Armstrong, J. L. (1986). *Planning effectively for educational quality: An outcomes-based approach for colleges committed to excellence*. San Francisco: Jossey-Bass.

Bergquist, W. H., Betwee, J., & Meuel, D. (1995). *Building strategic relationships: How to extend your organization's reach through partnerships, alliances, and joint ventures*. San Francisco: Jossey-Bass.

Bergquist, W. H., Greenberg, E. M., & Klaum, G. A. (1993). *In our fifties: Voices of men and women reinventing their lives*. San Francisco: Jossey-Bass.

Bergquist, W. H., Guest, S., & Rooney, T. (2004). *Who is wounding the healers? The four cultures of health care*. Sacramento: Pacific Sounding Press.

Bergquist, W. H., & Mura, A. (2005). *Ten themes and variations for postmodern leaders and their coaches*. Sacramento: Pacific Soundings Press.

Bergquist, W. H., & Phillips, S. (1975). *A handbook for faculty development: Vol. I*. Washington, DC: Council of Independent Colleges.

Bergquist, W. H., & Phillips, S. (1977). *A handbook for faculty development: Vol. II*. Washington, DC: Council of Independent Colleges.

Bergquist, W. H., & Phillips, S. (1981). *A handbook for faculty development: Vol. III*. Washington, DC: Council of Independent Colleges.

Bergquist, W. H., & Shoemaker, W. A. (Eds.). (1976). *A comprehensive approach to institutional development*. New Directions for Higher Education, no. 15. San Francisco: Jossey-Bass.

Best, F. (Ed.). (1973). *The future of work*. Englewood Cliffs, NJ: Prentice Hall.

Birnbaum, R. (1988). *How colleges work: The cybernetics of academic organization and leadership*. San Francisco: Jossey-Bass.

Birnbaum, R. (2000). *Management fads in higher education*. San Francisco: Jossey-Bass.

Birnbaum, R. (2004). The end of shared governance: Looking ahead or looking back. In W. Tierney & V. Lechuga (Eds.), *Restructuring shared governance in higher education*. New Directions for Higher Education, no. 127. San Francisco: Jossey-Bass.

Blake, R., Mouton, J. S., & Williams, M. S. (1981). *The academic administrator grid*. San Francisco: Jossey-Bass.

Bland, C., & Bergquist, W. (1997). The vitality of senior faculty members: Snow on the roof—Fire in the furnace. *Eric Digest* (ERIC Document No. ED 415733). Washington, DC: George Washington University.

Bledstein, B. J. (1976). *The culture of professionalism: The middle class and development of higher education in America*. New York: Norton.

Bloom, A. (1988). *The closing of the American mind*. New York: Simon & Schuster.

Boulding, K. (1968). *Beyond economics: Essays on society, religion and ethics*. Ann Arbor: University of Michigan Press.

Boulding, K. (1973). Intersects: The peculiar organizations. In K. Bursk (Ed.), *Challenge to leadership: Managing in a changing world*. New York: Free Press and The Conference Board.

Bowen, H. R., & Douglass, G. K. (1971). *Efficiency in liberal education*. New York: McGraw-Hill.

Bowen, H. R., & Schuster, J. (1986). *American professors: A national resource imperiled*. New York: Oxford University Press.

Boyer, E. L. (1990). *Scholarship reconsidered: Priorities of the professoriate*. Princeton: Princeton University Press and The Carnegie Foundation for the Advancement of Teaching.

Boyer, R., & Crockett, C. (1973). Introduction. *Journal of Higher Education* (Special Issue on Organization Development in Higher Education), *44*, 339–351.

Bringle, R. G., & Hatcher, J. A. (1996, March-April). Implementing service learning in higher education. *Journal of Higher Education, 67*(2), 221–239.

Brookfield, S. (1995). *Becoming a critically reflective teacher*. San Francisco: Jossey-Bass.

Brookfield, S. (2004). *The power of critical theory: Liberating adult learning and teaching*. San Francisco: Jossey-Bass.

Broom, M. F., & Klein, D. C. (1999). *Power: The infinite game*. Ellicott City, MD: Sea Otter Press.

Brown, B. L. (2000). *Web-based training* (Report No. EDO-CE-00–218). Columbus, OH: Center on Education and Training for Employment. (ERIC Document Reproduction Services No. ED 445234)

Brubacher, J. S., & Rudy, W. (1958). *Higher education in transition*. New York: HarperCollins.

Burke, J. C., & Modarresi, S. (2000, July-August). To keep or not to keep performance funding. *Journal of Higher Education, 71*(4), 432–454.

Cameron, K. S., & Quinn, R. E. (1999). *Diagnosing and changing organizational culture*. Reading, MA: Addison-Wesley.

Carr, R. K., & Van Eyck, D. K. (1973). *Collective bargaining comes to the campus*. Washington, DC: American Council on Education.

Chickering, A. (1969). *Education and identity*. San Francisco: Jossey-Bass.

Chickering, A., Halliburton, D., Bergquist, W. H., & Lindquist, J. (1977). *Developing the college curriculum: A handbook for faculty and administrators*. Washington, DC: Council for the Advancement of Small Colleges.

Clark, B. R. (1960). *The open door college: A case study*. New York: McGraw-Hill.

Clark, B. R. (1970). *The distinctive college: Antioch, Reed, and Swarthmore*. Hawthorne, NY: Aldine de Gruyter.

Clark, B. R. (1997, May-June). The modern integration of research activities with teaching and learning. *Journal of Higher Education*, 68(3), 241–255.

Coghlan, A. T., Preskill, H., & Catsambas, T. T. (Eds.). (2003). *An overview of appreciative inquiry in evaluation*. New Directions for Evaluation, no. 100. San Francisco: Jossey-Bass.

Cohen, A. (1998). *The shaping of American higher education*. San Francisco: Jossey-Bass.

Cohen, A. (2003). *The American community college*. San Francisco: Jossey-Bass.

Colbeck, C. L. (1998, November-December). Merging in a seamless blend. *Journal of Higher Education*, 69(6), 647–672.

College Institute Educators' Association. (2000, October). *Job Security for Temps in BC*. Retrieved May 21, 2007, from http://www.caut.ca/en/bulletin/issues/2000_oct/news_cieabc.htm.

Collins, J. C. (2001). *Good to great*. New York: HarperCollins.

Cross, K. P. (1990). Classroom research: Helping professors learn more about teaching and learning (pp. 122–142). In P. Seldin (Ed.), *How administrators can improve teaching*. San Francisco: Jossey-Bass.

Csikszentmihalyi, M. (1975). *Beyond boredom and anxiety: The experience of play in work and games*. San Francisco: Jossey-Bass.

Csikszentmihalyi, M. (1990). *Flow: The psychology of optimal experience*. New York: HarperCollins.

Daft, R. L., & Lengel, R. H. (2000). *Fusion leadership: Unlocking the subtle forces that change people and organizations*. San Francisco: Berrett-Koehler.

Deal, T. E., & Kennedy, A. A. (1982). *Corporate cultures: The rites and rituals of corporate life*. Reading, MA: Addison-Wesley.

Dennison, J. (1986). *Canada's community colleges: A critical analysis*. Vancouver: University of British Columbia Press.

Dewey, J. (1944). *Democracy and education*. New York: Free Press. (Original work published 1916)

Diamond, R. M. (1976). *Syracuse University: A systematic approach to curriculum and faculty development*. In W. H. Bergquist & W. A. Shoemaker (Eds.), *A comprehensive approach to institutional development*. New Directions for Higher Education, no. 15. San Francisco: Jossey-Bass.

Diamond, R. M. (Ed.). (2002). *Field guide to academic leadership*. San Francisco: Jossey-Bass.

Diamond, R. M., Kelly, E. F., Holloway, R. E., Eickmann, P. E., & Pascarella, E. T. (1975). *Instructional development for individualized learning in higher education*. Englewood Cliffs, NJ: Educational Technology Publications.

Donald, J. (1997). *Improving the environment for learning: Academic leaders talk about what works*. San Francisco: Jossey-Bass.

Douglas, J. M. (1988). Unionization among college faculty. In G. T. Kurian (Ed.), *Yearbook of American universities and colleges*. New York: Garland.

Drucker, P. F. (1999). *Management challenges for the 21st century*. New York: HarperBusiness.

Duderstadt, J. J., Atkins, D. E., & Van Houweling, D. (2002). *Higher education in the digital age: Technology issues and strategies for American colleges and universities*. Washington, DC: American Council on Education.

Duke, A. (1996). *Importing Oxbridge: English residential colleges and American universities*. New Haven: Yale University Press.

Duley, J. (1974). Editor's notes. In J. Duley (Ed.), *Implementing field experience education*. New Directions for Higher Education, no. 6. San Francisco: Jossey-Bass.

Durkheim, E. (1933). *The division of labor in society*. New York: Free Press. (Original work published 1893)

Egbert, D. D. (n.d.). *The architecture and the setting*. Retrieved September 12, 2006, from http://etcweb.princeton.edu/CampusWWW/Otherdocs/setting.html.

Eisler, R. (1987). *The chalice and the blade*. San Francisco: HarperSan Francisco.

Enos, S., & Morton, K. (2003). Developing a theory and practice of campus-community partnerships. In B. Jacoby (Ed.), *Building partnerships for service learning*. San Francisco: Jossey-Bass.

Euben, D., & Hustoles, T. P. (2001). *Collective bargaining revised and revisited.* Retrieved September 6, 2006, from http://www.aaup.org/Legal/info%20outlines/legcb.htm.

Feldman, K. A., & Newcomb, T. M. (1969). *The impact of college on students.* San Francisco: Jossey-Bass.

Foucault, M. (1965). *Madness and civilization.* New York: Random House.

Foucault, M. (1979). *Discipline and punish.* New York: Vintage Books.

Friedman, T. (1999). *The Lexus and the olive tree.* New York: Farrar, Straus and Giroux.

Gaff, J. G. (1978). *Institutional renewal through the improvement of teaching.* San Francisco: Jossey-Bass.

Gaff, J. G., Ratcliff, J. L., & Associates. (1997). *Handbook of the undergraduate curriculum: A comprehensive guide to purposes, structures, practices, and change.* San Francisco: Jossey-Bass.

Gappa, J. M., Austin, A. E., & Trice, A. G. (2007). *Rethinking faculty work.* San Francisco: Jossey-Bass.

Gappa, J. M., & Leslie, D. W. (1993). *The invisible faculty: Improving the status of part-timers in higher education.* San Francisco: Jossey-Bass.

Garcia, M., & Ratcliff, J. L. (1997). Social forces shaping the curriculum. In J. G. Gaff, J. L. Ratcliff, & Associates (Eds.), *Handbook of the undergraduate curriculum: A comprehensive guide to purposes, structures, practices, and change* (pp. 118–136). San Francisco: Jossey-Bass.

Gardner, H. (1993). *Frames of mind: The theory of multiple intelligences.* New York: Basic Books.

Gardner, H. (2000). *Intelligence reframed: Multiple intelligences for the 21st century.* New York: Basic Books.

Gardner, J. W. (1993). *On leadership.* New York: Free Press.

Gardner, J. W. (1995). *Self-renewal: The individual and the innovative society.* New York: Norton.

Garner, C., Pepicello, W., & Swenson, C. (2005). Faculty scholarship in a nontraditional university. In K. O'Meara & R. E. Rice (Eds.), *Faculty priorities reconsidered: Rewarding multiple forms of scholarship* (pp. 132–145). San Francisco: Jossey-Bass.

Gayle, D. J., Tewaire B., & White, Q. Jr. (2003). Governance in the twenty-first century. *ASHE-ERIC Higher Education Report, 30*(1).

Gilligan, C. (1982). *In a different voice.* Cambridge: Harvard University Press.

Gladwell, M. (2000). *The tipping point.* Boston: Little, Brown.

Glassick, C. E., Huber, M. T., & Maeroff, G. I. (1997). *Scholarship assessed: Evaluation of the professoriate.* San Francisco: Jossey-Bass and The Carnegie Foundation for the Advancement of Teaching.

Gleason, P. (1967). American Catholic higher education: A historical perspective (pp. 15–56). In R. Hessenger (Ed.), *The shape of Catholic higher education.* Chicago: University of Chicago Press.

Goffman, E. (1952). On cooling the mark out. *Psychiatry, 15*, 451–463.

Goleman, D. (2005). *Emotional intelligence*. New York: Bantam Books.

Goleman, D. (2006). *Social intelligence: The new science of human relationships*. New York: Bantam Books.

Greenleaf, R. K. (1970). *The servant as leader*. Peterborough, NH: Center for Applied Studies.

Greenleaf, R. K. (1972). *The institution as servant*. Peterborough, NH: Center for Applied Studies.

Greenleaf, R. K. (1974). *Trustees as servants*. Peterborough, NH: Center for Applied Studies.

Greenleaf, R. K. (1979). *Teacher as servant*. New York: Paulist Press.

Greenleaf, R. K. (1980). *Servant: Retrospect and prospect*. Peterborough, NH: Center for Applied Studies.

Group for Human Development in Higher Education. (1974). *Faculty development in a time of retrenchment*. New Rochelle, NY: Change Magazine Publications.

Grubb, W. N., & Associates. (1999). *Honored but invisible: An inside look at teaching in community colleges*. New York: Routledge.

Gumport, P. J., & Snydman, S. K. (2002, May-June). The formal organization of knowledge. *Journal of Higher Education, 73*(3), 375–409.

Guskin, A. E., & Marcy, M. B. (2002). Pressures for fundamental reform. In R. M. Diamond (Ed.), *Field guide to academic leadership* (pp. 3–24). San Francisco: Jossey-Bass.

Handy, C. (1994a). *The age of paradox*. Cambridge: Harvard Business School Press.

Handy, C. (1994b). *The age of unreason*. Cambridge: Harvard Business School Press.

Hanna, D., & Associates. (2000). *Higher education in an era of digital competition, choices and challenges*. Madison, WI: Atwood.

Harrington, J. (1883). *The Commonwealth of Oceania*. London: Henry Morley. (Original work published 1656)

Havelock, R. (1971). *Planning for innovation through the dissemination and utilization of scientific knowledge*. Ann Arbor, MI: Institute for Social Research.

Hill, J. (n.d.). *The educational sciences*. Oakland, MI: Oakland Community College.

Hillway, T. (1958). *The American two-year college*. New York: HarperCollins.

Hollander, E., & Hartley, M. (2003). Civic renewal: A powerful framework for advancing service learning. In B. Jacoby (Ed.), *Building partnerships for service learning*. San Francisco: Jossey-Bass.

Holub, T. (2003). Contract faculty in higher education. *ERIC Digest* (ED 482556). Retrieved May 17, 2007, from http://www.ericdigests.org/2005-1/contract.htm1/contract.htm.

Horn, M. (1999). *Academic freedom in Canada: A history*. Ontario, Canada: University of Toronto Press.

Hossler, D., & Anderson, D. K. (2005). *The enrollment management process*. In M. L. Upcroft, J. N. Gardner, & B. O. Barefoot (Eds.), *Challenging and supporting the first-year student* (pp. 67–85). San Francisco: Jossey-Bass.

Huber, M. T., & Hutchings, P. (2005). *The advancement of learning: Building the teaching commons*. San Francisco: Jossey-Bass.

Huber, M. T., Hutchings, P., & Shulman, L. S. (2005). The scholarship of teaching and learning today. In K. O'Meara & R. E. Rice (Eds.), *Faculty priorities reconsidered: Rewarding multiple forms of scholarship* (pp. 34–54). San Francisco: Jossey-Bass.

Industry Canada. (2003). *Canada's children in a wired world: The parents' view*. Retrieved May 21, 2007, from http://www.strategis.ic.gc.ca/epic/site/smt-gst.nsf/en/sf05376e.html.

Jacoby, B. (2003a). Fundamentals of service-learning partnerships. In B. Jacoby (Ed.), *Building partnerships for service learning*. San Francisco: Jossey-Bass.

Jacoby, B. (2003b). Building service-learning partnerships for the future. In B. Jacoby (Ed.), *Building partnerships for service learning*. San Francisco: Jossey-Bass.

Jencks, C., & Riesman, D. (1968). *The academic revolution*. Chicago: University of Chicago Press.

Johnson, B. (1996). *Polarity management: Identifying and managing unsolvable problems*. Amherst, MA: HRD Press.

Johnstone, R. L. (1981). *The scope of faculty collective bargaining*. Westport, CT: Greenwood Press.

Kanter, R. M. (1984). *The change masters*. New York: Simon & Schuster.

Kanter, R. M. (1994, July-August). Collaborative advantage: The art of alliances. *Harvard Business Review, 72*(4), 96–109.

Kanter, R. M. (2001). *Evolve! Succeeding in the digital culture of tomorrow*. Cambridge: Harvard Business School Press.

Katz, J., & Associates. (1968). *No time for youth: Growth and constraint in college students*. San Francisco: Jossey-Bass.

Kember, D., & McKay. J. (1996, September-October). Action research into the quality of student learning. *Journal of Higher Education, 67*(5), 528–554.

Kemerer, F. R., & Baldridge, J. V. (1975). *Unions on campus*. San Francisco: Jossey-Bass.

Kerr, C. (1963). *The uses of the university*. Cambridge: Harvard University Press.

Kezar, A., Carducci, R., & Contreras-McGavin, M. (2006). Rethinking the "L" word in higher education. *ASHE-ERIC Higher Education Report, 31*(6).

Knefelkamp, L., Widick, C., & Parker, C. (Eds.). (1978). *Applying new developmental findings*. New Directions for Student Services, no. 4. San Francisco: Jossey-Bass.

Koblik, S., & Graubard, S. R. (Eds.). (2000). *Distinctively American: The residential liberal arts college*. Somerset, NJ: Transaction.

Kolb, D. (1976). *The learning style inventory*. Boston: McBer.

Kotter, J. P., & Heskett, J. L. (1992). *Corporate culture and performance*. New York: Free Press.

Kreber, C., & Cranton, P. A. (2000, July-August). Exploring the scholarship of teaching. *Journal of Higher Education, 71*(4), 476–495.

Kuh, G., Kinzie, J., Schuh, J., Whitt, E., & Associates. (2005a). *Student success in college: Creating conditions that matter*. San Francisco: Jossey-Bass.

Kuh, G., Kinzie, J., Schuh, J., & Whitt, E. (2005b). *Assessing conditions to enhance educational effectiveness: The inventory for student engagement and success*. San Francisco: Jossey-Bass.

Kuhn, T. (1970). *The structure of scientific revolutions* (2nd ed.). Chicago: University of Chicago Press.

Ladd, E. C. Jr., & Lipset, S. M. (1973). *Professors, unions, and American higher education*. New York: McGraw-Hill.

Landrith, H. (1971). *Introduction to the community college*. Danville, IL: Interstate Printers and Publishers.

Lawler, E. E. (1986). *High-involvement management: Participative strategies for improving organization performance*. San Francisco: Jossey-Bass.

Lawler, E. E. (1992). *The ultimate advantage: Creating the high-involvement organization*. San Francisco: Jossey-Bass.

Leslie, D. W., & Gappa, J. M. (1994). Education's new academic workforce. *Planning for Higher Education, 22*(4), 1–6.

Lessem, R. (1990). *Managing corporate culture*. Brookfield, VT: Gower.

Levin, D., & Arafeh, S. (2002, August 14). *The digital disconnect—The widening gap between Internet-savvy students and their schools*. Retrieved May 21, 2007, from http://www.pewinternet.org/PPF/r/67/report_display.asp.

Lewis, M. W. (2000, October). Exploring paradox: Toward a more comprehensive guide. *Academy of Management Review, 25*(4), 760–776.

Lewis, M. W., & Dehler, G. E. (2000, December). Learning through paradox: A pedagogical strategy for exploring contradictions and complexity. *Journal of Management Education, 24*(6), 708–725.

Lick, D. W. (2002). Leadership and change. In R. M. Diamond (Ed.), *Field guide to academic leadership* (pp. 27–47). San Francisco: Jossey-Bass.

Lindquist, J. (Ed.). (1978a). *Designing teaching improvement programs.* Washington, DC: Council of Independent Colleges.

Lindquist, J. (1978b). *Strategies for change.* Washington, DC: Council of Independent Colleges.

Lippitt, R., Watson, J., & Westley, B. (1958). *Dynamics of planned change.* Orlando: Harcourt Brace Jovanovich.

London, H. B. (1978). *The culture of a community college.* New York: Praeger.

Lyotard, J.-F. (1984). *The postmodern condition.* Minneapolis: University of Minnesota Press.

Magnusson, J. (1997, March-April). Higher education research and psychological inquiry. *Journal of Higher Education,* 68(2), 191–211.

Malinowski, B. (1948). *A scientific theory of culture.* Oxford, England: Oxford University Press.

Mardis, M. (2001). Uncovering the hidden Web. Part I: Finding what the search engines don't. *ERIC Digest* (ED 456863). Syracuse, NY: ERIC Clearinghouse on Information and Technology. Retrieved June 8, 2007, from http://www.ericdigests.org/2002-2/hidden.htm.

Martin, J. (2002). *Organizational culture: Mapping the terrain.* Thousand Oaks, CA: Sage.

Martin, W. B. (1969). *Conformity: Standards and change in higher education.* San Francisco: Jossey-Bass.

McGregor, D. M. (1960). *The human side of enterprise.* New York: McGraw-Hill.

McKeachie, W. J. (1964). Research on teaching at the college and university level. In N. L. Gage (Ed.), *Handbook of research on teaching* (pp. 1118–1172). Skokie, IL: Rand McNally.

McNaught, C. (2002). *Implementing technology in higher education: The management of multiple dimensions.* Paper presented at the Association for the Advancement of Computing in Education conference. Retrieved May 21, 2007, from http://www.cuhk.edu.hk/clear/download/Paper/ED-MEDIAMcN_2002.pdf.

McNaught, C. (2003). Innovation and change in higher education: Managing multiple polarities. *Perspectives,* 7(3), 76–82.

Medsker, L. L., & Tillery, D. (1971). *Breaking the access barriers.* New York: McGraw-Hill.

Mentkowski, M. (2000). *Learning that lasts: Integrating learning, development, and performance in college and beyond.* San Francisco: Jossey-Bass.

Menzies Lyth, I. (1992). The functioning of social systems as a defence against anxiety (pp. 43–85). In I. Menzies Lyth (Ed.), *Containing anxiety in institutions.* London: Free Associations.

Meyerson, D. (2001). *Tempered radicals: How people use difference to inspire change at work.* Boston: Harvard Business School Press.

Meyerson, D. (2003). *Tempered radicals: How everyday leaders inspire change at work*. Boston: Harvard Business School Press.

Mezirow, J. (1981). A critical theory of adult learning and education. *Adult Education, 32*, 3–24.

Mezirow, J. (1997). *Transformative learning: Theory to practice*. New Directions for Adult and Continuing Education, no. 74. San Francisco: Jossey-Bass.

Millett, J. (1962). *The academic community: An essay on organization*. New York: McGraw-Hill.

National Center for Education Statistics. (1999). *Institutional policies and practices: Results from the 1999 national study of postsecondary faculty—Institution survey*. Retrieved September 9, 2006, from http://nces.ed.gov.

National Center for Education Statistics. (2003). *Digest of education statistics: Postsecondary education: Part 1*. Retrieved September 9, 2006, from http://nces.ed.gov/pubs2005/2005025c1.pdf.

Newman, F., Couturier, L., & Scurry, J. (2004). *The future of higher education: Rhetoric, reality, and the risks of the market*. San Francisco: Jossey-Bass.

Nielsen, R., & Polishook, I. H. (1985). Higher education and collective bargaining: Past, present, and future. *Journal of the College and University Personnel Association, 36*(2), 52–57.

O'Banion, T. (1989). The renaissance of innovation. In T. O'Banion (Ed.), *Innovation in the community college*. New York: Macmillan.

O'Driscoll, T., & Briki, P. (2006). *Adapt or die: The strategic role of learning in the on-demand enterprise*. Retrieved September 6, 2006, from http://www.learningcircuits.org/2004/may2004/odriscoll-briki.htm.

O'Meara, K., & Rice, R. E. (Eds.). (2005). *Faculty priorities reconsidered: Rewarding multiple forms of scholarship*. San Francisco: Jossey-Bass.

O'Neill, E. T., Lavoie, B. F., & Bennett, R. (2003, April). Trends in the evolution of the public Web, 1998–2002. D-Lib Magazine, 9(4). Retrieved May 21, 2007, from http://www.dlib.org/dlib/april03/lavoie/04lavoie.html.

Online Computer Library System (OCLC). (2002). *Web characterization*. Retrieved May 21, 2007, from http://www.oclc.org/research/projects/archive/wcp/.

Palloff, R. M., & Pratt, K. (2003). *The virtual student: A profile and guide to working with online learners*. San Francisco: Jossey-Bass.

Palmer, S. (1999). *A brief history of collective bargaining in higher education*. Retrieved May 21, 2007, from http://home.comcast.net/~HECollectBar.html.

Parsons, T., & Platt, G. M. (1973). *The American university*. Cambridge: Harvard University Press.

Perry, W. (1970). *Forms of intellectual and ethical development in the college years: A scheme*. Austin, TX: Holt, Rinehart & Winston.

Peters, T. (1988). *Thriving on chaos*. New York: HarperCollins.

Peters, T. J., & Waterman, R. H. (1982). *In search of excellence: Lessons from America's best-run companies*. New York: HarperCollins.

Pettigrew, A. M. (1979). On studying organizational cultures. *Administrative Science Quarterly*, *24*, 570–581.

Polanyi, M. (1969). Sense-reading and sense-giving. In M. Polanyi (Ed.), *Knowing and being*. Chicago: University of Chicago Press.

Prensky, M. (2001). *Digital natives, digital immigrants*. Retrieved September 6, 2006, from http://www.marcprensky.com/writing/Prensky%20-%20Digital%20Natives,%20Digital%20Immigrants%20-%20Part1.pdf.

Price, G., & Sherman, C. (2001). *The invisible Web: Uncovering information sources search engines can't see*. Medford, NJ: CyberAge Books.

Prigogine, I., & Stengers, I. (1984). *Order out of chaos*. New York: Bantam Books.

Pusey, N. (1963). *The age of the scholar*. Cambridge: Harvard University Press.

Quehl, G. H., Bergquist, W. H., & Subbiando, J. L. (1999). *Fifty years of innovations in undergraduate education: Change and stasis in the pursuit of quality*. Indianapolis: USA Group.

Rajagopal, I., & Farr, W. D. (1992). Hidden academics: The part-time faculty in Canada. *Higher Education*, *24* (3), 317–331.

Rhoades, G., & Slaughter, S. (2004, June). Academic capitalism in the new economy: Challenges and choices. *American Academic*, pp. 37–60.

Rice, R. E. (1986). The academic profession in transition: Toward a new social friction. *Teaching Sociology*, *41*, 12–23.

Rice, R. E. (2005). Scholarship reconsidered: History and context. In K. O'Meara & R. E. Rice (Eds.), *Faculty priorities reconsidered: Rewarding multiple forms of scholarship* (pp. 17–31). San Francisco: Jossey-Bass.

Riechmann, S., & Grasha, A. (1974). A rational approach to developing and assessing the construct validity of a student learning style scale instrument. *Journal of Psychology*, *87*, 213–223.

Riemer, S., & McKeown, J. (2003). Involving corporate partners. In B. Jacoby (Ed.), *Building partnerships for service learning*. San Francisco: Jossey-Bass.

Riesman, D. (1967). Foreword. In Robert Hessenger (Ed.), *The shape of Catholic higher education* (pp. i–viii). Chicago: University of Chicago Press.

Riesman, D., Gusfield, J., & Gamson, Z. (1970). *Academic values and mass education: The early years of Oakland Monteith*. New York: Doubleday.

Robst, J. (2001, November-December). Cost efficiency in public higher educational institutions. *Journal of Higher Education, 72*(6), 730–751.

Rogers, E. M. (2003). *Diffusion of innovations* (5th ed.). New York: Free Press.

Rorty, R. (1989). *Contingency, irony, and solidarity*. New York: Cambridge University Press.

Rowley, D. J., Lujan, H. D., & Dolence, M. G. (1998). *Strategic choices for the academy: How demand for lifelong learning will re-create higher education*. San Francisco: Jossey-Bass.

Ruben, B. (2003). *Pursuing excellence in higher education: Eight fundamental challenges*. San Francisco: Jossey-Bass.

Rudolph, F. (1962). *The American college and university: A history*. New York: Random House.

Ruesch, J., & Kees, W. (1969). *Nonverbal communication: Notes on the visual perception of human relations*. Berkeley: University of California Press.

Sanford, N. (Ed.). (1962). *The American college*. New York: Wiley.

Schein, E. (1980). *Organizational psychology* (3rd ed.). Englewood Cliffs, NJ: Prentice Hall.

Schein, E. (1985). *Organizational culture and leadership: A dynamic view*. San Francisco: Jossey-Bass.

Schein, E. (1992). *Organizational culture and leadership* (2nd ed.). San Francisco: Jossey Bass.

Schein, E. (1999). *The corporate culture survival guide*. San Francisco: Jossey-Bass.

Schein, E., & Bennis, W. G. (1965). *Personal and organizational change through group methods*. New York: Wiley.

Schön, D. A. (1983). *The reflective practitioner: How professionals think in action*. New York: Basic Books.

Senge, P. (1990). *The fifth discipline*. New York: Doubleday.

Siegel, M., & Sousa, G. (1994, September). Inventing the virtual textbook: Changing the nature of schooling. *Educational Technology*, pp. 49–54.

Sikes, W., Schlesinger, L. E., & Seashore, C. N. (1974). *Renewing higher education from within*. San Francisco: Jossey-Bass.

Sommer, R. (1969). *Personal space*. Englewood Cliffs, NJ: Prentice Hall.

Srivastva, S., Cooperrider, D., & Associates. (1990). *Appreciative management and leadership: The power of positive thought and action in organizations*. San Francisco: Jossey-Bass.

Stiehl, R., & Lewchuck, L. (2002). *The outcomes primer: Reconstructing the college curriculum*. Corvallis, OR: The Learning Organization.

Tagg, J. (2003). *The learning paradigm college*. Bolton, MA: Anker.

Tierney, W. G. (1988). Organizational culture in higher education. *Journal of Higher Education, 59*, 2–21.

Tierney, W. G. (Ed.). (1990). *Assessing academic climates and cultures.* New Directions for Institutional Research, no. 68. San Francisco: Jossey-Bass.

Tierney, W. G. (1993). *Building communities of difference: Higher education in the twenty-first century*. Westport, CT: Bergin & Garvey.

Tierney, W. G., & Minor, J. T. (2004). A cultural perspective on communication and governance. In W. Tierney & V. Lechuga (Eds.), *Restructuring shared governance in higher education*. New Directions for Higher Education, no. 127. San Francisco: Jossey-Bass.

Toma, J. D., Dubrow, G., & Hartley, M. (2005). *The uses of institutional culture*. San Francisco: Jossey-Bass.

University of the Arctic. (n.d.). *Welcome to the University of the Arctic.* Retrieved September 6, 2006, from http://www.uarctic.org/.

Watkins, J. M., & Mohr, B. J. (2001). *Appreciative inquiry: Change at the speed of imagination*. San Francisco: Jossey-Bass.

Watson, G., & Johnson, D. (1972). *Social psychology: Issues and insights* (2nd ed.). Philadelphia: Lippincott.

Watts G. E. (Ed.). (2002). *Enhancing community colleges through professional development*. New Directions for Community Colleges, no. 120. San Francisco: Jossey Bass.

Watts, M. M. (2005). The place of the library versus the library as place. In M. L. Upcraft, J. N. Gardner, & B. O. Barefoot (Eds.), *Challenging and supporting the first-year student* (pp. 339–355). San Francisco: Jossey-Bass.

Weber, M. (1947). *The theory of social and economic organization*. New York: Free Press.

Whitney, D., & Cooperrider, D. L. (2006). *The appreciative inquiry summit: An emerging methodology for whole system positive change.* Retrieved May 21, 2007, from http://www.all-in-one-spirit.de/lit/appinq/appinq05.htm.

Whitney, D., & Trosten-Bloom, A. (2003). *The power of appreciative inquiry: A practical guide to positive change*. San Francisco: Berrett-Koehler.

Wise, J. M. (1997). *Exploring technology and social space: Communications and agency at the end of the twentieth century*. Thousand Oaks, CA: Sage.

Zahorski, K. J. (2005). Redefining scholarship: A small liberal arts college's journey. In K. O'Meara & R. E. Rice (Eds.), *Faculty priorities reconsidered: Rewarding multiple forms of scholarship*. San Francisco: Jossey-Bass.

Zeller, W. J. (2005). First-year student living environments. In M. L. Upcraft, J. N. Gardner, & B. O. Barefoot (Eds.), *Challenging and supporting the first-year student* (pp. 410–427). San Francisco: Jossey-Bass.

Name Index

S

T

V

W

Z

Subject Index

E

F

G

I

J

K

L

M

O

P

Q

R

S

Printed in the USA/Agawam, MA
August 13, 2021

779569.001